The International Film Business

The International Film Business examines the independent film sector as a business, and addresses the specific skills and knowledge it demands. It describes both the present state of the industry, the significant technological developments that have begun to take place, and what changes these might effect.

The International Film Business:

- describes and analyses the present structure of the film industry as a business, with a specific focus on the film value chain
- discusses current digital technology and how it potentially may change the structure of the industry in the future
- provides information and advice on the different business and management skills and strategies
- includes case studies on a variety of films including *The Name of the Rose* (1986), *Cloverfield* (2008), *Pobby & Dingan* (aka *Opal Dream*, 2005), *Confessions of a Dangerous Mind* (2002), and *The Mother* (2003), and company case studies on EuropaCorp, Redbus and Zentropa.

Taking an entrepreneurial perspective on what future opportunities will be available to prepared and informed students and emerging practitioners, this text includes case studies that take students through the successes and failures of a variety of real film companies and projects and features exclusive interviews with leading practitioners in all sectors of the industry, from production to exhibition.

Angus Finney is a course director and visiting lecturer on film and media businesses at Cass Business School, City University London. He teaches at MSc and MBA level, and works with the UK's Regional Screen Agencies, the South African National Film and Video Foundation and the Abu Dhabi Film Commission as a trainer and consultant. He is Film London's Project Manager for the Production Finance Market, an annual event, and has had practitioner experience as Managing Director of Renaissance Films, a production, finance and sales company that was expanded with investment from the City in 1999. He has worked as a media specialist and journalist, and his previous books include: *Developing Feature Films in Europe: A Practical Guide* (1996), *The State of European Cinema* (1996) and *The Egos Have Landed: The Rise and Fall of Palace Pictures* (1996).

This really is the complete guide to today's film industry. Right up to date, but with a real understanding of the journey that the industry has taken to get here. Comprehensive and well researched; erudite and very readable. Quite simply the book that all practitioners and industry players alike have been waiting for. Many, I suspect, may pretend to themselves that they know it already, but privately will keep the book near at hand for constant reference and self assurance. I know I will.

Ken Dearsley, *Partner, DLA Piper Middle East LLP*

This book successfully accomplishes what many others on the same topic have failed to do. It not only captures the excitement of the international film industry, but it also delves deeply into its structure and practices. The author uses to full advantage his first-hand knowledge of the film business to develop a comprehensive analysis that will have enduring value for both film insiders and readers that are fascinated by this industry.

Joseph Lampel, *Professor of Strategy, and Entrepreneurship,*
Cass Business School, City University London

At last a book for the professional practitioners of filmmaking but accessible to the interested layman, full of insights into the digital age of distribution and production with a road map for the future development of the film business. If you are going to buy one book on the international business of film, this is it!

Sandy Lieberson, *Chairman of Film London,*
former President of Production, Twentieth Century Fox

The International Film Business

A market guide beyond Hollywood

Angus Finney

Routledge
Taylor & Francis Group

LONDON AND NEW YORK

First published 2010
by Routledge
2 Park Square, Milton Park, Abingdon, Oxon OX14 4RN

Simultaneously published in the USA and Canada
by Routledge
270 Madison Avenue, New York, NY 10016

Routledge is an imprint of the Taylor & Francis Group, an informa business

© 2010 Angus Finney

Typeset in Sabon by
Book Now Ltd, London
Printed and bound in Great Britain by
TJ International Ltd, Padstow, Cornwall

British Library Cataloguing in Publication Data
A catalogue record for this book is available from the British Library

Library of Congress Cataloging in Publication Data
Finney, Angus, 1964–
The international film business : a market guide beyond Hollywood / Angus Finney.
    p. cm.
Includes bibliographical references and index.
1. Motion pictures—Marketing. 2. Motion pictures—Distribution. 3. Motion picture industry—Finance. I. Title.
PN1995.9.M29F565 2010
791.43068'8—dc22
2009048663

ISBN10: 0–415–57584–2 (hbk)
ISBN10: 0–415–57585–0 (pbk)
ISBN10: 0–203–85114–5 (ebk)

ISBN13: 978–0–415–57584–3 (hbk)
ISBN13: 978–0–415–57585–0 (pbk)
ISBN13: 978–0–203–85114–2 (ebk)

For Michaela Eyston

Contents

PART 3
Business and management strategies

Illustrations

Figures

Tables

Preface

The inspiration for this book – which is not to be confused with any associated claims of 'inspirational' qualities – is born out of failure, not success. I spent an earlier decade of my career in journalism, consulting and book writing during the 1990s before being presented with the opportunity to cross the commentator/practitioner divide, and work as an entrepreneur and manager at the sharp end of the business. I ran Renaissance Films, a London-based film company, over a seven-year period, the first four with my former partner Stephen Evans. Ultimately, I was forced to close that company and place it into receivership in 2005. The challenge and associated pressures of combining development, production, finance, sales, marketing and the eternal search for distribution under one umbrella, while managing the expectations of institutional investors and later completing a sole management buyout of the company, were ultimately insurmountable. On reflection, however, that exposure and experience has been instructive. A large part of this book's purpose is to capture some of that knowledge.

During the process of personal and professional rehabilitation, it became clear that buried inside those years of practitioner activity was a rich seam of experience and potential case studies. Many less formal film books and lectures on the subject veer towards the anecdotal and focus often on 'successful exceptions'. This book attempts to use the majority of the case studies to explore the dysfunctional and often inefficient processes and people-generated problems rather than just throw a spotlight on the extraordinary and rare hits. It is also wide reaching across the industry's complex architecture, in a strategic effort to cut across the pervasive 'silo' mentality of the fragmented and divided industry in question. This text is aimed directly at both the specialized film student and also the broader media education sector (both undergraduate and postgraduate). The book has also been designed in a way to make much of the material relevant to practitioners in the international film business. When reviewing existing literature on the film business, many texts seemed to focus on Hollywood and the predominantly 'big six' Studio approach to production and distribution. Whilst it is understandable why academic research is drawn to the Studios – who offer quantitative data and historical trends in abundance – what is left untended is the international film industry as practised and experienced by all outside (although often connected to) the Hollywood hegemony. That exclusion has created a considerable knowledge gap. In addition, there exists a plethora of biographical books, alongside film theory, econometric, strategic and management-focused academic work, and a smorgasbord of production/finance/legal 'how to' texts. There are, however, remarkably few books that seriously address the industry that is termed 'Independent' – meaning everything outside the 'big six', and how that industry relates to Hollywood and the rapidly changing worldwide film business today.

The International Film Business – A Market Guide beyond Hollywood is split into three main sections: 1 The film value chain; 2 Users and the changing digital market; and 3 Business and management strategies. This book has been designed to enable the majority of the chapters and case studies to stand alone, and to be utilized for teaching and training purposes without the need to wade through the entire 100,000 word text in one linear session. However, the book is also aiming to be larger than just the sum of its parts. By analysing the horizontal and vertical structures that shape the film industry, in tandem with changing patterns of users and digital technology, I have aimed to concurrently examine the existing industry while acknowledging the high levels of current restructuring. When reviewing existing literature and exploring the above themes while teaching at MSc and MBA level at Cass Business School, City University London, it became clear that business, project and management skills needed to be welded into any industry and market analysis of the film sector. All too often those skills are an afterthought or deemed irrelevant to the creative pool, which is at best wrong-headed and at worst deeply damaging to the industry's future. And film, although not the largest of a number of key creative industries, remains one of the most visible. Indeed, feature film is not called a 'loss-leader' for nothing.

Acknowledgements

This book originated through discussions with Terry Ilott, Course Director at the Film Business Academy (FBA); Peter Bloore, then an associate director at the FBA and now an established academic at University of East Anglia and Bournemouth University; and Cass's Professor of Strategy, Joe Lampel. I subsequently received research support from the UK Film Council and Skillset, for which I am extremely grateful. John Woodward, Janine Marmot, Tina McFarling and others were extremely encouraging, and without their combined kick-start the process would have stalled.

Other practitioners and lecturers who have supported, aided and taught me much – often through joint lecturing, practitioner workshops and teaching/training sessions but also through general contact – include Stephen Evans, Jeremy Thomas, Mark Gill, Daniel Battsek, Andrew Macdonald, Simon Franks, Rebecca O'Brien, Peter Le Tessier, Michael Kuhn, David Kosse, Mark Beilby, Patrick Russo, Stewart Till, Kevin Loader, Sara Frain, Ashley Pharoah, Peter Bloore, Mike Kelly, Peter Broderick, Heather Mansfield, Pierre-Ange Le Pogam, Ian Hutchinson, Jake Eberts, Andy Harries, Geoff Gilmore, Philippe Carcasonne, Hilary Davis, Phil Hunt, Simon Bosanquet, Michael Henry, Nick Manzi, Alejandro Pardo, Simon Franks, Sean Steele, Howard Kaidaish, David Collins, Nik Powell, Stephen Woolley, Marc Boothe, Ralph Kamp, Charles Macdonald, Lars Hermann, Tina Sorensen, Soren Kragh Jacobsen and Kim Magnusson, to thank but a few I can recall. Those not listed who I've also learnt from – in particular during my trials and errors at Renaissance Films – thank you.

A number of organizations in the United Kingdom have indirectly helped shape my thinking, learning and the development of this book's themes. In particular, my associates at Film London, including Adrian Wootton, Sandy Lieberson, Helena Mackenzie, Libby Savill and Daniela Kirchner, have been extremely encouraging. My role as manager of the Production Finance Market on Film London's behalf has been instructive in the continual search for relevance and commercial realism, and hence thanks also to the PFM's co-ordinator, Chloe Laing, for her input. My intensive exposure to training and coaching outside the formal education system was made possible in part due to the FBA, but also thanks to South West Screen, Film Agency Wales, B3 Media and the Film Distributors' Association. My recent work has taken me far beyond the United Kingdom. Thanks are also due to the South African Film and Video Foundation – in particular Ryan Haidarian and Clarence Hamilton – the Danish National Film School (Ole John) and the Abu Dhabi Film Commission (David Shepheard), all of whom have exposed me to different film cultures and industries and forced me to work beyond my comfort zone.

The vast majority of this book was written, while my three children were asleep, on holidays, while my partner patiently encouraged (and at times pressed) me to keep writing. For them I am greatly indebted, although the chances of this particular book keeping my young sons up at night with a torch are slim. Lastly, significant additional and personal thanks is due to Terry Ilott, who played a critical role in advising and guiding this book's design, and in final editing notes; and my executive assistant, Eugenio Triana, whose outstanding research, academic flair and generational insight has been critical to this process reaching fruition. Thanks are also due to my editor, Aileen Storry, and her team at Routledge, and to Simon Gallant of Gallant Macmillian for his ever-reliable legal advice. Of course, all omissions, errors and mistakes remain my responsibility.

Angus Finney

Part 1
The film value chain

1   Global film: a changing world

> For centuries, mankind knew all there was to know about the shape of the Earth. It was a flat planet, shaped roughly like a circle, with lots of pointy things hanging down from the underside … .The oceans lapped against the sides of the Earth, and in places ran over, creating currents that would pull over the edge ships that ventured too far out to sea … .
>
> (The Flat Earth Society, Mission Statement, 2008[1])
>
> The word 'flat' … means equalizing, because the flattening forces are empowering more and more individuals today to reach farther, faster, deeper, and cheaper than ever before. … In my view, this flattening of the playing field is the most important thing happening in the world today.
>
> (Thomas L. Friedman, *The World Is Flat*[2])

The world's changing shape

Reference to the long-held yet fantastical notion of a flat earth may appear a strange point to begin an opening chapter of a book about the international film market. Yet the image of a horizontal planet, covered in firm earth and choppy seas, with lots of vertical, 'pointy things hanging down' offers an arresting visual image that serves the following analysis more appropriately than a perfectly formed sphere.

Why does the visual image fit the analysis? Because the film market can be analysed from a horizontal perspective, which assists us in understanding global, multi-national, and territory-by-territory strategies, and the respective values of scale and reach. As such, the horizontal approach allows us a degree of 'macro' analysis, taking into account global trends, key territorial distinctions and, in the rare instance of a film that hits worldwide, an extraordinary penetration and super-returns resulting from Slumdog-style universal exploitation. Big stuff. Sounds exciting, huh? Well, the use of the word 'rare' is advisory, and applies as much to the Hollywood Studio system as it does to the independent industry that works alongside the global machine. As we shall see all too soon, a 'hit-driven' business is normally predicated on the vast failure of the majority.

The film market can also be approached from a vertical perspective, which enables us to analyse specific film media characteristics and their relative values and roles within the film value and exploitation chain. Each film product is capable of being delivered and viewed a number of ways by the end-user. Up until recently, and still predominant, is the exploitation chain:

1   theatrical release window;
2   DVD window;
3   pay-TV window; and
4   free-TV window.

It is this chain, when analysed from vertical link-to-link, that helps us towards an understanding of how film can be valued and the business analysed on a 'micro' basis. Film exploitation remains somewhat dependent on both the vertical and horizontal aspects, and they tend not to mesh neatly on a regular basis to form the perfect sphere or circle. Up until recent times, it would be accurate to state that a film is nearly always released first in its domestic country of origin and then subsequently exploited in additional territories. It was also accurate to state that a film has been released first theatrically (if it succeeds in being booked), and then through DVD and then television. But as this book explores, much is set to change.

Why has the film industry followed such rigid, structured forms? The first reason is historical as the film industry was initially less global at the start of the last century. The first few cinemas catered to local passers-by.[3] It was only with the development of the motion picture, and the associated costs in production and marketing, that the need to expand to new markets arose. The theatrical window is also the first vertical form because it was the first to be invented for transmitting films.

But the second reason lies at the heart of the economic structure of the business: it is no secret that the Hollywood Studios dominate the world film industry. These are the six major distributors[4], based in Los Angeles but with worldwide exploitation systems that consistently hold the greatest share of the world film market. They utilize the vertical economic approach by releasing their films theatrically first, and ensuring increased revenues and profits through creating a system of 'windows' where the film is not released onto the next form of media until the exploitation in its previous one has been exhausted.

They also strategically apply the horizontal approach to the business of film by typically acquiring rights to any possible territories in which a film could be exploited (if not laying off risk by sharing territories with a partner). Any revenue returns are then governed by 'cross-lateralization' – meaning that high returns in some territories are evened out by losses in others. In Hollywood legalese, the Studios use the word the 'Universe' to avoid any later misunderstandings about new encounters with a third kind – meaning of course potential markets and audiences yet to be discovered (i.e. planets yet to be colonized – such an example might be extraordinary but it helps drive the point of the absurdity of 'Universe' in a more visual, almost cinematic way).

Increasingly, over the past decade in particular, the Studios have seen their dominance over both conduits of exploitation – horizontal and vertical – under increasing pressure and in certain cases, market erosion. As this book explores in detail, an increasing degree of flexibility between a vertical and horizontal landscape is now lifting off and expanding: the ball is beginning to take on an interesting shape.

The economic challenge facing film

The international film business stands on a delicate cusp. Changing technology and user demands are radically challenging the established 'windows' structure so favoured by the Studios and other leading gate-keeping distribution incumbents.

Local audiences and communities are rising up, demanding culturally specific stories that explore their own communities. Even the Studios are conceding that American 'world series' (sic) sports movies or homogenized, formulaic romantic-comedies set in Long Island are failing to rock audiences from Angora to Zagreb.

The current dynamic changes – numerous examples of which are addressed in the second and third sections of this book – need to be set against economic factors that are specific to the film industry's characteristics. On the positive side, key statistical drivers indicate a strong growth rate and a promising horizon. Increases in productivity, the advent of new markets and the introduction of new media platforms have led to a compound annual growth rate in filmed entertainment of between 7.5 and 9 per cent since 1985, with a growth rate triple that of the rise of the underlying economy as a whole.[5]

This impressive expansion reflects film's resilience in the fight for consumer leisure time. Competition for leisure time is intense, and whilst leisure time has increased in most countries since 1945, there is evidence that since 1980 it has been decreasing in the USA, some of Europe's largest territories, including the United Kingdom, Germany and France, and parts of the Far East, where there is significant growth and volatility of employment. It can be argued that consumers compare the marginal utility of leisure time against the marginal cost of foregone earnings: hence they weigh up the trade-off between spending more money and earning more money, with the later increasingly dominating. The 2007–2008 world economic crash, the volatility of employment trends and an overall increase in saving rather than spending will also be making their mark on film's immediate future. As people work longer hours, leisure time decreases and competition for leisure time becomes highly competitive.

Popular media remains obsessed by the high-end spectacle of the feature film business, but it is important to note that cinema and DVD occupy just under 2 per cent of total leisure time, compared to TV's 40 per cent plus figure. The share, however, is under increasing pressure, in particular within the 12–24 demographic age group. In most industries, demand and supply are typically mediated by the price mechanism. But film does not provide differential pricing (except between locations, e.g. rural versus urban). In a given location, cinema tickets cost the same whether the film is a hit or a dud, expensive to make or cheap to make. A ticket to *Paranormal Activity* costs just the same as *Avatar* even though there is a $200m plus production cost differential. On the supply side, the absence of a movable price mechanism to mediate demand is compensated for by built-in excess capacity.

The elasticity of capacity is only possible because, although film has very high sunk costs, there are very low marginal costs associated with increased supply. In cinema and TV, whether one person watches or 10,000 it makes very little difference. Even in DVD, the marginal costs are very low compared with other industries. While supply is mediated by excess/variable capacity and low marginal costs, demand is mediated mostly by production values and marketable elements such as stars, and the uncontrollable 'x' factor of word of mouth. These characteristics explain the constant upward pressure on costs and the search for the zeitgeist break-out hit.

Film has a fairly unique combination of characteristics: prototypical production, high sunk costs in development (R&D), very high unit costs of production, high (and rising) costs of marketing, a huge rate of failure, a short and competitive shelf life in the primary marketplace and no price differentiation. There are other industries that share some of the above characteristics: biotechnology, oil and gas exploration and high-end sports. As Terry Ilott notes in his Cass MBA lectures, all operate business models that are hit-dependent and therefore predicated upon failure.

> The average sunk cost in production and initial US marketing for a studio film is now more than $100m. Yet demand is entirely unknown. The unpredictability of demand explains why *Star Wars*, *Raiders of the Lost Ark*, *Jaws*, *Home Alone* and *Back to the Future* were all initially rejected by studios. Once the sunk costs have been recouped, there being minimal marginal costs, films can be very, indeed increasingly, profitable.

However, the combination of upward cost pressures (to remain competitive), the historic transfer of power and economic benefit to talent (again, the result of competitive pressures) and the relatively poor rates of return in increasingly important ancillary markets of TV, DVD and the Internet, have led to a decline in operating margins, which, for the Hollywood Studios, have fallen from around 15 per cent in the 1970s to around 5 per cent today, according to *Screen Digest* data. More bluntly, the repercussions are starting to become disruptive. *Variety*'s Peter Bart pointed out, that

> the explosion of the DVD business helped fuel a spectacular boom in Hollywood, one that lifted the community's expectations and appetites. But the air has gone out of the DVD balloon, and the gap between the demands of the corporations and those of the artists who contribute the content is causing a toxic atmosphere.[6]

In part, the economic characteristics of the film industry have, historically, been the consequence of the capacity constraint in exhibition. Films have to be screened in real time. There are a fixed number of cinema screens. Film releases are competing for those screens in real time. It is arguable that this circumstance has resulted in, or contributed to, the market failure that is evident in the 'natural' monopoly enjoyed by the six Hollywood Studios (acting as an oligopoly, there being nothing to distinguish one from another), the asymmetry of information, whereby only the Studios have access to reliable market data, and the phenomenon of increasing profits (super profits) once a film has achieved break-even.

Market failure is also apparent through the plethora of subsidies, soft equity/ licence broadcaster support, non-repayable and soft loans, grants, fiscal incentives and other measures designed to rectify market collapse and Hollywood's hegemony in many markets, particularly in Europe over the past 30 years.[7]

The oligopoly of the Hollywood Studios is the film industry's response to the economic characteristics of the business. Mitigation of risk is achieved by vertical and horizontal integration, portfolio investment, syndication of risk via off-balance sheet finance, capital concentration and clustering. The movie business is concentrated in a single location, Hollywood (or more accurately today, Los Angeles), dominated by the six Studios, around which cluster a host of specialist service providers, from visual effects companies to banks, insurers, accountants and law firms. Each Studio has a large catalogue of intellectual property rights and each enjoys very considerable barriers to entry that have ensured that no major Studio has joined the ranks since Fox in the mid-1930s. The Studios have a symbiotic relationship with the independent sector, upon which they rely for creative and commercial innovation, cost reduction, identification of new talent and connection with evolving consumer tastes.

Studios keep all the risks of development, production and distribution and thus keep all the margins (to date). Independents offload the risks and forego the margins. The film economy is significantly contra-cyclical. But, being a global business with significant capital requirements and local cash generative qualities, it is heavily influenced by interest rates and exchange rates as well as local fiscal incentives. Technological advances, regulation, demographic change and changes in consumer behaviour (as between media, for example) also have a big influence.

Bill Mechanic pointed out in his 2009 Independent Film & Television Alliance (IFTA) keynote speech:

> You can see that there is a 21 per cent drop in film going amongst the core target audience and a 24 per cent drop in the next key category, 25–39 year olds … . If the audiences are shifting, why isn't the product shifting as well? Name five mainstream films this year that successfully targeted an over-30 year audience? In that way, Hollywood in the broadest sense of the word is much like Detroit. It's a manufacturer's mentality that reigns, seemingly indifferent to the consumer it serves. Ignore whether the consumer likes our product as long as they buy it. Market it and they will come. And don't worry if they don't come back. Accept 60 per cent drop off rates as the norm, saying it's all about wide openings.[8]

Change has almost shot past us, while incumbents struggle to turn their tankers around, and smaller independent players find themselves caught in a V shape: declining distribution advances, a lack of bank appetite for lending and declining DVD revenues, yet no clear way to monetize future video-on-demand (VOD) exploitation models. There is increasing pressure to create new business models, but many remain hybrid experiments rather than clearly sustainable new business platforms. That is not to criticize entrepreneurs' efforts but the only clear thing about the future is its uncertainty.

According to Ilott, we can expect the film industry to take on the aspects of a flexible, network economy,

> with great fluidity in terms of capital flows among the studios and between the studios and the independents. We might also expect the film industry to become less 'special' and more like other industries as larger parts of the value chain, freed from capacity constraints and able to implement differential pricing, take on 'normal' commercial characteristics.[9]

Specifically the Internet, with its global reach, is a leading example of a horizontal world delivery system capable of disseminating volumes of information and media at light-breaking speed. However, specific media traffic on the Internet can also be broken down in terms of vertical exploitation. Net access via phone and wireless lines can now be traced and billed on a territory-by-territory basis.

Contemporary currents are definitely pushing ships close to the edge, and some are bound to fall off. And new digital technologies have also shrunk and opened up the vertical chain model. Increasingly, films are distributed at different stages of the old value chain, and move on from there. The windows system is breaking up.

What is the current state of the independent (non-Hollywood) market? How might digital technologies change this in the near future? And what business skills will the future entrepreneur of film and digital media need to navigate this whole round world of distribution? The primary aim of this book is to answer the above three questions, and help both the emerging student and the practitioner, in mid-storm, to take stock and consider the future before it is too late.

2 The film value chain

> Always go up, not down …
>
> (Samuel Goldwyn)

The underlying and created rights

The primary products of the film industry are often described as a group or 'bundle' of rights. This group of related rights that constitute a movie product can be broken down into three key parts: 1) the underlying rights; 2) newly created copyrights; and 3) exploitation rights. Before examining the broader implications of the film value chain, it is essential to ground the analysis in a legal and practical framework.

The underlying rights to a film normally kick off in a pre-existing book, script (original or adapted), play or other source of material that has to be acquired, along with any underlying rights that are created or used within the film, including elements such as character, image and music, etc. These rights normally belong to third parties, and have to be legally acquired before they can be incorporated into a film. Secondly, the right to utilize and exploit the work of writers, actors, directors, designers, has to be acquired by legal contract. Writers, directors and creative artists normally are contracted through standard formatted contracts that are agreed across the industry. Thirdly, it is often required that permissions must be sought and cleared from third parties – most notably when shooting on location. Service agreements have to be entered into for the use of studios, laboratories, visual effects houses, etc.

Once a film has completed production and post-production, an entirely new right is created: the film copyright. Other copyrighted elements may be included within the film, such as the soundtrack, costumes or characters. The film copyright and related copyrights are then exploited by the licensing of various sales, distribution and merchandising rights to third parties active in film sales, distribution, exhibition, home entertainment, merchandising, etc.

The Hollywood Studio approach

The Hollywood Studio system is essentially composed along the lines of a vertically integrated model. The Studio develops (and normally owns and therefore controls) the underlying rights; it produces – with the assistance of producers 'for hire' – the physical film; and its marketing and distribution operation set about positioning and exploiting the product through the varying windows available. The distribution phases starts with cinema exhibition (viewed from Hollywood as theatrical 'domestic' and 'foreign' windows) followed by home video and DVD, pay-TV, free-TV, syndication and possible video gaming and merchandising opportunities. These windows have made up the stages of the exploitation phases, but as we shall examine later in this chapter, the windows are set to change radically over the next period of film business activity.

Studios have mitigated risks inherent in production and distribution of feature films, in part through the above 'vertically integrated' approach. This has allowed them historically to control and own as much of the profit margins as possible in the distribution and exploitation value chain. They also exploit through 'horizontal integration', which allows them to cover a range of production and different types of audiences, maximized by taking on film, television and game production and distribution, rather than narrowing their consumer base to one sector or demographic. Studios also apply traditional investment tools, including slate or portfolio management, whereby they spread the risks of investment across many projects (now typically 15–30 new features and falling per annum, but complemented by a range of ancillary production exploitation). A key strategy harnessed to the previous approaches includes the need to achieve critical mass.

This has historically enabled the Studios to act as gatekeepers, so that they can attract the top talent and the best projects, while controlling costs by negotiating best terms from suppliers and clients where possible. Access to capital, and its concentration in one location, allows the Hollywood Studios to dominate the world's top film talent, and act as a magnet for leading international filmmakers and stars to gravitate towards the Hollywood system. The Studios utilize complex financial instruments, such as off-balance sheet financing, which attract third parties who are not strategic players in the film value chain to share the risk of production and distribution investment, and enable the Studio to protect repayment of its significant overheads and reduce the cost of financing. They are also well placed to compare and ultimately maximize tax and other local, regional and national production incentives. The Studios syndicate rights to lower exposure to an element of their slate. This is sometimes carried out by two Studios splitting domestic and foreign rights respectively; and sometimes achieved by utilizing either an associated foreign sales operation (e.g. Universal/Focus Features), or a separated foreign sales agency/company that matches the negotiated balance of the production cost.

In order to attempt to further mitigate risk versus the costs of production and distribution/marketing (north of $120m for most typical studio productions, and as high as $300m for tent pole releases), Studios have focused on franchises based on properties that have demonstrated their appeal in the domestic or global marketplace. Studios are capitalizing on brand equity, and are making investment decisions on previously known-quantities – both in-house and to the consumer.

The fragmented independent chain

The independently structured film industry rarely makes and delivers to a final audience a product developed, produced and distributed by a single company or entity. Of course, there are exceptions, with national 'studio-style' structures and international companies operating outside Los Angeles, but here we are concentrating on the typical independent system. In contrast to the above analysis of the Hollywood

Table 2.1 Film value chain model (independent model, by activity)

Element	Players	Support
Consumer	First time product is seen by end-user, and where true value can be assessed and realized. Time and money have been sunk at high level before this final contact with the consumer marketplace.	
Exploitation	Exhibition/cinema release, DVD sales/rental, VHS, sales/rental, pay-TV, video-on-demand, Internet, download, free-TV, Syndication Library rights: ongoing exploitation opportunities for producer, financier; distributor's licence window. Remake, prequel/sequel rights. Long tail opportunities.	*Marketing* By territory (distributor and separately by exhibitor).
Distributor	International sales agent; producer's representative producer. Marketing and selling distribution rights and in return receiving commission.	*Marketing* By sales agent. International markets.
Shoot/post	Production company/producer, director, cast, crew, studio locations, laboratories support services, post-production, supervision, facilities. (Director, producer and financiers normally involved in final cut and sign off of product.)	*Marketing* Use of PR. On shoot.
Financing	Producer(s); production company; package (including the script, director, cast, national and international pre-sales (if available), co-production. Funds/partners, national subsidy finance, national broadcaster. Finance, equity, bank, gap finance, tax financing. Executive, associate and co-producers. Talent agent, talent manager, lawyers. Completion bond. Insurance.	Lawyers, talent agents.
Development	Concept, idea, underlying material producer (creative), writer, development executive, script editor, development financier, talent agent, talent manager, director (as developer with writer or as writer/director). Private equity support is rare at this stage.	Regional and national subsidy support and/or broadcaster support.

Source: A. Finney.

Studios' integrated approach, the independent business consists of a chain of connected companies, individuals and freelancers, all working on different elements of the filmmaking and exploitation process, at varying stages of the process.

Table 2.1, which demonstrates the independent film value chain structure(s) and interlinking stages, is fruitful as a tool to examine the inherent problems, challenges and weaknesses of the fragmented system. The strategic effect of what could be termed a 'disintegrated model' is that each element in the chain is heavily dependent on the next player/operator's partnership and co-operation in order to drive a project forward. A network of varying interacting players has to be attracted, managed and, in many cases, forced into focusing and delivering specific commitments and activities in order for a film project to proceed. The risks are extreme. In addition, the seed idea, and early sunk costs in a concept, idea and writer's work to produce a realizable screenplay, is six, highly complex stages away from contact with the end-user, the film consumer.

Finding effective ways to capture the 'returns' or 'value' to an initial concept (or innovation), and to create and exploit a structure that compensates for the risks taken, are few and far between. Unfortunately for producers and writers in the early stages of development and financing, there is no guarantee that they will extract or create any value flowing from their work and ideas.

In Table 2.1 and the above analysis, what is in question is the 'architecture' or set of templates within which the different players interact. Some are socially motivated, and some are economically driven, but it is then complexity and lack of transparency that leads to assumptions and inherent inefficiencies that beleaguers the independent business.

Another way of examining the shape of the film value chain is by expanding the players section and looking at the links over a horizontal sequence, as seen in Peter Bloore's paper 'Re-defining the Independent Value Chain'[1] (see Table 2.2). Bloore's paper also explores the history of value chains and its application to the film and TV sector.

The problem of a production company's size and longevity

Independent film production companies operate an inherently weak business model. The independent industry's modus operandi requires them to invest in the development of film projects and pay their associated overhead costs at their own risk. The business plan will normally follow a route whereby they assume that if they can develop a sufficient level of projects that can be placed into production, they can both recoup their development costs (with an industry standard premium of say 25–50 per cent) and create sufficient production fees to cover both the work in producing and delivering the film, along with the sunk costs in overheads to date.

Ironically, the independent production community has few to no barriers to entry. So alongside the high level of risks associated with this 'innovative' stage of project development comes a high level of competition from rival producers and projects. To be genuinely competitive, the producer has to invest not just in the best projects and top writers, but at a level of volume that ensures, even with a low rate of conversion, there is enough production activity to cover historical, immediate and future overhead costs.

Independent producers hope that by investing in high-quality projects, assisted by strong talent attachments, that they will achieve not just a break-even conversion ratio, but that they will remain in business long enough for a project to 'break' and receive net profits in addition to recoupment of development costs and a production fee. Net profits are effectively the 'upside' of the independent producer's business.

'The reality is that the above equation is exceptionally difficult to sustain over a significant period' explains author and Film Business Academy director Terry Ilott.

Table 2.2 The independent film project value chain, © Peter Bloore, 2009 (by activity; conventional European/US indie, non-Studio)

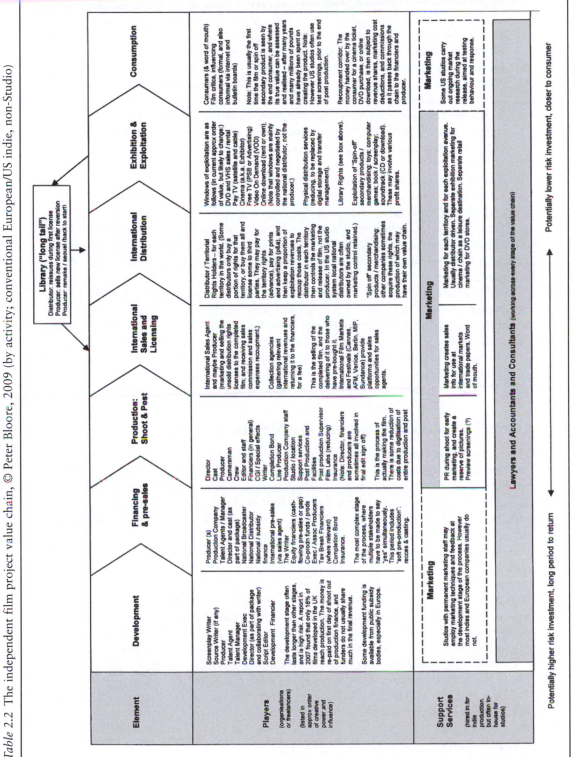

Library ("long tail")
Distributor: reissues during first license
Producer: sells new license after reversion
Producer: remake / sequel (back to start)

Element	Development	Financing & pre-sales	Production: Shoot & Post	International Sales and Licensing	International Distribution	Exhibition & Exploitation	Consumption
Players (organisations or freelancers) (listed in approx order of creative power and influence)	Screenplay Writer; Source Writer (if any); Producer; Talent Agent; Talent Manager; Development Exec; Director (as part of package and collaborating with writer); Script Editor; Development Financier. The development stage often lasts longer than other stages, and is high risk. A report in 2007 found that only 18% of films developed in the UK reach production. The money is re-paid on first day of shoot out of production finance, and funders do not usually share much in the final revenue. Some development funding is available from public subsidy bodies, especially in Europe.	Producer (s); Production Company; Talent Agents / Manager; Director and cast (as part of package); National Broadcaster; National Distributor; National / subsidy finance; International pre-sales (via sales agent); The Writer; Equity financiers (cash-flowing pre-sales (as gap) in Co-profit funds / prods; Exec / Assoc Producers; Tax Break Financiers (where relevant); Completion Bond; Insurance. The most complex stage of the process, where multiple stakeholders have to be made to say 'yes' simultaneously. This period includes "soft pre-production": recces & casting.	Director; Cast; Producer; Cameraman; Crew; Editor and staff; Financiers (in general); CGI / Special effects; Writer; Completion Bond; Line Producer; Production Company staff; Studio / location; Support services; Post Production and Facilities; Post production Supervisor; Film Labs (reducing); Insurance. (Note: Director, financiers and producers are sometimes all involved in final edit sign off). This is the process of actually making the film. There is some reduction of costs due to digitisation of entire production and post	International Sales Agent and maybe Producer (marketing and selling the unsold distribution rights licenses to the completed film; and receiving sales commission and sales expenses recoupment.) Collection agencies (gathering relevant international revenues and returning it to the financiers, for a fee) This is the selling of the completed film, and the delivering of it to those who have pre-bought it. International Film Markets and Festivals (Cannes, AFM, Venice, Berlin, MIP, Sundance) provide platforms and sales opportunities for sales agents.	Distributor / Territorial Rights Holders – for each territory in the world. (Some distributors only buy a portion of rights for that territory, or buy them all and license some to third parties. They may pay for the territory rights (advance), pay for prints and advertising (p&a), and then keep a proportion of exploitation revenues to recoup those costs. The distributor in each territory then controls the marketing and release of the film, not the producer. In the US studio system local national distributors are often owned by the studio, and marketing control retained.) "Spin off" secondary products / merchandising: other companies sometimes acquire some rights, the production of which may have their own value chain.	Windows of exploitation are as follows (in current approx order of value, but likely to change): DVD and VHS sales / rental; Pay TV (satellite and cable); Cinema (a.k.a. Exhibitor); Free TV (PSB or Advertising); Video On Demand (VOD); Online download (rent or own). (Note that windows are mainly controlled and negotiated by the national distributor, not the producer.) Physical distribution services (reducing, to be replaced by digital storage and transfer management). Library Rights (see box above). Exploitation of "Spin-off" secondary products / merchandising: toys; computer games; book / screenplay; soundtrack (CD or download). These may involve various profit shares.	Consumers (& word of mouth) Film critics, influencing consumers (formal, and also informal via internet and bulletin boards) Note: This is usually the first time the film or spin off secondary product is seen by the end consumer, and where its true value can be assessed and realised – after many years and many millions of pounds have already been spent on creating the product. Note: However US studios often use test screenings, prior to the end of post production. Recoupment corridor: The money handed over by the consumer for a cinema ticket, DVD purchase, or online download, is then subject to revenue shares, marketing cost deductions, and commissions as it passes back through the chain to the financiers and producer.
Support Services (hired in for indie production, but often in-house for studios)	**Marketing** Studios with permanent marketing staff may employ marketing techniques and feedback at the development stage of the process. However most indies and European companies usually do not.		**Marketing** PR during shoot for early marketing, and create a reserve of pictures. Preview screenings (?)	**Marketing** Marketing creates sales info for use at international markets and trade papers. Word of mouth.	Marketing for each territory and for each exploitation avenue. Usually distributor driven. Separate exhibition marketing for cinema / chain as a leisure destination. Separate marketing for DVD stores.		**Marketing** Some US studios carry out ongoing market research during the release, aimed at testing behaviour and response.

Lawyers and Accountants and Consultants (working across every stage of the value chain)

Potentially higher risk investment, long period to return ←→ Potentially lower risk investment, closer to consumer

Source: P. Bloore, 'Re-defining the Independent Film Value Chain', London: UK Film Council, 2009.

Independent production companies that do not have an early hit, quickly run out of capital. Those that have an early hit stay in the game longer, but must have another hit before they too run out of capital. While the conversion ratio and the hit ratio cannot be predicted, the expenditure on development and overhead will be relatively constant if the company is to stay in business. Most companies will, sooner or later, find that the generation of development premiums, production fees and profit shares lags behind the cumulative costs of development and over-heads. If they cannot recapitalise, they will go out of business. If they can recapitalise, they re-enter the treadmill until, once more, the need for recapitalisation reoccurs. Few companies can recapitalise more than once.[2]

In addition to this damning analysis, it should be stressed that given the pressures on producers when closing finance, many are pushed and forced to defer either a part or the majority of their fees. And many are forced to forego their development repayment, or at least the premium attached to these sunk costs. In many instances, financiers force the producer to place such costs and/or deferred fees well back in the film's financial recoupment order as a way of protecting their investment – higher up the repayment system.

Finally, Ilott suggests that the alternative model to the above portfolio approach to development is to reduce the scale of activity and overhead to a minimum in order to run the company on a 'cottage industry' basis. Such companies remain very small and often have long periods of inactivity between productions. 'It used to be called a cottage industry', explains industry producer veteran Stephen Evans (*Much Ado about Nothing, Madness of King George*). 'Being an independent producer is now like working out of a cupboard, inside a bedroom, at the top of the cottage.'

Distribution role set for change within the film value chain

Historically, film distribution has been the main risk-taker in the film value chain. It has acted as a 'gatekeeper', essentially selecting and determining which films get made, marketed and distributed. The distributor – whether a Hollywood Studio or a powerful integrated foreign company – has invested (or co-invested rather than putting up 100 per cent of a budget) in production costs, and has borne the majority of the prints and advertising costs (e.g. marketing costs). In turn, the distributor has been the principal beneficiary of success in the marketplace. Distributors enter into sliding-scale deals in exhibition, royalty deals in home entertainment and perform-ance-related deals in pay-TV, etc. A studio recovers its marketing costs in first position and takes significant distribution fees before passing any revenues back to the producer or his/her sales agent. This pivotal role has arisen because of the specific economic characteristics of the film industry. Huge rising costs on production and marketing, the high failure rate and, until recently, the capacity constraints in exhibition, have all enabled the distributor to remain a powerful gatekeeper: the key lynch-pin that dictates the majority of what gets made, and who gets what.

The above model is under increasing pressure to change. The arrival of direct links between the producer and the consumer, in particular via the Internet, is now fundamentally changing the economic characteristics, but also its architecture. Production and publishing roles, as per the music and book publishing models, are becoming increasingly important at the cost of distribution's previously dominant position. Just as television broadcasters are being forced to adapt to a consumer who wants a pro-gramme instantly, rather than follow a forced schedule (or anachronistically copy a show for later viewing), so too is the distributor finding pressure on what the film consumer demands within their own pressurized leisure time zones, rather than what suits the distributor's time scale of delivery.

The potential transformation is unlikely to have a significant impact on all sectors of the film business. For example, mainstream studio product is likely to continue to be produced and distributed in a similar manner over the next decade – in particular product aimed at the core 16–24-year-old market. But it is the potential tightening of the film value chain, whereby the producer is brought much closer to the consumer (and hence the revenue streams being recouped), that is of significant interest. Niche audiences, once able to be tapped and marketed directly, have significant value if able to be reached less expensively. Communities offer the potential for fan bases and, on occasion, significant commercial core audiences.

The new industry architecture

Alongside the 'opening' of the market, with the distributor's role potentially being taken over on either side – by both the producer and the exhibitor – it is reasonable to surmise that new kinds of investors may become interested in investing in film and content. These new opportunities are of interest to large, retail brands, for example, looking for new sponsorship and marketing opportunities.

Ultimately, Internet marketing and its growth in sophistication and specific demo-graphic reach, will encourage end-users such as cinema owners and chains, pay-TV operators and even video game operators to enter the production market themselves. Global aggregators, such as Google and Apple, may also decide to prime the pump. A world where these players commission development and feature films which in turn help drive their respective platforms will cut out third-party distribution completely. The cost of marketing will be borne by the production financier rather than be carried over to the distributor.

The new film value chain is likely to become considerably truncated and simplified. Theatrical release of feature film product will continue to play a dominant role. However, the complex system of connected windows for exploitation is going to look considerably flatter. Within a few years, it is going to appear as in Figure 2.1.

The architecture of making a film, from development to exploitation, is a key way of analysing the value chain. Extreme uncertainty underlines the recoupment struc-ture. A number of academic studies have concluded that the distribution of sales, profits and returns in the film business looks odd. Actually, they follow a 'power law' of distribution: the 80:20 rule. This was first applied to the distribution of income, where the economist Vilfredo Pareto noted that 20 per cent of the population earned around 80 per cent of the income. Since that observation, the regularity of this unequal distribution has been noted in many other spheres of activity, in particular recently in analysis of Internet traffic. For example, the top 5 per cent of Internet blog sites account for around 50 per cent of the total blog traffic.

Power law distributions look very different to normal (often referred to as 'bell curve') distributions. Extraordinary and exceptional events that dictate and affect the performance and awareness of product help dictate the power law environment. Standard risk management procedures do not apply to film investment models.

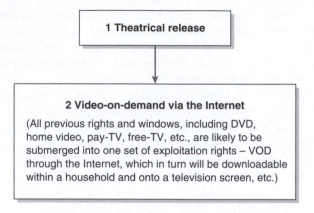

Figure 2.1 New film exploitation value chain.

A further significant barrier to investment and growth is the structure of the film exploitation value chain with regards to recoupment. The author, when pitching to a merchant banker a business model for a film production and sales company, was taken to one side, and politely drawn on a blackboard a bucket. From that bucket sprang numerous leaks. What the merchant banker explained is that while the sales arm of the production company was higher up the bucket, the overall business model was unattractive due to the inherent high commissions, lost incomes and 'leakage' in the model.

Taking the merchant banker's observations further, it is instructive to consider the cost of recoupment (Table 2.3).

Players within the value chain

All major global industries are dominated by key players, whether they take the form of powerful individuals, significant companies or multi-national corporations. The film business offers three significant magnets to potential high-fliers: its global scope and reach; its thirst to find and develop creative talent; and the oft-stated but rarely realized potential of hit-propelled profits. This heady mix tends to attract a volatile and eclectic crowd. Very few make it to any kind of elite.

Real influence is relative and ever shifting, and can range from those players who command territorial domination in a key sector, to those who control multi-nationals that operate a wide range of media interests, of which film is just one arm. Whether these 'key players' are creative individuals, leading industry principals, independent companies or multi-national corporations, a grasp of 'who does what' in which sector(s) is fundamental to a wider understanding of how the 'the business' operates.

In our current information-loaded, celebrity-focused media environment, major studio heads, top executives and leading filmmakers garner considerably more press attention when compared to the founding players of the Hollywood Studio system a century ago. It is important, therefore, to continue to distinguish between powerful individuals, and dominant companies and major corporate entities.

Individuals and in certain cases, smaller companies, can react quickly and, if required, reinvent themselves. The larger the corporate entity, the longer it can take

Table 2.3 The leaking bucket: the value chain's cost of recoupment

Model: an independent movie

Assumptions:

i) US distribution is through Major specialist arm
ii) Foreign sold/handled by an international sales company
iii) Back end is a 50–50 split between financiers and producer re net profits (after negative cost of the film has been repaid and all fees/costs have been paid out....)

	US side of exploitation	Revenue flow
Fee	US distributor: interest and overhead charge on advance (override): 10% minimum, can be as much as 18–20%.	
Fee/cost	TV sales (30–40% of income given to distributor).	
Fee/cost	DVD duplication and marketing costs (royalty to you of 15–20% unless you can achieve a better deal).	
Fee/cost	Prints and advertising costs against the theatrical release in all territories with interest and override.	
Fee	35% distribution commission against rental figure of between 40 and 50% income stream to distributor.	
	Foreign sales side of exploitation	
Fee	10–25% sales commission on all foreign territories, 5–10% against the US sale.	
Fee/cost	$150,000 minimum sales and marketing costs in foreign (but likely to be $200,000).	
Fee	1–1.5% collection agent on all revenues collected.	
	Individual distributor deals in 'foreign'	
Fee	Distributor: interest and overhead charge on advance (override): 10% minimum.	
Fee/cost	TV sales (30–40% of income given to distributor).	
Fee/cost	DVD duplication and marketing costs (royalty to you of 15–20% unless you can achieve a better deal).	
Fee/cost	Prints and advertising costs against the theatrical release in all territories, with interest and override.	
Fee	35% distribution commission against the rental figure of approximately 30–45% income stream, but as low as 25% in the United Kingdom.	

Source: Angus Finney (from a range of industry sources).

for its principals and Board to move the ship and point the behemoth in a different, more profitable direction. However, companies 'built to last' far outrun the individuals who steered them for a period to, or at, the top.

The filmmakers

Significant players' influence may have originated, and sometimes continues to be, enshrined in the specific filmmaking process. Leading writers, producers and directors who create intellectual property rights and have the business acumen to control and exploit their brand, properties (and in particular franchises) can wield considerable power.

Top directors such as Steven Spielberg, George Lucas, Ron Howard and James Cameron are regular Hollywood names in power lists. Their power rests not solely as a result of their directing skills, but in their roles as producers, rights owners, shareholders, and, for some, their executive and non-executive board memberships. Most crucially, it is their place as market 'operators', who can heavily influence the filmmaking process and wider value of the companies or corporations that they either own or are attached to, that sets them apart from other dedicated filmmakers. By that same token, fully fledged movie stars who 'operate' across more of the business than their next movie, hold enormous sway, far beyond their daily media profile.

Leading producers share similar skills and spheres of influence. Hollywood has a small cadre of distinct A-list producers, including players like Jerry Bruckheimer, Brian Grazer, Larry Gordon, Joel Silver and Scott Rudin, who wield great influence over which films and product get made. In contrast to the executives who manage a worldwide studio operation, the above film producers/players certainly have *more* influence over specific film product green-lit each year than the apparatchiks who run the overall studio could ever manage to focus on.

The Studios and the barbarians

The persistence of a 'natural monopoly' in the form of the six Hollywood Studios, which continue to dominate the majority share of the worldwide production and distribution markets for movies, is under considerable pressure today. Historically, the Studios' access to heavyweight distribution has provided them with control over the film value chain. They have represented the tallest, strongest 'gatekeepers' of the system. The Studios have long had to suffer barbarians at their gate, in the form of a significant independent sector. But those gates are currently being beaten more firmly than ever before in the shape of digitization and the global Internet. The first fundamentally changes the economics of who can afford to make a film; the second changes the way the audience can reach and see it.

While the above debate is scrutinized in considerable depth in later chapters of this book, the independent sector is a hugely significant player in the market. More than $3bn of independent film sales is made each year outside the Hollywood Studios' production sector. The independent sector, according to Cass's Terry Ilott, performs three key functions:

> First, it increasingly provides productions for distribution, whether by the Hollywood Studios or by independent distributors. Second, it accounts for a significant proportion of the distribution market for English language films (including American independent productions) around the world. Third, it dominates the production and distribution of local-language films, the popularity and profitability of which is growing in some key territories.[3]

The European surge

Specifically, Europe's leading film production and distribution companies, some of which are now reaching maturity, offer a significant challenge to the Hollywood Studios' traditional hegemony over the Continent and the United Kingdom. Such companies include players like the international player Lionsgate (although its parent is Canadian), Momentum, Entertainment Film Distributors and most recently Optimum (owned by Studio Canal) in the United Kingdom; Constantin and Tobis in Germany; Studio Canal, Pathe, Gaumont, EuropaCorp, Metropolitan and Wild Bunch in France; Sogedesa and TriPictures in Spain; A-Film in the Benelux countries; and Scanbox and Nordisk in Scandinavia. Each of them is addressing a changing, expanding market and they are taking the Studios on, head to head.

On a wider scale, over less than a generation, the change across Europe is most marked by domestic films attracting local audiences in a manner that many could only dream of in the mid-1990s. According to the European Audiovisual Observatory, many countries reporting strong growth in admissions in 2006 also registered excellent performances by domestic films. As a result the overall market share for European films in the European Union reached 27.6 per cent, compared to a marginal 15 per cent in 1996.

Breaking down the players

As a device for exploring and analysing key players, ten groups examining different leading film-related sectors are shown in Table 2.4 (overleaf). The groups are certainly not exhaustive, but when taken together, they serve to provide a framework that introduces the major players.

Table 2.4 Key players in the film business: a breakdown

1 Creative players	2 Company players (small/medium)	3 Vertically integrated companies	4 Finance players	5 National powerhouses that have wider international market impact
Authors and screenwriters Directors (and writer/directors) Creative producers Talent 1 – stars/ actors Talent 2 – creative producers, e.g. director of photography, editor, etc. [Agents and managers, as representatives of key creative talent]	Production companies – led by business/creative producer or team Sales companies (aka sales agents or international distributors) Distribution companies (normally within a 'national' territory) Specialist cinemas, screens/chains	Production/finance/sales/ marketing/distribution companies Distribution/exhibition companies Specialist ancillary distribution companies TV production/film production companies	Equity players – as investors Equity players – as financiers Tax/cash flow financing players Banks – as financiers Subsidy players/pan, national and regional/ US state specific Broadcasters Distributors –aka as 'buyers' [Agents – as packagers] [Lawyers – as producer/financier tool] Note: 'finance' and 'equity/investment' are often mixed up. Certain finance players are pure 'investors' in film in return for rights/income streams. Others are 'financiers', meaning that they assist with cash flow through discounting and gap funding rather than direct equity investments (e.g. banks). Broadcasters normally acquire licence rights, but some also invest equity.	Leading non-Hollywood companies – normally vertically integrated. Examples within the European Union include Pathé, Europa, Svensk, Gaumont, UGC, Rai Cinema, Egmont Nordisk, etc.

(Continued)

Table 2.4 (Continued)

6 Public funds – national and pan-European	7 Hollywood Studios	8 Leading international independent players	9 Major exhibition chains	10 New players emerging via 'connected' market delivery systems
The European Union's MEDIA programme – loans for development, sales, distribution, etc. The European Commission's Eurimages co-production support mechanism for production loans National film subsidy bodies, e.g. UK Film Council, Irish Film Board, Centre National du Cinéma (France), Dutch Film Fund, the national Scandinavian/ Nordic funds (territories), the Nordic Film Fund (pan-Nordic), etc.	MPA members SONY (controlling Columbia Tristar, MGM, United Artists, Sony Pictures Classics, etc.); DISNEY (including Walt Disney, Touchstone, Buena Vista, and most recently, Pixar); WARNERS (controlling New Line, HBO Films); PARAMOUNT (controlling DreamWorks, MTV, Paramount Vantage); UNIVERSAL (controlling Focus, Working Title); FOX (including Fox Searchlight), etc.	The Weinstein Company, Lions Gate, Summit Entertainment, Village Roadshow, Overture, The Film Department, Metropolitan, Gaumont, Pathé, Studio Canal, Nordisk, Sogetel, Scanbox, Entertainment Film Distributors, Momentum, etc.	US: AMC (American Multi-Cinemas), Regal Entertainment Group, Century, Loews Cineplex, Carmike Cinemas (lead in digital), Redstone (National Amusements), UltraStar, Cinemark and Marcus Corporation. European Union: Europalaces, Odeon/UCI, Cineworld Cinemas, Kinepolis, Egmont/Nordisk Asia Pacific: Toho (Japan), Hoyts (Australia), PVR (India), CGV (South Korea)	To include: Apple, Google, Yahoo, AOL, British Telecom, Amazon, Netflix, Ericsson, Nokia, Vodaphone, Motorola, etc. Advancing conent web players – YouTube, MySpace, etc.

Source: A. Finney.

3 Film development

> I always look for a good story. That sounds very simplistic, but you'd be surprised – it is the most difficult thing to find.
>
> (Producer Kathleen Kennedy, president
> of Amblin Entertainment)
>
> The basic art of motion pictures is the screenplay; it is fundamental, without it there is nothing.
>
> (Raymond Chandler)

Introduction to film development

Development is the chronological starting point for all producers, writers, writer/directors and many directors who do not actually 'write' screenplays when embarking on the film process. It is the place that ideas, stories and projects start their lives. From there, early-stage conceptions need to be stimulated and nourished, and driven forwards through a range of different stages. As such, the development stage of a film project is the bedrock to subsequent film activities, including production, financing, packaging, distribution, marketing and the subsequent film exploitation process.

When professionals refer to 'development' in most industries, they are normally referring to 'R&D', meaning 'research and development'. This can be described as an upfront, long-term investment normally involving considerable sunk costs that are unlikely to be returned quickly, or in many cases, at all. Nevertheless, long-term planning and the opportunity costs associated with building a strong product and an occasional discovery are deemed critical to a healthy industrial model. However, development within the film industry – and in particular development outside the Hollywood Studio system – operates within a much more precarious infrastructure.

For the purposes of this book, development activity is defined as the work that surrounds the initial concept or story idea, the acquisition of that idea, the screenwriting process, the raising of development finance and the initial stage of production planning. In addition to the seeking out of either original ideas or secondary source material (meaning books, articles, etc.), development is traditionally considered to encompass the writing of treatments. These are normally documents consisting of around ten pages of story outline without dialogue. A treatment is used to map out a story or concept, and for potential parties to consider if that story or concept is of interest to develop further into a screenplay.

Following a treatment, some writers opt to develop a step outline, which blocks out each scene of a screenplay but does not include (normally) dialogue of the characters. This helps provide a further guide to the writer when they come to flesh out the story into a full screenplay. However, the document most used to raise development support (partners and money) is the treatment, rather than a step outline.

Once a writer embarks upon the screenwriting stage, they are normally commissioned in a series of 'steps'. A typical deal would be for a writer to be commissioned to write two drafts and a 'polish'. At that point the producer (and development financier, if separate) has the option to appoint a new writer. However, the standard UK Writers Guild agreement has seven stages of payment: two for the treatment (commencement and completion), two for the first draft, two for the second draft and one on principal photography. Only 20 per cent of the overall payment structure is dedicated to the treatment stage, a factor that some industry analysts raise as a real barrier to the seriousness of the story and concept being written out and tested as fully as possible prior to the script being written.

In addition to the screenwriting process, it should be noted that the raising of finance and the initial planning of production (in particular the stage prior to formal pre-production) are all essential elements of the development process. Development activity includes the time (a key factor that is nearly always underestimated) and the money spent in building a project into a package, which requires attracting talent, including the marketing of the concept to potential directors (if not attached already), cast and financiers. Technically, locations, casting and line budgets are not normally seen as part of the development process, but often a project will need, for example, at least one lead actor, in order to drive the project from development into pre-production.

The early stages of development

The initial idea stage is a loosely structured area with a considerable number of possibilities. An idea may take a variety of routes towards a full screenplay commission. The flow system in Figure 3.1 shows some of the different routes that are often taken.

The initial idea of a script [1] can be an idea, a treatment, or a first draft screenplay. Unsolicited scripts from unknown (or unrepresented) writers [2] will in the majority of instances move through to a reader first [3]. Readers are professionally employed script 'reviewers' who have to follow a set of relatively standardized rules and form-filling. These normally include: a logline; a one-page synopsis; and then a critique of the script that includes the relative strengths and weaknesses of the story, the commercial appeal, the dialogue, the time and setting, the pace and emotional value of the script, etc.

Most unsolicited screenplays will be rejected. A very small percentage will come through as an idea [1] from development. Ideas also come from contacts [4]; a pitch by [5] or commission to [6] a known/established screenplay writer; or from the buying of book option [7]. A large number of creative producers generate ideas themselves [8]. The producer will then normally assess the essential idea/concept through a combination of taste, creative assessment, 'hook', possible cast, director, locations,

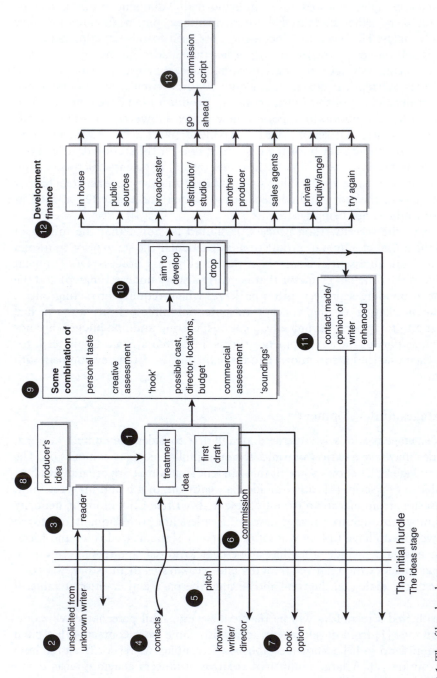

Figure 3.1 The film development process
(Source: National Film and Television School / A. Finney).

interiors and budget [9]. On this basis, the producer may decide to go ahead with the development, or to drop the project [10]. His/her decision often depends on whether the idea and writer can be 'set up' at a development home (in the independent market, this would include a broadcaster or subsidy player; in Hollywood it would mean a Studio or well-financed independent production company) [11].

To develop an idea, a producer will either have access to their own finance or secure third-party finance [12]. This can come from an in-house source, from a public development fund, a broadcaster, a private financier, a distributor or the producer themselves. It should be noted that certain independent producers prefer not to set up projects at the early stage of development, as this ties both them and the rights to a particular financier. 'It's always better to see if you can either convince a writer, or find the money to kick a screenplay off, rather than depend on a third party from the outset', explains producer Andrew Macdonald. 'That way you really are the producer of the screenplay.'[1]

The producer also has to make a commitment in terms of time, energy, planning and focus; often incurring considerable expense through travelling to potential partners, financiers, markets and festivals. He/she will have to put a development budget together at an early stage. In addition, another producer or potential co-financier may assist with development finance. Once the finance structure has been at least part-raised, the idea will normally move into a fully fledged development stage. This normally includes a first and second draft, one polish [13] and the active raising of awareness and a potential 'package' prior to formal financing.

Development as a high-risk activity

Figure 3.1 appears to provide the impression that there is a straightforward, standardized route for developing ideas into screenplays, and then on to the market. However, the fact is that feature film development is an inexact and high-risk activity. Most production companies are, by their nature, heavily involved in the development process. And most film projects that start their life in active development fail to make it to the principal photography stage. While there are many different ways and routes to move a film project towards production, one element remains consistent throughout the independent film business: development is a high-risk stage of film production. There are no guarantees of a project's successful journey from idea through to treatment and subsequent drafts, from screenplay that is signed off by a director, and on to production – then distribution and exhibition, and finally to what should be the ultimate goal: an audience.

Development of feature film projects is a relatively expensive area of risk investment. With reference to Chapter 2, The film value chain, we see how far the development activity and initial seed money is from the final end-user. Not only is the development stage distanced from the exploitation stage, but it requires considerable sunk costs to even bring a project to the point of potential financing. For example, a European film with a budget of around €2–4m may cost between €50,000 and €150,000 at a minimum to develop to the point of official pre-production. Larger budget films of around €7–10m may cost as much as €300,000 to move through development and into production.

The US independent marketplace, by contrast, tends to be more ad hoc and opportunistic: many writers and directors in the early stages of their career are more set on getting a first feature into production than following a linear, albeit limited, development structure. And with the absence of public funds and broadcaster support systems, the US independent filmmakers' entry points are on the one hand harder regarding the lack of financial support, but more open to the commercial whim of the open market. Within both approaches, the surrounding but strategically central elements to the scriptwriting process itself tend to be ignored or at least downplayed. These include research and acquisitions of rights for source material (often ignored or treated casually at the early stage by new writers and filmmakers, at their peril often later down the line), treatment development, the building of a 'package', the raising of finance, the positioning of the package to the relevant part of the international market, and the costs of paying script editors or hiring additional writers.

Independent film producers have traditionally seen development costs and time spent on the process in relation to their projected return from production fees (if not forced to be part or fully deferred) and potentially retained rights. The preoccupation with production has mainly stemmed from the fact that when producers are in production, they are being paid. This approach has tended to obscure the financial and practical elements essential to a concrete and healthy development process. Crucially, it has also led the producer to take a less realistic, hard look at the projected 'value' of a project, and how to realize that value in the marketplace.

In addition to the fragmented economic model referred to previously, the European producer has also had to deal with the 'auteur' challenge. Part of Europe's idiosyncratic blind spot regarding development is an historical one, and stems from a very heavily developed 'auteur' culture, where film directors have enjoyed the majority of the power in the filmmaking process. This is particularly the case in France and French-speaking territories, and to a large extent in Spain, Italy and many smaller territories. The results of this dependence have led to feature films tending to be rescued in the cutting room by film editors rather than script editors before the main budget was spent. European writers, in particular, have tended to be marginalized by the auteur system, while producers have arguably lost out and have been seen as financial servants for the directors.

The Studio model

Most comprehensive models that offer a fully fledged, integrated development process are generally found within the Hollywood Studio system. Nearly all independent filmmakers lack Hollywood-type studio infrastructures. The independent sector rarely attracts the capital or larger entities with which to invest and manage development in an industrial manner. Individually run companies are forced to drive their ideas and screenplays from the bottom up and the potential for a 'national' film producer to recoup the costs of a production from that one territory alone is normally unfeasible. Most individual territories, in particular in Europe, are not large enough to recoup the negative cost of a film's budget. And those international territories that are large enough to fund and recoup within – including for example Japan and South Korea – tend to drive highly domestic product that rarely sells or travels across the global market.

'On-the-block' development deals – where a production company is attached to a studio – hardly exist in Europe, mainly because there are no studios operating on the same scale as Hollywood. A major studio or major film production company with direct links to distribution normally treats development as a fixed cost within its overall annual budget and longer term business plan. A portion of this expenditure is allocated to each film as an above-the-line cost. In Hollywood, the Studios tend to place development costs at around 8–10 per cent of a film's total budget. Hollywood's development to production success ratio is very low, with estimates placing it at around one in twenty projects making production. By contrast, around one in five or six screenplays is placed into production with the European system.[2]

At its simplest, hit films that go on to make a profit repay the costs of unmade screenplays and projects. Profits are then pumped back into the development system, and the cycle of production is continued. Estimates place the Studio system's annual spend on development at more than $1bn. 'That is what Europe is competing with', producer David Puttnam points out. 'It is administered by very experienced executives working at an energy level almost unknown in Europe. It is fed by a very aggressive and well-run agency system at every level. The process is on a different planet.'[3]

On closer examination, the Studio system and its approach to development is far from linear. A typical Hollywood development department would generally be handling around 20–30 solicited ideas and scripts from numerous sources. These ideas would emerge from movies, TV shows, books (fiction, non-fiction and biography), articles, plays and comic strips, etc. Executives working within this system have their own approach to seeking out material: some are 'pitch driven', and want a story or idea told to them during a meeting; others are material driven, and want time to read a treatment or story outline along with background material. Some act like producers and come up with new ideas for which they then find a writer to come on board and commission.

One senior Studio executive described the aspects of her job as follows:

> I spend every waking hour thinking about what might be a good movie. I talk to as many people as I can to find new ideas. People call all the time with pitches. If certain people call me with a specific movie pitch, I schedule an hour with them to hear the story … . I have found over the years that there is no sense in buying something that I'm not personally invested in. We spend so much time developing these ideas into scripts and then movies, that it is important to love the idea. After buying an idea, the next step is developing a workable script. That can take months, or even years. We work closely with the screenwriter and help line up the director and key actors, as the script gets closer to completion.[4]

The social network of contacts, friends, and the flow of information within the Studio system is essential glue to this industrialized development process. But there are inherent pitfalls and dangers within this highly pressurized and competitive sector. Stay too close to the same people, and the ideas may become less fresh. Become dependent on the same teams of talent and you can run the risk of becoming tired and uninventive. 'When you stick to the same collaborators for too long you may run out of creative frictions', observes director Peter Weir.[5]

Whilst the above structures, all tightly organized around weekly development and approval meetings, appear solid and focused, there are well-documented (both formally and informally) weaknesses in the above system. By taking into account the recent history of each film's performance, and, crucially, by depending on a marketing department's assessment of a package and previous data on starts, director, genre, etc., there is a pervasive tendency for development executives to either say 'no', or fire writers and hire a new one, or veer at the start of the process to distinctly homogenized fare for fear of stepping outside the wagon circle. They need, after all, to look as if they are doing something.

Independent producers close to the Studio system tend to treat independent sources of finance in a similar manner to a Studio, albeit at a different level of financial support. While an on-the-lot, in-house producer will normally have an office, an overhead, a 'quote' price for his/her production fee, and a development budget agreed with a Studio, an independent producer off-the-lot will seek a development fee (normally in the range of $25,000–$40,000) as they prepare to work with a financier/indie house on an agreed project. No such system operates in this manner outside the mature independent marketplace in the USA.

The writers' place in film development

The key starting point for every feature film is the 'idea'. The creative concept of what will make a potential film lies at the centre of development. In turn, the writer is at the heart of the creative development process. In many cases, he/she will either initiate an idea for an original screenplay, or suggest an adaptation of an existing book or work. The writer may develop an outline of 1–2 pages, or a more fully fledged treatment of 10–15 pages before approaching a producer. (Sometimes the producer will write out the outline and then seek out the appropriate writer.) More experienced writers are approached by producers to adapt their ideas for a film or to work on a story for which the producer owns the adaptation rights. In contrast to the Studio system, few non-Hollywood writers work on teams or even in pairs. Many writers in Europe have emerged from television or theatre, and have often written long-form literature such as novels and non-fiction books.

Above all, many writers for independent cinema are isolated and unconnected from the main arteries of the film business. Few are 'networked' into the channels that would help move their projects through development and into production. Above all, they often lack close and trusting relationships with film producers capable of stable conditions both creatively and economically. Indeed, according to the Federation of Screenwriters in Europe:

> it is often the case that writers write scripts 'on spec' (without a specific commission), and often accept low or non-existent payment for early stage development in order to try to assist projects into development. Fees paid for actual development or production rarely take into account the level of high-investment by writers into projects which often do not even go into production. In effect, writers often subsidise project development.[6]

By way of contrast, it is relevant to compare the television fiction development process that is normally followed by the Anglo-centric model. Generally, the producer initiates an idea, and then commissions a writer to draft both an outline and screenplay drafts. In order to facilitate both payment and a potential market for the project/series, the producer normally sets the project up with a national broadcaster after they have approved the outline. No director is considered at this point. Only after considerable drafts, during which the producer gives significant creative input, is a director even considered to be attached to the project. This process is not to denigrate the role of the director – but underlines the critical importance of the concept, script(s), and the overall creative thrust of the project as derived by the partnership of the producer and writer (or writing team). 'The director is of course vital once they come on board, but they don't guide and shape the creative material from the start, ' explains *The Queen* and *Wallender* TV and film producer Andy Harries. 'It's the producer's responsibility.'[7]

Script editing

The role of the script editor is generally embraced within the Hollywood system. In the United Kingdom, script editors are often used, but they tend to be trained and employed only within the broadcast sector, and are normally working in this discipline as a route up the ladder to writing, producing or directing. Experienced script editors are not generally employed on the Continent for feature film work, although work through the MEDIA's ACE and EAVE programmes has lowered some of the resistance with positive effect. Programmes adopted by some emerging territories, such as the South African National Film and Video Foundation's screenwriting strategy, have championed the stepped approach and actively included the role of the script editor, with interesting results regarding the improvement of screenplay quality emerging from the Foundation's slate.

A strong script editor can quickly spot structural holes in a screenplay. Problems with a screenplay can be solved earlier with the help of an editor, saving both time and money later in the production and post-production process. 'A script that is far too long and ends up being shot is a disaster', says producer Bernd Eichinger. 'Of course you can shoot it, and cut it in the editing room, but in the case of a big, $30m film, you are cutting away $10m that you could have saved in the first place.'[8]

Professional script editors are not executives or freelancers who simply provide 'coverage'. The coverage, normally executed in the form of a generally standardized script report, is used by executives, producers and even directors to pre-select (or pass on) material that they may be interested in working on or taking to a further stage of investment. Strong, high-marked coverage may simply mean that a project has been brought to an executive or producer's attention. It does not necessarily mean that they have read the screenplay themselves.

The varying roles of the film producer

While the screenwriter is at the heart of the development process, the producer should be right there next to him or her, supporting and driving the process. Producers often initiate films, raise the money for rights to adapt ideas and material, hire the screenwriter(s) and during the process, constructively analyse and develop the script drafts in partnership with the writer(s). Producers rarely write or heavily re-write screenplays. Ideas, and in certain cases, editing or restructuring is one task; fully fledged writing is quite another. One of the key jobs of a producer is to work out how to make his/her writer write better.

The film industry tends to divide producers into two vaguely defined camps: the 'creative' producer and the 'financial' producer (see Chapters 16 and 17 for further analysis). Few practitioners are uniquely talented in both disciplines. Theoretically, an effective producing combination is one where two people – one creatively skilled and one financially astute and capable – work together on developing and producing projects, and building a sustainable company. Other experienced producers build a team of varying talents around them that complement and enhance their operation. For example, Jeremy Thomas has built a team that includes a highly capable manager and financial operator in Peter Watson; an experienced creative development executive in the late Hercules Belville; and a leading sales executive in Tim Haslam, who manages Hanway, the sales arm of Thomas's film activities. Whilst Thomas drives the selection of ideas, projects, writers and directors, he is constantly in touch with these key executives, who in turn help shape his slate and future business. That said, Thomas tends to always develop with a director attached from the start of the development process – making the director the central filmmaker from the start.

The term 'executive producer' is often applied to the producer who takes a specific role in co-financing a feature. However, over the past decade the term has become much abused. Executive producer credits have been insisted upon in return for early development commitments, or early attachment without active responsibility for the filmmaking process. Credits are insisted upon for relatively small and straightforward contributions to a film's overall financial package. American independent films sometimes credit more than half a dozen executive producers or more, somehow denigrating the credit itself. Public funds and their executives can also be an issue. Heads of funds can elect to either take a credit or pass on a credit. Above all, lead film producers should know the details of the financial aspects of their project and not delegate ultimate financing responsibility to an executive producer.

The creative producer

One of the key functions of the creative producer is to develop a strong set of relations with talent. Whilst directors and actors are important, the writer is where the development process kicks into action. Producers normally build up a trust and understanding over a considerable period of time with writing talent. Whether it comes through story ideas, structural suggestions or an ability to help the writers improve their work, the producer needs to have the writer's respect and trust.

Creative producers read solicited, and in many cases, unsolicited scripts, treatments and story outlines. These normally come to them either through writers, writer/directors, talent agents, contacts or friends. In addition, the producer will have his/her own ideas and sources. The creative producer develops relationships with publishers, and attempts to see advance book lists and upcoming proofs and work as soon as possible. It they think that a book has potential for a screenplay, an option may be paid to the author of that work to protect the right to adapt it for a film. Normally, that option is for a specific period, after which the option lapses and the screenplay rights revert to the author of the original work. Many producers take out a two to three year option on a work, or option for less time but with automatic renewals. Options are normally renewed because the development process has demonstrated progress and the producer believes that the project can reach fruition.

The creative producer also develops strong relationships with writers, actors and directors (and agents and managers who represent such talent). Above all, it is their flair and competence when dealing with and attaching talent that helps them develop successfully. This area marks out the importance of the balance between the producer, the writer and the director (if the writer is not also the director). The skill of passing a project from a writer on to the appropriate director lies at the heart of the producer's role. Managing creative egos and sensibilities is a highly complex task, and the producer will often need to keep the writer and the director separate for a period of development, rather than expose a director's viewpoint too directly upon the writer. In addition, no writer wants to hear solely from a head of development or a script editor; he or she wants to have the attention of the producer and direct feedback where possible.

The financial producer

The 'financial' producer is the person responsible for bringing together the different elements of the film's budget. Like the creative producer they too are aware of the relative 'value' of the project. That means that they need to know how much the different 'elements' , including the book or source material, the writer, the director, the cast and the genre if appropriate, are worth in the marketplace. The financial producer will have a strong understanding of previous performance of the aforesaid elements; and will have box office and sales figures on previous films, genres and performance around the world. All this information helps the producer build a convincing 'pitch' for the positioning of a film in the financing and distribution marketplace.

It is the financial producer who should know all the different international sales companies, key distributors in different territories, private equity and banking finance sources, public subsidy funds – both national and supra-national – and key executives within the medium and larger film production/distribution companies around the world. They need to know how different institutions and business cultures operate, and, critically, which people make decisions within them. This will include not just chief executives, but assistants, script editors, development executives, marketing executives, etc. All projects need support and champions to gather momentum, and a strong producer needs to build a case for a project.

A key element of this process is 'testing' in the marketplace. This process requires considerable contacts, and the ability to gauge the right time to launch a project. The objective is to determine whether the marketplace will support a project, or whether a screenplay and package do not add up. This is not to suggest that the market's determination is universally empirical or scientifically 'correct'. Many world-famous hit projects that went on to box office success were widely rejected at their early or packaged stages. Others that appeared to appeal can fall at the final financing stage due to inherent problems and weaknesses that only become apparent at the point that financiers and distributors are forced to become partners and make commitments in order for a film to enter production.

Financiers and distributors only tend to read once. Sending out incomplete, early drafts, or projects without crucial elements such as a director or key cast attached, wastes executives' time. A producer normally only has one bite of the cherry. Waiting until a screenplay is well developed, with strong attachments, will normally pay considerable dividends. As Nick Manzi, an experienced head of acquisitions at Lionsgate points out: 'I won't look at a film until it's got everything I need to make an assessment – including the cast, the director and the budget. Otherwise I am wasting everyone's time, including my own.'

Case study: *The Name of the Rose*

The *Name of the Rose* is a $30m European film, based on the classic novel by Italian author Umberto Eco. The film remains one of the most complex European productions ever financed and produced, and also became one of the most commercially successful – notably across the Continent. Producer Bernd Eichinger and director Jean-Jacques Annaud provided a European Film Academy Master Class about the development and making of the film, which the author attended.

The background to the film

The story of the making of *The Name of the Rose* – a screenplay adaptation of the highly complex novel written by Umberto Eco – is almost as overwrought as the near-600-page book itself. French film director Jean-Jacques Annaud became aware of the novel's existence while promoting his film *Quest for Fire* in the Caribbean in 1982. He read an article in *Le Monde* about the novel, which caught his attention because the subject matter was similar in nature to his studies, which had focused on medieval history. Through a friend, Annaud succeeded in getting hold of a translation of the book, and after 60 pages of reading, he was personally convinced that he wanted to make a film from the story:

> I flew immediately to Rome, because I knew that the rights were owned by RAI television, so I went to see the president of production. I asked him who the director was for *The Rose*, and he said that they didn't know. I said, 'It's me.'

Annaud initially worked with a French producer, but the relationship fell apart when it became clear that the producer was a frustrated director and was not able to focus on developing *The Rose*. Despite this handicap, Annaud had to honour the deal, and he started to work on the initial screenplay version of the book.

Meanwhile, German producer and distributor Bernd Eichinger had read the novel in German, and was keen to acquire the distribution rights. He was too late to compete for the option, but he pursued the project and tracked Annaud down to enquire about the project's progress. (Annaud and Eichinger knew each other through *Quest for Fire*, which Eichinger's company, Neue Constantin, had distributed in German-speaking territories.) Although it was clear at that stage that the film was likely to be a French-lead production, Eichinger left the door open, saying that if Annaud ran into trouble later, he should come back to him.

'I sensed that this project would be very large and complex to shoot because it was a sophisticated and entirely European subject matter, involving murder and comedy derived from Aristotle', explained Eichinger.

> There were many elements that were not obviously commercial, including the monastery setting in the fourteenth century; and yet it was clearly a very expensive movie, so you had to think about the American market. I thought that Jean-Jacques would come back. Fortunately for me, but sadly for him, his French producer was shot.

Adapting the novel

Annaud worked on nine initial screenplay drafts, but he found the novel extremely difficult to adapt. The 560 pages of complex material did not lend itself obviously to a movie-going audience. 'I hated my first scripts, because there was no emotion. It was too complex, and it was too long', recalled Annaud.

> By script draft nine, I knew I almost had the movie because I felt the major emotions, but there were still a number of scenes that had no muscle. If you start shooting a scene that doesn't read well, then it doesn't edit well. You can try to cut it, but that often doesn't work because you need the information. People might not have seen the difference between the screenplay number nine and eleven, because the story, order and characters are still the same. But the rhythm's different.

Annaud also faced a somewhat ironic problem. When the book rights had originally been optioned 'for peanuts', he had been certain that the book would remain a largely unknown treasure. However, the book took on a literary fame and life that made it famous in itself, even though many buyers were not actually reading the book from start to finish; laughed Annaud, 'It was the most unread best-seller ever.' Even Eco, by this stage a friend of the filmmaker, would agree that many people never actually completed the entire book.

Hence Annaud was already facing considerable problems by the time his French producer was shot down in a car park. The project was taken over by another French producer, who was uneasy about the state of the screenplay and the high budget, by now set at $35m. 'Everybody looked at me and said that I could make it for $12m', recalled Annaud. 'I said "No".'

A team was already scouting for locations by draft eleven, but they were proving impossible to find. Meanwhile, the director's life was gradually grinding to a halt. 'We're talking about two years of my life. Not being paid. Unable to pay taxes, or even go to restaurants any more. Then one day my producer sent the script to Bernd in Germany.' Eichinger came back with three options: 1) a distribution advance for German speaking rights; 2) a major advance to set the project up as a fully fledged co-production but involving German talent; or 3) for Eichinger and Neue Constantin to produce the entire film.

Further screenplay development in Germany

Annaud moved to Munich for 18 months. He recalls that this time was one of the best experiences in his life. 'This was because I was working with people who wanted to make the same film, and they weren't afraid of this monster movie. So I went in to see Bernd with the tenth draft of the screenplay. He said, "You know what, this screenplay isn't all that good."' Annaud agreed, and the writer/director and producer went to work on ultimately seven further versions, working with two writers, including Andrew Birkin, who later directed *The Cement Garden*.

The main problem that inhibited progress was the length. By draft ten, the story was still running at an epic three-and-a-half hours long. It was agreed that the length had to come down to two hours. 'Nobody can stand a three-and-a-half hour movie. Only the director thinks it's good enough to be that long, but most people don't. And it's very difficult to compress a story', explained Annaud.

By draft 11, Annaud had started to work on a storyboard for the film. Up to draft nine, the script was written in French. From draft nine to the final seventeenth screenplay draft, Annaud and his writing collaborators worked in English. Annaud stressed that while getting the script right is absolutely critical, the hard part is thinking in images rather than worrying about dialogue:

> European screenplays tend to have too much dialogue, and this is the reason why Continental European writers say that they cannot write in the English language. I don't think that is a problem. If the story is carried by images then you need to write with the right ones. Dialogue is important to an extent, but not as much as music, for example.

While Annaud worked on the screenplay drafts, Eichinger was finding it very difficult to raise finance for the production. The strength of the project, however, was that the natural story and its locations genuinely lent itself to a true European co-production – with monks from all over Europe coming together under one monastery's roof – and offering strong roles for British, French and Italian actors:

> Bernd had many moments when he must have thought I was crazy, when the only thing to do was to build this monastery. We knew that we couldn't compromise on quality, but at times he had to calm me down and make me realize the reality: there was a limit of money for this production in the international marketplace.

Eichinger stressed that although the raising of the film's budget was hard, the really long struggle was getting the screenplay into shooting shape:

> My respect for Jean-Jacques was growing. If you have a director who is writing the screenplay himself, then he gets tired and doesn't want to hear anything for a while. And he'd already done nine drafts before we'd met.

To help get the screenplay into shape, Eichinger hired two more writers, but it was still a year before it was ready to be sent out to financiers. Even at that point, Eichinger was nervous that it had been sent out too early, pointing out that distributors only read a script once and then have to bite. They never read any screenplay twice.

The importance of picking up the tempo is critical to a project at the packaging and financing stages. 'What you need is a "Yes" from actors and distributors around the world', something that is virtually impossible without a strong, fully completed screenplay. What *The Name of the Rose* had managed by this stage was some verbal commitments, but most of these only translated into actual pre-sales or financing deals once the script had been nailed. While the script was being further edited on a 24-hour basis, the monastery was being built on a hill near Rome, taking half a year, and costing more than $3m alone in build. As Annaud pointed out,

It's very unusual for producers to have the balls to invest so much money upfront, trusting that the screenplay will be right in six to eight months' time. And at the same time as writing, I was supervising the construction of this huge set.

The technological failure

Writing the script day and night on an Olivetti computer proved problematical, because the writing team did not have a computer print-out. One evening, Andrew Birkin hit the wrong button, and lost the entire screenplay. In a desperate effort to recover the pages, he pulled the plug out. When he plugged it in again, the script was gone. Efforts were made to open up the computer to retrieve the draft, but the script was not on the hard drive and was irretrievable.

Annaud and Birkin went downstairs to tell Eichinger about the fifteenth draft that now no longer existed. They had plane tickets to Los Angeles, meetings planned, and not even a relatively recent screenplay version available. 'You're just joking guys', laughed Eichinger. Birkin nearly passed out. Guilty, tired and depressed, Annaud and Birkin slunk off to a local nightclub. On their return to the office, they found a note, a big bunch of flowers and fruits from Eichinger, commiserating and encouraging them to start again. 'They did a great job, because they started right away on the new draft and it was completed in just two weeks', said Eichinger, pointing out that they were now printing out as they went along. At the point that the new draft was completed, no one was allowed to assume it was on a computer. The team used scissors and glue, and they 'carried the movie in a box full of paper'.

But the script was by now far more than just the lines on paper. Annaud has always storyboarded his films:

My films are already in my head, and if they're not, then I'm not ready to shoot. Some say this means that I can't possibly be inspired on set. That it's not artistic. But this mythology of the inspired director on set is all wrong. If it is all on paper, then my 250 people working for me know what each day is going to be about. It takes more time, but I feel that the film I have completed is the one I saw before shooting. Architects don't build skyscrapers without a drawing.

Eichinger managed to clinch a deal with Twentieth Century Fox for North American theatrical and television rights, along with worldwide video rights. The remaining financing was raised through pre-sales across the world and an equity investment by Neue Constantin. This might appear fairly uncomplicated, but this level of major pre-sales and a US partner upfront is very rare indeed in the current market. More than two decades ago, a North American deal was extremely hard for Eichinger to pull off on such unusual, European-centred material and cast. 'The phone calls were always "No"', Annaud recalled, 'Even though we still had a good time together, I knew Bernie hurt inside. In Europe, a lot of people are frightened by money, but it's the freedom to make a movie you really want.'

Annaud argued that the issues that so often come up about control over the script and ultimately the final edit of the film simply highlights the extremes between the European and American approach to filmmaking:

In Europe we have long said that it's the director alone; in America they say it's the producer alone. The truth doesn't lie on one side or the other, but in a harmonious mixture and understanding between the two. Most of the artistically and commercially successful movies ever made have been undertaken by a producer and director who understand each other, and have fought for the making of the movie for the same reason. Directors must never take the wrong producer, because the project will go nowhere. The extreme is in America, where there are ten producers all fighting over the same movie. Only the people who've created the movie know what it's going to be like – the writer, the producer and the director.

Starring Sean Connery and a youthful Christian Slater, *The Name of the Rose* opened on 14 September 1986 in North America, but the film attracted very mixed reviews. 'We were very disappointed', recalls Eichinger. 'It was the film's first territory, and it was a very cold shower for us.' A month later the film opened in Germany and it took off, attracting six million German-speaking admissions and taking more than $45m – and at that time breaking many box office records. The French release won more than seven million admissions; and Italy took a further five million. The film's performance across Europe was hugely successful, and the total box office gross topped $120 million, despite the nominal US performance.

4 Green lighting films

There is no such thing as an independent producer. There are dependent producers. Dependent on distributors, financiers and bankers, and distribution channels that understand the market even less than the corporations that own the studios ... . Perhaps even more than the studios, those with the controls over whether or not a movie gets made independent of the studios do so almost with less attention to the movie itself.

(Bill Mechanic, president/CEO of
Pandemonium LLC and former chair/CEO of
Fox Filmed Entertainment, IFTA keynote, 2009)

An introduction to green lighting

The film industry uses the term 'green lighting' for the moment a financier or set of financiers decide to move ahead, commit investment and place a film project into production. In a perfect world, that moment normally happens at a formal meeting, whose attendants in turn consider a set of criteria prior to taking a formal decision. Such a process would seem to be a rational approach to managing risk-investment decisions often in the many millions. The reality is rather different, and the actual process varies considerably from studios to mini-majors, and through to the myriad of sources of finance that make up the typical independent film's structure. This chapter explores some of the typical mistakes so often made in the independent system through the case of the author's former company, Renaissance Films.

For a Studio, most often responsible for 100 per cent of the budget (or at least 50 per cent through a split-rights deal), the decision will have taken place with all key heads of departments, including worldwide territory managers, who will supply revenue projections for their global regions. The one-stop shopping approach entailed by the Studio's ability to fully finance a film makes the green light process reasonably straightforward although there is still considerable resistance and second-guessing from owners and powerful executives along the way. By contrast, independent films are rarely triggered in such an orderly process, as their financing relies on a variety (sometimes a multitude) of sources of finance and investment. This complex web makes the task of 'closing' a film's finance particularly challenging when working in the independent sector.

Any green light decision requires information upon which a decision can be made. Prior to investing or committing finance, financiers will demand full details of a project's budget, cast, director, producer, finance plan, pre-sales, remaining sales estimates (or distribution projections, territory by territory, if a Studio) and estimated timing of delivery. If a recoupment order has been proposed by a producer, this too will form a critical part of the assumptions; but often financiers tend to use the exercise (colloquially referred to as 'running the numbers') in order to negotiate their recoupment position re other investors. This range of information is then placed into a spreadsheet (aka a 'control sheet') that relies predominantly on the sales estimates or territory projections, as these combined revenue streams are the key route to an investor/financier's being repaid.

Many independent sector green light decisions will include further hurdles that the management and the specific film project have to overcome before drawdown of investment is allowed. At times, a green light meeting's 'yes' decision may mean only a part of the film's finance is triggered, and the film's final move into principal photography is still dependent on other deals or green lights from other co-financing sources being closed or approved.

Many independently financed features crawl haphazardly through a vague green light stage, where in the words of Stephen Woolley, one of the most experienced UK producers, 'the producer starts, and everyone else catches up'.[1]

The practice of 'management by committee' and the wisdom of collective decision-making attract much criticism. The way current and previous Studio heads, by contrast, refer to their jobs speaks volumes about the centralized power they exercise to make decisions. 'My job running a studio was to make money', explained Bill Mechanic, former chairman and CEO of Fox Filmed Entertainment:

> My goal was to make good movies. When I did my job well, I made good movies that made money. The key to making decisions that don't blow up in your face is to understand the aims of the film and the filmmakers.[2]

The following in-depth case study examines some of the inherent problems, issues and consequences that arise when key green lighting decisions are made through a collective committee.

Case study: green lighting film productions at Renaissance Films

The call came in from Renaissance Film's finance director to Angus Finney; the company's co-managing director, just as he was set to board a plane in Malaga Airport following a summer break:

> We need to call a green light committee meeting as soon as you are back. I think we're going to need to do this film *Morality Play*. We're under a lot of pressure from the Board to use the investors' money and get productions going.

As his plane took off, Finney pondered the numerous issues and variables that would inevitably be raised and considered at the upcoming meeting. *Morality Play* (aka *The Reckoning*) was the third Renaissance film to be brought to the green light committee over the past year, but by far the most ambitious both in terms of production and budget.

Rules for how Renaissance Films placed films into production had been clearly mapped out in a business plan written by Finney and his partner Stephen Evans the previous year. The green lighting rules had been discussed at length by the management and the investor, Hermes, and they had been refined before the investment of £24.5m had been finalized. The investors and the management (also at risk for a combined £500,000 in shares) had jointly recognized that the green light system formed a critical part of the risk management of their investment decisions in movie productions.

Renaissance's green light committee was comprised of four executive directors, including the company's co-managing directors; the finance director and the director of sales; and three non-executive directors, including the Investor's representative and the company's chairman. Four votes (a simple majority) in favour of a green light decision would carry the day, as long as the film fulfilled *all* criteria within the rules. The Investor's representative had the power of a 'veto' if the four executive directors voted for a film, while the three non-executive directors voted against. The intention was that the committee operated a 'checks and balances' system. It was assumed that the existence of a veto would effectively guard against the management 'railroading' its film choices into production.

If a film that failed the criteria was to still receive a green light (albeit with one or more of the rules effectively broken), all seven committee members would have to vote in favour of going ahead. The rules as written out in the company's Articles of Association covered the following points:

- A film under consideration had to present a package containing the following elements: a script, budget, producer track record, director and two main cast actors. The package had to be satisfactory to the Committee. These documents needed to be made available at least ten days prior to the committee meeting.
- A reputable Completion Guarantor needed to have issued a letter of intent to bond the film's production and delivery at the budget level (less standard exclusions) submitted to the Committee.
- A minimum of 30 per cent of the film's total budget needed to be covered in either pre-sales to distributors, and/or co-financed by third-party investors. Such co-financing had to be in place prior to the green light decision.
- Satisfactory minimum sales projections from available territories indicating no less than a straight 100 per cent return on investment had to be provided by Renaissance's sales team.
- Any bank involved in cash-flowing a section of the finance, and/or 'gapping' up to 25 per cent of the film's budget, had to be pre-approved by the Committee.
- The Committee could not commit more than 50 per cent of a film's total budget; nor approve an investment of more than $10m in any one single film production.

Previous green lighting decisions

The two films previously green lit by the committee were *The Luzhin Defence* and *Disco Pigs*. *The Luzhin Defence* was a project already in advanced development when the new investment was secured. A 'go' project was deemed attractive by the investors. To their eyes, the film was a 'kick-start' to investment and production activity, and the chairman had agreed to 'shepherd' the film through the green lighting committee.

In terms of the green light criteria, *Luzhin* was well positioned. The screenplay was adapted from a classic novella. The producers were 'in-house'. The director and cast was deemed attractive enough for an $8.8m budget; and more than 30 per cent of the finance was originating from three co-production partners – France; The Netherlands and Italy.

(The Netherlands was later replaced by Hungary following a dispute between Renaissance and the Dutch producer, but the film still qualified as an official co-production under the European Convention on Cinematic Co-productions, thereby not collapsing the complex structure of co-finance from the different territories.) These co-financing sources were not strictly 'pre-sales' to commercial distributors; but this point was quickly glossed over. Film Finances, a reputable completion guarantor, had issued a letter of intent to bond the film; and Société Général, with an experienced film finance arm, was lined up to discount and cash-flow nearly 40 per cent of the film's financing. A UK sale and lease-back tax arrangement was in place for around 12 per cent of the film's budget. Sales projections showed acceptable minimum sales from around the world (excluding the United Kingdom, where Renaissance had secured a guaranteed theatrical distribution deal with a leading independent distributor, Entertainment, on an ongoing basis). However, no hard pre-sales had been achieved on the back of the script and package prior to the committee's decision to go ahead with the movie production. Renaissance was investing $4.4m of the *The Luzhin Defence*'s $8.8m budget, thereby complementing the 50 per cent maximum investment rule under the green light rules.

Almost as soon as the film had been green lit; Evans and Finney secured a co-financing deal with Clear Blue Sky, a deep-pocketed US independent company. However, Clear Blue Sky, a development, production and finance company, had been attracted to the screenplay for *Luzhin* and admired the package. Critically, Clear Blue Sky was keen to do business with a company that could match its financial resources, rather than be tapped by third-party productions where it was not a full and equal production and finance partner. The deal stated that when deciding to proceed on a film investment, each party would put equal amounts of money into the production. Additional fees and commission were agreed which allowed Renaissance to charge for its sales and marketing services. Clear Blue Sky wanted the deal to include a joint investment in *Luzhin* albeit that it was a retrospective arrangment. Renaissance's investment subsequently was offset a further 50 per cent, dropping from $4.4m to $2.2m.

Prior to completion of the *The Luzhin Defence*, sales activity based on the package and a 12-minute promotional video, had proved the committee had little to worry about. A pre-sale was achieved to Japan for the $1m 'asking price'. This is the 'high' or 'Ask' sales estimate rather than the minimum 'Take'. The pre-sale was made during the MIFED film market in Milan (while the film was in post-production), and it helped to provide confidence within the Board that the film was on track.

Disco Pigs, the other film the green light committee had already approved, was a low-budget Irish production adapted from a theatre play. A promising first-time director was attached, alongside one of Ireland's most interesting and prolific film producers. The green light decision rested on the following criteria:

- The film was supported by Ireland's state subsidy body, the Irish Film Board with an investment worth 25 per cent of the budget.
- A further 14 per cent was to be raised by the Irish tax deferral system, Section 481.

This left Renaissance needing to put up around 61 per cent of the budget, 11 per cent more than its 50 per cent rule. All other criteria had been fulfilled, with the exception of pre-sales or investor finance covering more than 30 per cent of the budget. It was deemed by the committee that the combination of two sources of 'soft' financing was applicable to cover the 30 per cent rule. As the film was seen, in the words of the chairman, as a 'baby' project, *Disco Pigs* went ahead, backed unanimously by the green light committee, with Renaissance investing just under $2m of the $3m budget. Little notice was taken of the fact that the rules had effectively been sidelined in order to place the film into production.

Morality Play

Like *Luzhin*, *Morality Play* had been in lengthy gestation at Renaissance Films prior to the arrival of the Hermes £24.5m investment. A dark tale set in medieval Britain adapted from Barry Unsworth's admired novel, the script had gone through a number of drafts, and had been considered and rejected by a range of UK and European directors. That spring prior to the August green light meeting, a former photographer and second-time director, read the screenplay and responded positively to the material. Although his first film had not scored at the box office it had won some critical acclaim and he had discovered a new 'hot' UK actor. The film offered an insight into the director's ability to handle tough material and attract strong performances from his actors. When Renaissance showed interest in this director, the new actor in turn showed willingness to play the lead role in *Morality Play*.

During that year's Cannes film festival and market, Renaissance held a number of meetings with prospective co-production and finance partners for *Morality Play*. These included numerous potential German co-production partners and a German tax fund that showed keen interest in the project. However, no distributors showed any appetite for pre-buying the (then) $10m budgeted project. A meeting with Clear Blue Sky focused mainly on a different, US independent film that the companies ended up co-financing later that year. *Morality Play* was given scant attention by Clear Blue Sky.

Talks with a German tax fund partner had continued during the summer prior to the August green light meeting. Finney had travelled to Los Angeles in July in an effort to close a deal, but no commitment in writing had been issued by the tax vehicle's representative. Meanwhile, with no interested German co-producing partner, the lead producer looked to southern Spain as a region to shoot the film. A large and expensive set was to be built, with the ultimate intention to burn it down at the end of the shoot, as per the narrative in the screenplay. An experienced Spanish co-production partner was brought in, contributing the minimum 20 per cent under the Anglo-Spanish Bilateral Co-production Treaty rules. However, while the contribution on paper needed to be 20 per cent of the budget, the hard cash contribution from the Spanish partner was $800,000 – just 8 per cent of the $10m budget. It was also going to be cash-flowed by the co-producer against future distribution and TV deals rather than discounted and guaranteed by a bank.

A UK sale and leaseback partner was contracted, contributing a further 12 per cent of the budget. By the first week of August just 20 per cent of the $10m budget had been raised. Major territory distributors, including North American buyers, who had read the screenplay and held meetings with the Renaissance sales team during Cannes, all, without exception, chose to wait rather than pre-buy rights in the movie. A number of them stressed their concern about the subject matter when compared to the relatively high budget. And no German tax deal had been secured by Finney.

The film's budget, following the appointment by the producer of a top director of photography and an ambitious production designer, had meanwhile swollen to

$12m. Both heads of department had worked with the director on his previous film. 'I'm not interested in compromise', the director had indicated forcefully at a meeting with the production team and the executive producers. 'This is the film we're making and there's no point in going ahead unless we've got this budget.'

Meanwhile, the film had been formally presented to Clear Blue Sky under the co-financing deal they had already partnered on *Luzhin*. Despite a leading US independent actor joining the cast, Clear Blue Sky elected to pass on *Morality Play*. At this stage, one of the co-managing directors had chosen to place the new, rising actor on a 'pay-or-play' deal. Evans's intention was to stop a rival film 'stealing' the actor away that autumn and pushing *Morality Play* back into a shoot the following year. This meant that the relatively new actor would be paid his fee even if film did not go ahead. In addition to the development and pre-pre production costs, which by August amounted to some $300,000, Renaissance was going to be penalized a further $250,000 payable to the actor if the green light committee decided not to go ahead with the film. While the UK sale and lease-back deal was able to remain at 12 per cent of the new budget ($1.44m), the Spanish contribution in hard cash remained at $800,000, or 6.6 per cent of the budget.

The Finance Plan for *Morality Play*, as presented to the committee in August, is shown below:

	Percentage
UK sale and leaseback contribution:	12
Spanish co-producer contribution:	6.6
Renaissance Films:	*81.4*
Total:	100

The green light meeting

Finney had only 24 hours from the moment his flight landed to the green light meeting. He had a series of meetings and conversations, including with one of the in-house producers of *Morality Play*, who cogently argued that a decision to go into formal pre-production was critical if the production was to hit its actors' and location dates. Deposits and crew contracts were being made on a daily basis. A delay or postponement of a decision would effectively have collapsed the film, an argument that was made forcefully by Evans and the finance director to Finney just before the meeting. Finney was also worried about the lack of pre-sales and indeed real interest in the project from the independent distribution market. He recalled how difficult the film had proved with regards to pre-sales and potential co-financiers only three months earlier at the Cannes Film Festival. However, he was potentially compromised if he went up against his senior co-managing director in front of the green light committee. If he became the 'veto' vote from within the executive director management team, he was aware that he might well be 'vetoed' out of the company all together.

The management decided to divide the presentation into two key parts. Part of the management team put forward the creative case for the film going ahead. This argument highlighted the cast, script, subject matter, production values and director's vision. Once this 'pitch' had been made, the second part of the presentation concentrated on the financials. The point was underlined that not doing the film was going to cost the company more than $800,000 dollars. Heads of departments had been placed on contracts that would have to be met; bookings would need to be cancelled with associated kill fees; the lead actor would have to be paid his full $250,000 fee; and Renaissance's historical costs would be effectively lost and ultimately written off. In addition to the financial hit, Evans stressed that a 'no' decision would cause considerable damage to Renaissance's reputation, a valid concern given the slow start the company had experienced post-Hermes. He fleshed out his concern by explaining that agents, talent and existing and potential partners would lose confidence in the company's ability to green light investment decisions. Renaissance, in his mind, needed to 'walk the walk, and not just talk the talk'.

The finance director presented the investment case for the film, but this part of the meeting was already under the shadow of the 'hit' that Renaissance would have to take if the green lighting committee was to say no to the film. Financing actually in place by this date totalled 18.6 per cent of the budget. No pre-sales had been achieved. This in turn meant that no bank had been approached to 'gap' a percentage of the budget against remaining available territories (as had been the case in *Luzhin*). All film finance banks demand a 'market test' in the form of hard pre-sales to significant territories before lending against remaining estimates. Of the film's negative cost, 81.4 per cent would need to be guaranteed by Renaissance if the decision was made to go ahead.

The minimum estimates from the international sales team amounted to around $7m, some $5m lower than the (then) negative cost of the film (excluding the value of the UK distribution rights). The estimates would not cover Renaissance's exposure of just under $9.76m. The argument, however, was once again put by the management to the committee that the difference between writing the film off and risking losing $2.76m on the downside of the minimum sales estimates (with the possible boost of a strong UK performance to help mitigate any losses) was a reasonable way to gauge the investment decision at hand. Much was made of the production fees, at around 8 per cent of the $12m budget that would also partly mitigate the risk.

Finney, who had recently returned from Los Angeles prior to his Spanish break, also unwisely stressed the likelihood of the company closing a German tax fund deal, which in turn would bring a co-financing partner worth 20 per cent of the film's overall budget. If such a deal was closed, it would bring a further $2.4m to the production, and Renaissance's contribution would effectively drop to $7.36m, still higher than the 50 per cent of a total budget green light rule and still below 100 per cent coverage on minimum sales estimates, but significantly more acceptable in the eyes of the committee.

Lastly, the director of sales presented what in view of hindsight was an optimistic view of the cast, script and his ability to close sales at MIFED as the film proceeded through production. This was despite a poor reception at Cannes and a straight 'pass' from nearly all the French and German independent distributors who had reviewed the project over the proceeding four months. Part of the problem facing the sales team at Cannes had been an incomplete package and the wrong script draft for distribution to buyers.

Film Finances, a reputable completion guarantor, had issued a letter of intent to bond the production at the agreed budget of $12m. The guarantor had a strong relationship with Evans, and felt comfortable at this stage about bonding the production. However, Renaissance's production fees and historical costs were excluded, as is usual, from the overall delivery guarantee.

The green light committee had no Renaissance films that had completed their first full cycle of sales with which to compare the estimates and 'ultimate' results presented on the behalf of *Morality Play*. However, *The Luzhin Defence* had premiered at the Cannes film market in May that year. The film had sold to North America during Cannes, but for a $300,000 advance. The minimum estimate from the sales team prior to the film being green lit had been $1m.

The chairman asked the management what risks North America presented to the film's success. Evans explained that it was his intention to try to sell the film to a North American distributor as the film was shooting. 'They will take the film seriously once the cameras are rolling.' The minimum (Take) figure for North American value had been stated at $1.5m by the sales team. Hermes's Investor Representative had indicated during recent Board meetings that the Investor was growing somewhat frustrated that the company was not using its financial resources to make more films. The company was well behind in its stated aim to produce or acquire four to five films per annum, as set out in the business plan.

During the green light meeting, which formally voted unanimously to green light *Morality Play*, the Investor concluded the meeting with the words: 'It's good to see the company is finally making films.'

But was it the right decision to green light the film?

Ramifications of the Renaissance green light decision

Morality Play, which was finally released as *The Reckoning*, underwent the following:

a) Further overspend: the final budget was $14.2m, and the additional $2.2m overspend was excluded by Film Finances at the point of closing the bond. Renaissance received no production or financing fees for the film.
b) No further partners: the German tax deal was never closed, in part due to the agents representing the tax fund falling out with their partner – something that only became clear in late August, two weeks after the green light decision had been made.
c) No further pre-sales were made until completion and screening to buyers in August 2001.
d) The Spanish deal was to remain stuck at $800,000 despite the budget overspend.
e) Final sales (ultimates) were significantly lower than the minimum sales estimates. On screening, Paramount Classics bought North America, Japan, Latin America, South Africa, and the Middle East for $1.75m, but demanded a new music score, and significant edits and a two-day re-shoot. The additional 'cost' of the deal was around $130,000, which was to be split 50–50 between Renaissance and Paramount. Overall sales on the film remained at around $2.5m, compared to the low estimates of $7m, despite the North American multi-territory deal.
f) The film was rejected from all the major film festivals, including Toronto, Venice and Berlin. It premiered in Taormina, in Sicily, in the fall of 2002, some 12 months after completion. It premiered in North America at the Tribeca Film Festival a further 8 months later, and sunk at the box office. The UK theatrical release lasted two weeks.
g) The corporate impact of the film being green lit: Renaissance lost more than one third of its available capital for film investment due to its decision to green light *The Reckoning*.
h) The green light rules were never properly revisited.

5 Sales and markets

> You bring me a picture like this and want money for it? You may as well put your hand in my pocket and steal it. It isn't commerical. Everyone in it dies ...
>
> (Hollywood mogul, Adolph Zucker,
> passing on *Broken Blossoms*)

The territorial picture

A film is a product that can potentially be exploited throughout the entire world in a range of media. Before examining the sales sector and specific functions of a sales company, it is important to consider the way that the film business refers to rights and footprints, as these heavily shape sales activity. 'Territory' as a definitive term has a variety of uses: it can apply to one country, but it can also be applied as a term of ownership or licensing footprint across a number of territories. For example, it can be applied to describe a range of rights, from worldwide, to a cluster of territories, to just one small country or even state within a country.

World markets break down in the film business into five key sectors:

1   'North America' – USA (and normally Canada). When referred to together, the term 'domestic' is used to define 'North America';
2   Europe – which can be further broken into Western Europe, and Eastern Europe;
3   South East Asia (often described as Asia/Pacific, in which case Australia and New Zealand are included);
4   Latin America;
5   Others (Middle East, Israel, South Africa, etc.).

A further way the business considers the world market is to take the globe as its starting point, and then divide it into 'domestic' and 'foreign' (also known as 'international', which can be confusing). For example, sales operations and Studios use 'foreign' (or 'international') to describe all territories outside North America (or 'domestic'). Alternatively, a typical 'territory' often applied in transactions is 'English Language' (or 'English speaking'). This definition would normally include North America (including Canada), the United Kingdom (including Ireland), Australasia (including therefore New

Zealand) and South Africa. English language or English speaking takes on the legal form of a 'footprint' territory by shared language definition.

The business breaks the term 'international' down further into subsections, and then typically allocates specific territories within each subsection heading. For example, Western Europe is divided into the 'big five', which include France, Germany, the United Kingdom, Spain and Italy; and the smaller Western European territories, which include the Benelux countries, Scandinavia (including Nordic territory Finland, but excluding Iceland), Iceland, Greece, Portugal and Switzerland.

Table 5.1 is familiar to international sales agents and the Studios' international distribution departments, including, crucially, their marketing departments. For example, the territories, and their groupings, dictate the kind of footprint a multi-territory deal might encompass. Or a marketing department may need to strategize an international roll-out, determining which key territories will be released when, and in what particular order. For any independent film business concentrating on the buying and selling of film rights, territories help break down complex sets of rights, their relative pricing, and assist in the organization and strategic priorities of an international sales or distribution entity.

The relevance of territories and their groupings has a wider impact than on just the sales and distribution markets. How territories are acquired, defined and exploited play a critical role for film financiers and film investors, risk managers and film producers. After all, if a film is able to be financed by a producer through the resources of its home territory alone, that film, theoretically, can subsequently go on to be distributed, marketed and exploited in every territory in the world.

The sales sector

The international film sales sector grew exponentially during the late 1970s and early 1980s with the advent of a new ancillary platform, video rental in the format of VHS tape, which famously beat out the technically superior rival Beta. As the video rental market matured during the 1980s, the ancillary revenues were so strong that 'video rights' were sometimes sold separately as a horizontal right across territories, or split out from vertical rights in specific territories. It was in part due to the considerable rise in prices and revenues that the concept of 'pre-sales' emerged, where a film's rights in different territories (or as one world territory) could be sold in advance of the film being produced and delivered. On the back of this system, the need for cash-flowing of contracts became critical, and hence the emergence of the specialized film banking sector that 'discounted' contracts and advanced finance for the making of film product. On delivery of the film, the bank lender would receive the balance of the distributor payment, and so the most dominant independent system of financing film product was born.

The sales sector has a formal trade organization, the Independent Film Trade Association (IFTA), formerly known as the American Film Marketing Association (AFMA). IFTA actively promotes independent film and monitors market developments on behalf of its membership cohort, whose product ranges from mainstream commercial fare to niche specialist films. Collectively, IFTA members produce more than 500 independent films and significant levels of television production every year. Levels of international sales (not including the USA) have risen from $1.6bn in 1996 to $3.276bn in 2006, but IFTA membership does not fully reflect the global level of film sales, as many companies outside its group are active in the sales arena. London

Table 5.1 World breakdowns of territories

Western Europe
United Kingdom (including Ireland)
France (including French-speaking Belgium and a range of African states)
Germany (including Austria)
Italy
Spain

Smaller Western European territories
Benelux countries (Holland, Flemish-speaking Belgium, Luxembourg)
Scandinavia (Sweden, Denmark, Norway and Finland)
Greece
Portugal
Switzerland
Iceland

Eastern Europe
Russia
Poland
Czech Republic
Serbia/Croatia/Slovenia
Hungary
Bulgaria/Romania/Baltics

Latin America
Argentina
Mexico
Brazil
Colombia
Chile
Venezuela
Peru/Ecuador/Bolivia
Central America
West Indies, Dominican Republic

South East Asia
Japan
South Korea
Thailand
Hong Kong
Singapore
Philippines
Malaysia
Indonesia
China
Taiwan
India

OTHERS

Australasia (Australia and New Zealand)

Africa
South Africa (most other African territories are included specifically in French, Benelux and
German contracts. A sales company/lawyer will know all the precedents)

Middle East
Israel, Middle East
Turkey
Additional rights: Airlines, shipping, etc.

Source: A. Finney/Renaissance Films

has proven to be a leading centre for international sales companies outside Los Angeles, in part due to its global time-difference position but also to do with the critical mass of film business-savy executives and established legal knowledge in the entertainment sector. However, for many years the UK sales sector was fragmented and disunified, with companies tending to be secretive and unhelpful to each other, despite their need for pooled information and critical mass as a lobbying body. That has fortunately changed since the advent of Film Export UK (FEUK), which has more than 30 active members and has greatly improved cross-fertilization, training, sharing of information and lobbying.

The specifc activities within a sales company

Many players outside the sales sector remain unclear about the functions and strategic role of a sales company. The key functions can be broken down into five main areas of activity: acquisitions, sales, publicity and marketing, business affairs and technical delivery.[1]

Acquisition of product

The key driver for a sales company is a flow of new films to sell. Acquisition executives or main sales staff in smaller companies will actively track projects and talented film-makers for the company to pursue. A controlled Tracking Document is normally maintained, with new potential films, tracked films and older product still being monitored all listed with notes on script, director, talent and budget, etc. When the company has established a relationship with a producer they nurture it and provide a conduit for information and feedback regarding development of the script and the talent package. Sales companies read scripts, treatments and other written submissions and provide coverage (reviews) and recommendations with specific regard to the commercial prospects of the package. They will be aware of the credits, reputations and career paths of filmmakers, actors, producers and financiers. They also screen completed product – often at festivals but also on screeners and at private screenings – and report on their suitability for the company. A basic knowledge of budgeting and financing as well of the production process is useful for acquisition executives, but the most important role is developing a strong network of producers.

The sales department

Sales executives negotiate a licence with the distributor (the buyer) for one or more films in one or more territories, negotiating the terms of commercial exploitation in one or more vertical media (theatrical, DVD retail and rental, VOD, pay-TV, free-TV, airlines, etc.) for a fixed licence period. These 'rights' are licensed in return for a consideration which is normally a share of revenue and usually involves an upfront advance against that share. Because the rights are normally licensed exclusively to only one distributor in a territory, a very strong film – either on package or on viewing – is normally the subject of major competition. Sales veteran Ralph Kamp explains that 'selling a "hot" film is actually fairly simple. The hard part is explaining to a number of unsuccessful distributors why their bids did not win, and how you can maintain good relations with unsuccessful bidders going forwards.'

Identifying the 'optimum deal' requires a high degree of knowledge of the territory in question, about the bidding companies, their expertise, track record, credit rating, and their future plans. It also requires knowledge of the distributor's plans for marketing and releasing the film and how those fit with the specific market and product. This is always important particularly to the producer. Often the sales person ensures that required approvals for the deal are obtained from producers and/or financiers and prepares a preliminary deal memo for the distributor to sign.

The critical role of the sales team is to compile sales 'estimates' – a set of numbers that estimate the value of a film in each territory in the world (see case study: *Pobby and Dingan* below). Normally, numbers are run in two columns – an 'Ask' and a 'Take' set. The 'Ask' numbers are ignored by financiers and in particular banks. Instead, lenders focus on the accuracy of the 'Take' or 'Low' figures. In addition, estimates cover all territories available, while in practice, many films fail to be sold to more than five to ten territories around the world. (Note: some sell to none outside their home market and/or co-producing territories.) A strong result for a film's sales is more than twenty territories, while a full sell-out across the world is an optimum result.

Producers often need a set of estimates in order to attract and start negotiations with financiers and investors at the financing stage of a film. Agents understandably are torn between proving positive estimates upfront in the knowledge that they may be competing, whilst remaining realistic about the film and market value of the film in question. The reputation of the sales company almost exclusively comes down to its ability to meet the majority of its 'Take' estimates – as these are the currency they compete and trade in.

Marketing and publicity

The marketing department in a sales company is responsible not only for the image and positioning of each film on the company's slate but also for branding the sales company corporately. The marketing department will read and report back on scripts, and on film packages. A member of the team will normally be present at the acquisitions meeting and monitor the tracking document.

As a film is prepared for the market prior to, or during, production, a concept poster is commissioned and designed, often by an outside agency. A promo, teaser or trailer is also commissioned. The marketing department is also involved in preparing information for the trade and press, in the form of B2B websites, press kits and materials that distributors can use for local markets. On-set 'unit' publicity is normally appointed by the producer but the sales company will have a relationship with that person, ensuring that set photography and the production notes are of the required standard for worldwide delivery. Additional publicity responsibilities include the commissioning, preparing, editing and occasional writing of material for publication.

The preparation for markets (for example, Berlin, Cannes and the American Film Market), and festivals, in particular where films are being launched, is a major part of the marketing department's responsibilities. The booking of the appropriate office, technical equipment, poster hanging, screens for trailers and promos to run, etc., are functions all too easily taken for granted by CEOs of sales companies and their producer clients.

Business affairs

Whether predominantly handled in-house by qualified lawyers, paralegals or experienced contract executives, or by external lawyers, business affairs is a pivotal function because the film sales business involves numerous documents and agreements that tend to lack consensus on 'standard terms and conditions'. This extends to definitions of media rights to be granted (e.g. new digital media) and territories granted (e.g. satellite footprints) even before hard commercial and financial points are reached.

The sales company's role in closing a film's financing, even if that company is not a direct investor, is tantamount to acting as the 'glue' that binds many different elements together. Producers come to depend on the estimates – and live in hope that serious pre-sales are possible to achieve. The producer also depends heavily on the numerous functions the sales company supplies in reaching distributors and the international marketplace. The financiers, in turn, depend on the sales company's reliability, experience and reputation to deliver; and for investors, the sales company is the entity they look to first for recoupment of their monies. Business affairs executives will be involved in many contract negotiations that involve a high degree of contention (not just triggered by the value of the deal). Among the transactions and relationships they will cover are: inter-party agreement (recoupment order, co-production agreements); acquisition (agreement to obtain rights in films from producers or financiers, e.g. sales agency agreements); sub-licences granting exploitations rights to distributors (sales); what should be covered in negotiations on terms and conditions of use of copyright materials.

Technical and servicing

Until a film is ready to be fully delivered to a distributor, a sales company remains unpaid in commission or in repayment of its advance. With the exception of North America and increasingly Germany, most distributors pay the balance of their advance on Notice of Acceptance of Delivery – but the role of delivery is critical for both producer and sales company, and their interests are fully aligned in this aspect of film production and finance. A technical department (or out-sourced company which is the most usual method) is responsible for the physical materials necessary to exploit the film, including film and digital, video and audio, foreign language tracks, marketing elements and documentation. All this flows from obtaining the correct elements from the production. This includes preparing all the necessary paperwork and keeping accurate records. Because irreparable defects or omissions in these elements can terminate agreements, meticulous care is needed in their gathering, duplication, storage and shipping. Servicing executives develop in-depth technical knowledge of different (and proliferating) formats and interact with laboratories and distributors to ensure the timely and cost-effective provision of all necessary materials. They will manage supplier relationships in order to ensure that the company's time-sensitive communications are reliable, including material shipments, couriering of legal documentation, and delivery of marketing materials to trade shows and other events.

Sales strategy

An international sales company's strategic task is to build a slate, cement a brand, and attract a set of distributors that they can regularly sell films to in key territories around the world. They need to keep their product flow appropriate to the size, scale and demands of their particular area of the market. For example, certain boutique operations can survive by handling just four to six films or so a year. They do this by keeping overheads low and through steady relations with appropriate distributors who appreciate their taste and specialist skills. Other major sales companies handle up to 20–25 films a year, sometimes with different labels to differentiate product. The standard level of product carried by most medium-sized companies is at 10–15 films in play at different stages of development, financing and distribution at any given time.

Sales outfits need to market their companies to producers, talent and financiers, as these form their key sources of product. They do this by displaying their track record (in particular recent and current product), circulating recent sales deals through the trade press, developing their profile in the market (sometimes by advertising, but normally through word of mouth), and promoting their own personal approach to the role. For example, a sales company that provides helpful script reports, strong financing support – in particular, excellent bank relationships, healthy distributor relationships and detailed territory-by-territory knowledge – is offering compelling reasons to producers and suppliers to bring product to them.

The producer's needs

From a producer's perspective, their relationship to the sales company *should* be very important. The producer needs to feel confident of the sales company's enthusiasm and dedication to the film in question, and that the film fits appropriately in the sales company's slate. Sales companies can position a film and introduce it to appropriate distributors – hence their specialist contacts and track record with key 'types' of distributors is vital. A seller that tends to take on a wide range of films, and has a slate of say 20–25 films at any time can place producers at a disadvantage. If the specific film in question does not spark interest quickly, the busy sales outfit will tend to move on to what is selling rather than work hard at additional angles.

Boutique, highly specialized outfits have the advantage of time and focus, and can work a film hard in terms of appropriate festivals and markets. However, they do not have the advantage of 'weight' – meaning the ability to trade off other successful films coming through their pipeline – in order to glean advantage with buyers, or in particular to force collection of unpaid monies. Ultimately, producers would do well to learn about the different range and styles of sales operations in detail, and to do considerable research on their history, track record and current slate before committing into a contract. There is considerably more to the business relationship than just the exchange of sales estimates in return for representation of product.

In addition to the role of the sales agent, there has also been a trend in the North American market for 'producer's reps' to take on the key strategic, negotiating and contracting role. John Pierson, experienced producer rep and author of *Mike, Spike Slackers and Dykes,*[2] and John Sloss, of Sloss Law and founder of Cinetic, are two striking examples of such creatures. Their experience of handling challenging indie product, and positioning it effectively in not just the right festivals, but specific slots and screening times, are invaluable. Experienced reps know all the studio, mini-major and independent buyers – from CEOs to junior acquisition executives, and they have forensic knowledge of contracting terms, from payment structures to revenue shares all the way to TV costs. They can manage expectations on films that may not spark commercial interest, but when a film breaks out, their expertise is critical between a film not just picking up an impressive advance, but going on to benefit from a distribution plan across both North America and Foreign.

The business-to-business marketing stage

Once a sales company is up, running and armed with product, it will have two key marketing tasks. First, it needs to market its films to distributors at various different stages in the cycle (this work will also depend on, of course, at which stage it acquired rights). Second, it will need to create a range of marketing materials that a distributor will have access to if they acquire rights to the film. Areas that require marketing attention include:

1   Book/synopsis/screenplay to distributors
2   Script, budget, talent, cast (the full package to distributors)
3   Clips from rough footage (to distributors, often at film markets)
4   Promos shown to distributors (often at film markets)
5   Concept posters (shown at film markets)
6   Website with clips, news and links
7   Trailers and release posters for international distributors
8   Teaser trailers, TV clips
9   Press notes (supplied by producer to sales company)
10 Still photography
11 Early press coverage, e.g. set visits
12 Press pack
13 Electronic Press Kit (EPK)
14 Festivals
15 Press junket/launch (mainly for large budget films)
16 Market screenings
17 Trade press: releasing of deals, information, photography
18 Order of release territories – often controlled by USA and/or the lead producing territory.

Many of the marketing tasks and roles above are specifically designed to help each territorial distributor understand, prepare and release the film in their own territory. To summarize, the marketing tasks include the development of concepts, creative tools and materials, event management (in particular festivals and markets, see Table 5.2 below) and a plan for the film's roll-out across the world. The sales company's job is never to market directly to the audience, but it should always be thinking about the final intended audience at all stages that it is involved in handling a film.

Markets

There are currently three major film markets each year – Cannes (May), Berlin (February) and the American Film Market (AFM, November). These are key annual events that last from five main business days at the AFM to the two-week media hoopla of Cannes. They offer market platforms where producers, financiers,

Table 5.2 The film market calendar (festivals)

	Jan.	Feb.	Mar.	Apr.	May	Jun.	Jul.	Aug.	Sept.	Oct.	Nov.	Dec.
America/Australia	Sundance		Cartagena	Buenos Aires		Sydney	Melbourne	Montreal	Toronto		AFM, Santa Monica	
				Tribeca						New York		
Europe/Asia		Berlin	Brussels	Hong Kong	Cannes	Edinburgh	Karlova Vary	Sarajevo	Venice	London, PFM		
		Rotterdam						Locarno	Pusan	Sitges		
									San Sebastian			

investors, sales companies, independent distributors, agents, producer reps, publicists and Studios all meet to finance, promote, buy and sell films. Each has their own distinct character, and of course the two European markets are run alongside major film festivals.

Studios and a wide range of different kinds of independent distributors from around the world utilize the markets to 'track' upcoming films, to screen films, to buy product, and to help plan their future release strategies over the next 24 months or so. Leading market distributors will often send teams to cover Cannes, screening a broad selection of films that are not necessarily appropriate for their company. They screen and track in order to keep on top of directors and actors, and collect counter-programming information about rival acquisitions. This activity is also carried out at the major festivals, including Venice, Toronto, Sundance *et al*.

Pre-market information, preparation and working out a market strategy are critical for both sellers and buyers. Sellers tend to focus on their latest product; and market premiere screenings, and hence prepare buyers accordingly. Given that many sales executives will hold 30-minute meetings with buyers around 15–20 times on each market day, they have a limited amount of time to get their key information across. For producers (and financiers) the experience can be frustrating, as their film is only one of a number that the company is handling during this intense period. Films that have already screened at previous markets tend to fall off the end of the sales pitch, a contentious issue between the filmmaker and the sales agent.

Buyers will want to read screenplays before the market has begun; and will draw up a shortlist of films they intend to compete for, or at least consider acquiring. For larger budget films where, for example, distributors may need to pay significant advances for the rights to their territory, they will 'run numbers'. This will involve the compilation of a spreadsheet (aka a control sheet) with high, medium and low box office (and corresponding ancillary) estimates. Against these numbers will be a range of anticipated prints and advertising spends, and standard video and television sales costs. Overhead and interest will be added. The goal driving these calculations is the point that the film will break even; which in turn allows the distributor to consider an appropriate level of minimum guarantee (Advance).

In addition to the major markets, more specialized and targeted events have emerged over the past 20 years. Rotterdam Film Festival holds the Cinemart, a market aimed at broadcasters, public funds and smaller, lower budget feature filmmakers. The festival's programming is particularly strong in Asian cinema and includes a range of documentary as well as feature films. Cinemart holds a grid of meetings between producers and financiers, predominantly from the public fund and broadcasting sector. The structure and organization has been highly praised, providing producers from around the world with an opportunity to pitch and present. Pusan holds a market aimed at South East Asian feature film product in tandem with its international film festival. In 2007, Film London launched the Production Finance Market (October) to run alongside the London Film Festival. This highly focused market (which the author manages for Film London) is aimed at attracting commercial financiers and new sources of money to meet established producers keen to finance single projects and slates of films and company expansion. Financiers have found the event to be of significant value as it offers them an opportunity to meet each other, and to exchange notes on deal structures, emerging markets and changing revenue formats and income streams.

Festivals

The festival circuit plays an essential role in the discovery and launching of independent films. Festivals offer a platform to promote a film towards buyers, critics, entertainment press and audiences; and competitive festivals add the marketing hook of potential awards. Film festivals are one of the few marketing and positioning platforms outside the Studio release system that the rest of the film business has to make people aware of their film.

The precise positioning of a film within a festival can make a considerable difference to its ability to maximize the exposure. The specific playing time of the product matters, not just for the film's programming time, but also the counter-programming. Many expert sales and marketing veterans like their films to be screened later if playing in competition at Cannes, for example. Experienced film marketeer John Durie explains:

> If you play between the last Thursday and Saturday, when the festival is peaking, and the level of adrenaline is building, it will be much fresher in the minds of the jury. Unless your movie is absolutely stunning visually and is so strong it stays in the jury's minds, early screenings are at a disadvantage.[3]

Part of the key is for producers to learn their way around the complex clutter of film calendar events – competitive, non-competitive, market-driven or press-driven – and maximize their chances of improving their film's profile or lifting their film from post-completion obscurity. Experienced sales companies are the producer's ally in working through this challenge.

Exactly how a particular festival invite (and which section does the inviting) helps a film's overall sales and marketing strategy, in particular the event's timing and profile, are important questions for both a sales company and producer to ask before accepting. Many films, in particular US independent films that have not made the top American festival circuit such as Sundance, Toronto, New York, Tribeca, etc.; cannibalize their international festival opportunities by accepting the next US festival that invites them. This stops the film being able to be offered as a 'world premier' to, say, an interested European festival. Most top festivals are intensely competitive, and vie for the most promising, interesting and often the most controversial films every year.

The press is the critical element of the festival process, and all events need to be assessed in terms of industry attendance and foreign press presence. All festival directors design their selections and schedules with both contingents in mind. The leading trade papers will review a film only once, normally when it appears at an event they are covering. Consequently, the producer's role is to try to ensure that coverage is appearing in the right place, and that the film is going to secure a review next to considerable competition from other films. Beyond the critics, it is essential to be able to bring the appropriate and most compelling talent to the festival table. Just as a studio junket delivers director and key stars for an entire day in a major European city, so too must an independent film try to ensure that it takes maximum advantage of the launch festival marketing window. Talent that can only make dates prior to the film's screenings leaves the press at a major disadvantage when interviews are scheduled. An experienced publicist is a must.

For new talent, in particular directors, a film's successful embrace from the circuit can require them to make upwards of 15–20 international trips to support their film. Normally actors attend the launch festival, but the director needs to stay with their film. This can mean an entire year or so being spent on the move, rather than working on their follow-up film.

The sales company needs to wield considerable strategic skill when weaving together complex festival-and-market events. When is the right time to launch a film in advanced development to the market? When is it right to attempt to close pre-sales? At what point should a film be held back from distributors (and offers) until fully completed and ready to be formally launched? Films that are completed and screening pre major festivals may have already been rejected by those festivals – something that many producers are not transparent about. Above all, teamwork between the producer, sales company and financiers is critical if the festival system is to prove effective for sales and marketing to triumph.

Case study: *Pobby and Dingan* (aka *Opal Dream*)

This case study examines the compiling of pre-sale estimates for world rights; comparisons of those estimates with sales made at the different points during the process; and the problem that arises when different film versions are cut.

Background: the film

Pobby and Dingan (aka *Opal Dream*) is an $8m UK–Australian co-production, directed by Peter Cattaneo (*The Full Monty*), produced by Academy Films and financed by BBC Films, the UK Film Council, Invicta, New South Wales Film and TV Fund and the Royal Bank of Scotland. The story is about a little girl growing up in the opal mines of New South Wales with her brother and parents, and the loss and ultimate death of her two imaginary friends, Pobby and Dingan.

The pre-sales

Renaissance International, a London-based foreign sales operation linked to the former Renaissance Films Ltd, bid against other competing sales and financing operations for world rights in January 2004. The company's competitive advantages included its enthusiasm for the screenplay, a very quick response to the script and project, and a determination to undercut other sales companies in terms of rate of sales commission. The script, however, submitted to the distributors included the young girl dying at end of the story. Renaissance's support for the highly emotional ending was a key reason why Academy and the director chose them as the sales company representing the film.

As part of the negotiation to acquire world rights to the film outside the United Kingdom, Renaissance had to provide a full set of sales estimates for the world to the producer. At this stage, no cast was in place, so Renaissance was estimating the film's 'Ask' and 'Take' prices and designing a pre-sale strategy for the film against the screenplay, the material, and the track record of the director, Cattaneo. No star names were expected to be attached, and the leading roles were to be played by children. Renaissance also had to take into account the budget, which was at approximately $8m when it ran its sales estimates.

The sales figures in Table 5.3 demonstrate a heavy dependence on Western Europe, Japan and Australasia. The prices (divided into 'Ask' and 'Take' columns) record the maximum amount Renaissance decided it could ask distributors to pay, and the minimum it felt could be accepted without undermining the recoupment of the film's budget. It is the minimum prices (or 'Takes' or 'Lows') that any bank takes to be the potential indicator of a film's value, territory by territory, not the 'Asks' or sometimes euphemistically refered to as the 'Highs'.

A key element of the deal agreed with the producer included the requirement for Renaissance to achieve no less than £1m of pre-sale contracts by the close of the AFM in February 2004. As no advance was paid for world rights, the producer understandably included a 'performance' clause to protect the film's potential sales if Renaissance failed to deliver. This strategy was potentially risky to the producer. If Renaissance's efforts fell flat, the project would have been badly damaged commercially in the marketplace, possibly fatally.

The AFM was relatively slow that year, with few quality or 'hot' screenplays in circulation. The combination of Cattaneo's track record and finely written and emotionally sensitive screenplay worked to Renaissance's advantage, despite the potentially negative material around a climax focused on a plethora of deaths (Adolph Zukor may well have had some issues here). Indeed, a number of distributors passed on the project due to the girl's passing away in the final pages.

Territories sold included Australasia ($500,000) – which was made available rather than controlled by the Australian co-producer – Italy ($500,000), the Benelux countries (plus Indonesia) ($160,000) and Japan ($750,000 – for which permission had to be granted as it was $50,000 lower than the take price). Renaissance also turned down (unwisely on reflection) an offer for the United Kingdom ($250,000) for theatrical and video rights only (which would have allowed room for a BBC Films deal, taking pay-TV and free-TV under a licence deal that had yet to be concuded).

Renaissance went on to pre-sell a further $700,000 approximately of sales at Cannes in May 2004, including France, Switzerland, Greece, Israel and Middle East. The Royal Bank of Scotland (RBS) discounted the pre-sale contracts, and lent a further 12 per cent of the budget against remaining 'Take' sales estimates. However, Japanese distributor Gaga, who was experiencing acute cash-flow problems that summer, attempted to cancel their contract during July just as their first 'deposit' payment of 20 per cent of their contract was falling due. Had the pre-sale fallen through, the film would have collapsed. A new set of payment percentages and terms was agreed with Gaga, with Lee Beasley, then head of RBS's media banking arm, proving very flexible in cash-flowing the adjusted deficit. The finance was finally closed in August 2004, and a further major territory (Spain at $500,000) was sold on script and rough footage screened at the second AFM in November that year. A total of $3.2m of pre-sales had been made prior to the film's delivery, a significant contribution from the commercial marketplace towards the film's total budget.

When to screen the film?

Renaissance's sales team saw the film between February and March 2005 throughout a number of editing stages. The investors, including BBC Films, the UKFC and

Table 5.3 Renaissance sales estimates and pre-sales for *Pobby and Dingan* (19/02/2004)

Film title	Pobby and Dingan	Director	Peter Cattaneo
Film budget	TBC	Writer	Peter Cattaneo, Ben Rice
Producer	Lizie Gower		and Phil Traill
	Nick Morris	Cast	TBC
Territory	Asks	Takes	(Achieved)
	($)	($)	($)
North America			
USA/Canada/Fr Canada	3,000,000	1,000,000	
Total	**3,000,000**	**1,000,000**	500,000
W Europe			
UK	1,200,000	750,000	
Germany	1,200,000	750,000	
France	1,000,000	500,000	500,000
Benelux countries	175,000	125,000	125,000
Scandinavia	250,000	175,000	
Italy	1,000,000	500,000	500,000
Portugal	60,000	40,000	
Spain	700,000	400,000	500,000
Greece	100,000	60,000	
Iceland	10,0000	5,000	
Switzerland	175,000	100,000	100,000
Total	**5,870,000**	**3,405,000**	
Japan			
Japan	1,250,000	800,000	750,000
Total	**1,250,000**	**800,000**	
Australasia			
Australia/New Zealand			500,000
Total	**0**	**0**	
Africa			
S Africa	80,000	40,000	
Total	**80,000**	**40,000**	
Middle East			
Israel	60,000	40,000	40,000
Middle East	100,000	40,000	40,000
Turkey	50,000	30,000	
Total	**210,000**	**110,000**	
Eastern Europe			
CIS	200,000	75,000	
Poland	50,000	30,000	
Czech Republic	30,000	20,000	
Serbia/Croatia/Slovenia	50,000	25,000	
Hungary	30,000	18,000	
Baltics/Romania/Bulgaria	50,000	30,000	
Total	**410,000**	**198,000**	
SE Asia			
South Korea	300,000	125,000	
Thailand	50,000	30,000	
Hong Kong	60,000	25,000	
Singapore	s/d	s/d	
Philippines	30,000	10,000	

(Continued)

Table 5.3 (Continued)

Film title	Pobby and Dingan	Director	Peter Cattaneo
Film budget	TBC	Writer	Peter Cattaneo, Ben Rice
Producer	Lizie Gower		and Phil Traill
	Nick Morris	Cast	TBC
Territory	Asks	Takes	(Achieved)
	($)	($)	($)
Malaysia	25,000	12,000	
Indonesia	60,000	20,000	*(with Benelux territories)*
China	quota	quota	
Taiwan	125,000	60,000	
India	30,000	15,000	
Pay-TV	75,000	30,000	
Total	**755,000**	**327,000**	
Latin America			
Argentina	70,000	30,000	
Mexico	125,000	60,000	
Brazil	80,000	40,000	
Colombia	30,000	15,000	
Chile	30,000	15,000	
Venezuela	15,000	10,000	
Peru/Ecuador/Bolivia	25,000	15,000	
Central America	20,000	10,000	
Dominican Republic	7,000	5,000	
West Indies	7,000	5,000	
Pan-Latin pay-TV	250,000	150,000	
Total	**659,000**	**355,000**	
Airlines	300,000	150,000	
Total	**300,000**	**150,000**	
Total ($US)	**12,534,000**	**6,385,000**	

the sales team felt that although the film was uneven – and would be improved with certain re-shoots and a new editor – these could not be achieved under the time constraints of the Cannes market in May 2005.

The foreign distributors who had already bought the film from Renaissance were insisting on seeing the completed film at Cannes. They were prepared to see the film at a private screening, or at a market screening. The RBS insisted on the film screening during the Cannes market to all buyers as it had an outstanding gap of 12 per cent to be repaid. The producer and director did not want to show the film. BBC Films and the UKFC, who together had put up more than 40 per cent of the film's finance and mindful that the film could quickly be dubbed a 'problem' movie if delays became public, decided ultimately that the film should screen.

A North American distribution deal

Pobby and Dingan had a poor reception at its market screenings during Cannes that year. But Focus Features, a key US distributor, made an offer for North American rights. James Schamus, a very experienced filmmaker as well as the then joint managing director running Focus, asked to talk to the director about potentially changing the ending. Focus made an offer to buy the film and to contribute 50 per cent towards re-shoots, initially without insisting that the existing ending, where the girl dies, should be changed.

As the North American deal dragged out, however, the ending was changed at Focus's insistence. There were now two versions of the film – a North American version and a foreign version. What should the sales company do?

1   Agree to try to deliver the two different versions by offering foreign distributors a choice? What problems would this create?
2   Insist that foreign distributors have to take delivery of the foreign version.
3   Try to convince foreign distributors to all take the North American version.

What actually happened?

1   Focus insisted on changing the title from *Pobby and Dingan* to *Opal Dream*.
2   Renaissance went into administration two months after Cannes 2005. The film's sales duties were taken over by Becker Films, who took the position of trying to convince all distributors that the Focus version was the most commercial and the only real option available.
3   The film was marketed specifically as a children's film once the ending was altered. It played in the Children's section of the Berlin Film Festival in 2006.
4   Many of the original buyers who pre-bought the film from Renaissance lost interest in the film, and have rolled it out straight to video.
5   The balance of the $500,000 advance from the Spanish distributor was not paid to RBS, leaving the bank with a problem recouping its 12 per cent gap.
6   BBC Films pointed out to Focus that they had invested in a script where the lead girl dies at the end of the story, and that they had no intention of screening the US version. Two versions of the film exist as of today.

6 Film finance

> We should all make a killing in this business. There's so much money in the pot.
>
> (Irving Thalberg, production chief,
> MGM Studios)

> The film industry is a lousy place for the private investor. They might as well
> shove their money down a rat hole.
>
> (Jake Eberts, producer)

Introduction

The majority of independent films financed outside the Hollywood Studio system depend on a myriad of sources of finance and investment to enter film production. Industry texts and analysts talk about 'jigsaw puzzles' and often suggest that there are 'no rules' to independent financing of films. Beyond the fact that the film production business is prototypical – meaning that each film is unique (even sequels) – there have evolved certain structures and risk-managed approaches that continue to underpin the independent film finance business. But just as no films are the same creatively, few independent films are ever financed in precisely the same way (or repeated) with regards to the specific detail of partners, financing, investment, recoupment and profit share positions.

This chapter looks at the key difference between finance and investment, and examines the range of sources of finance available in return for varying demands and recoupment positions (see Table 6.1). We then move on to examine risk and risk management issues. For more detailed information on specialized forms of film funding, such as tax, see the sources and bibliography, as this chapter is designed to deal with general principles and practices rather than a forensic 'how to' guide.

Finance versus investment

Building on the strategic recoupment issues raised in Chapter 2: The film value chain, which places film investment in an often challenging place in terms of its respective recoupment position in the exploitation chain, it is important to first distinguish between 'finance' and 'investment'. Many independent films rely on both sources of cash towards their budgets, but it is often assumed that finance and investment are

Table 6.1 Finance and investment sources for film

Within the value chain

Exhibitor – needs product to fill cinemas, especially in order to sell concessions (popcorn and soft drinks, etc.).
Distributor – needs films to be in business, has the power to book and market product.
VOD/DVD distribution – the critical area of change in the independent business and key revenue earner with historically high profit margins.
Sales – needs films, volume, revenue for costs and overhead, commission fees for profit.
Broadcaster – needs to license films for schedule/eyeballs/audience.

Outside the value chain

TV – cultural/quota reasons for investment – often 'pubcasters' driven by political mandates rather than commercial imperatives.
Banks – security against all rights where possible. The aim is make significant fees and get money lent at high interest levels and then get it all back.
Hedge funds – paying back their own bank loans is important, but equity return is the real motivator, and 'super profits' the ideal. Private equity – wide range of incentives from pure speculative return to lower risk positions discounting receivables, now replacing bank finance on occasions.
Angel investors – want upside and involvement and link to creative element and lifestyle.
Tax based investors – tax relief/deferment for individuals or companies.
Public funds – talent and industry promotion, career support, political and cultural mandate.
Regional funds – inward investment, development of talent/local industry.

Source: Mike Kelly and Angus Finney, SEDIBA Producer Training Programme, NFTVF, South Africa, 2009.

essentially similar tools. They are not: each form an element of cash contribution that is governed by different objectives and end goals.

Film 'finance' is normally accessed in the form of a loan towards a film (or slate of films). It is provided in return for as high a position of security as possible. Finance is normally made available on the condition that there is a binding assignment of rights to the financier against all available assets of the film, enshrined typically within the special purpose vehicle (SPV) set up to make the filmed product. Specifically, bank loans are normally provided on the condition of their repayment being placed first in the recoupment agreement. The bank will consider accepting a collection agent's fee at say 1–1.5 per cent, agreed sales and marketing costs of normally between $100,000 and $200,000 depending on the size of the film and the timing of the sales company's involvement, and a nominal fee towards the sales agent of typically 5 per cent, while the bank's loan is being paid out.

Against these conditions, bank finance takes no ongoing position in the underlying rights of a film once repaid: e.g. the bank takes no net profit position. Once fully repaid, it releases its charge against the film, leaving the producer and investors relieved of their responsibilities to the financier. Net profits are then, if available post cash break-even, divided up on a typical 50–50 basis between the investors and producer if industry norms are used. Some investors drive a harder deal against the producer, demanding 60–70 per cent of net profits, but the standard remains 50–50.

Film investment – often referred to as 'equity' – is typically forced to sit behind film finance in the recoupment order. Film equity will normally recoup behind a bank, but prior to the producer receiving net profits. At the point of cash break-even, the investor then shares in the profits of the film. This way the investor becomes a co-owner of the film negative and normally shares in any value (i.e. cash flows) in perpetuity. Naturally, an investor will be keen for a film to 'break even' as quickly as possible, and for worldwide revenues to be as significant as possible over a long duration, hence sharing in as large a profit as possible alongside the producer's share. However, investors – in particular over the last decade – have insisted on significant fees within the film budget in addition to net profit participation. Aggressive fee positions effectively push other players back in the recoupment chart and make cash break-even hard to reach. From the investor's perspective, however, budget fees help to 'hedge' their risk.

Equity can be cash, but it can also be placed into a film as 'in kind'. For example, a 'facility deal' whereby the investor provides facilities in return for certain sharing of rights to a film, would also be termed an equity deal. Many of these deals are a mix of equity and reduced cash paid by the producer to the facility house. Equity can also be an alternative to salaries, such as the producer's and director's fees (or part of), which may be deferred and recouped after all financiers and investors are 'out' (meaning fully repaid).

Equity investors will typically take an aggressive approach to 'soft' investors – including state public subsidy funders and broadcasters putting up equity in addition to licence fee payments. It is in their interest to recoup ahead of these investors, accelerating the speed of their repayment, but specific details always come down to negotiation and the final contracted agreement. Overall, independent film recoupment structures normally adhere to the rule of pro-rata, pari passu in relation to the total budget – meaning they recoup at the same time and share 50–50 on each euro/dollar paid into the 'pot'. The area that differs is the position of the co-producer and his/her financiers – as they recoup typically from their own territory and corresponding rights, and not the recoupment pot.

Rights-based financiers and licensors within the value chain: sellers, distributors and broadcasters

Agreements for the exploitation of licence rights across horizontal and vertical territories and media form a critical component of independent film income. For a sales company, an advance (minimum guarantee) may be paid in return for the acquisition of a territory. This may be foreign, or English-speaking, or world, which would include both foreign and domestic, but not the producing territory and co-producing territories, as these rights are unavailable for sales/distribution apart from possibly servicing duties by the sales agent on behalf of the producer.

Technically, a sales company putting up a cash advance becomes the 'international distributor' of the film, as it has bought and owns rights (and is subsequently licensing them to third-party distributors), rather than representing the film and playing the role of 'agent' for the producer, who remains in ownership of the rights. Sales operations that have access to a line of credit (meaning their own source of finance to acquire rights, which still has to be repaid on agreed terms) or their own capital will often put up significant funds in advance in order to become a co-financier of projects, in return for a territory of rights to sell. However, there are considerably more commercial terms at stake than just the sales aspect if an agent puts up an advance, including the term of the deal in order to exploit for a much longer time (or, in cases, perpetuity); an executive producer position on the film; a share in the back-end profits; and a greater creative say in the production and marketing campaign.

Until the point that a sales company's advance, sales and marketing costs along with associated commission is recouped, the sales company remains in a position of almost complete control over each deal done within its agreed territory, unless of course a bank is sitting in front of its advance. This situation rarely occurs as both the bank and the sales agent is looking to get up to the top of the recoupment order to protect their position.

Distributors agreeing to make a pre-sale for a specific territory normally are required to pay 20 per cent on signature of long form, and 80 per cent on delivery of the film. It is the 80 per cent that generally has to be discounted by a financier (e.g. a bank) in order to cash-flow the commitment and direct those monies towards the production budget. Distributors tend to dislike having to sign a notice of assignment to a financier, which provides the bank ownership/security over their rights until either, a) the distributor has fully paid the contracted price or, b) if the distributor goes out of business or fails to pay. In this instance, the rights revert to the bank to exploit in order to recoup its financial position.

Broadcasters committed to film activity tend to be organized around development/ acquisitions and production financing – typically at the 20–30 per cent level of a film's overall budget in return for licence rights and a tranche of equity – but they rarely distribute theatrically themselves. Key European-based broadcasters such as BBC Films, Film Four, ARTE and RAI Cinema play an important role in propping up the predominantly culturally driven EU film market and in supporting new, emerging talent.

The market's precarious characteristics

The film business has been characterized as a high-risk investment. There are strong arguments and facts to support such a case. Sunk costs in product prior to income streams are very significant. There are major completion and final product delivery risks in film production; there are acquisition and marketing risks in film distribution; and there are performance risks (in cinema exhibition, DVD/VOD, pay-TV, free-TV, etc.). Given the creative judgements required in development, production and distribution, and given also the complex task of meshing together complex creative talents, there are, in addition, significant management risks, including the risk of failing to secure sufficient viable product to cover overheads. Furthermore, the marketplace is hard to read: only a minority of developed projects are converted into production; not all productions achieve a scale of release commensurate with their production costs; and only a minority of those so released make money. Outsiders who know nothing about the creative decision-making process tend to fall at the first hurdle. To paraphrase William Goldman, 'nobody knows anything', but outsiders know considerably less.

The combined production and US marketing costs of a Hollywood Studio movie now averages more than $120m. Studio budget escalation, to ensure the competitiveness of the product in a crowded leisure marketplace, is a constant pressure, prospectively increasing risks and postponing break-even. Contributing to this pressure is the unique leverage enjoyed by leading talent, which can sometimes extract fees from revenues as well as production budgets and profit participations. For how much longer remains a serious debate, given the economic pressures on the value chain.

Within the film value chain, income can be generated from budgets (e.g. fees paid to producers, executive producers, investors, financiers and talent), from revenue streams (e.g. fees retained by cinemas exhibitors and film distributors) and from profits (in the event that a film recoups its production cost). Various fee corridors are available within revenue streams, and profit definitions can favour one party over another. Too often, incoming investors, especially those who invest in the overhead and development expenditure of independent production companies, find that their investment is effectively 'first in-last out' money, in direct contrast to sophisticated financiers, who lend in a 'last in-first out' position.

The culture of the industry also has discouraged investors. Most links in the value chain appear to be ruled by creative teams driven by project vision, not enterprise vision, according to FBA director Terry Ilott:

> The projects themselves are dependent upon unpredictable talents, mostly employed on a temporary, freelance basis. Although the industry has enjoyed rapid growth, there has not been appropriate concentration of ownership and the companies within it are mostly small and highly volatile. They tend to have weak financial skills and low creditworthiness. The industry has a shortage of entry points and career paths, and this favours the emergence of maverick creative and commercial entrepreneurs who can be both brilliant but often unreliable. Most independent enterprises are small, non-hierarchical and dependent upon enthusiastic as well as industrious employees.[1]

Risk management and alignment of interests

Film investors have often misread the market, misunderstood the risks, or simply missed the appropriate point of entry – for example, by investing in development and production. As such, their commercial performance has been dependent on project conversion and on deriving net profits from successful films from which to gain a return. An ongoing concern for investors in film is whether their interests are aligned with those of the studio, distributor, and/or with the producers and co-financiers in the case of an independent film. Financiers have historically found it more straightforward to secure alignment through collateral and/or commissions, fees and interest charges. They have held the leverage to price risk relatively effectively; while often, investors have found it much harder to exercise leverage. Often, it has been the case that investors have fundamentally misunderstood the structure of the film business and its proximity to a 'market-failure model,' as opposed to a 'hit-driven' model, which sounds exciting but should really be for only the very brave and well informed.

As entrepreneur and finance specialist Mark Beilby points out, the wealthy individual or equity investor has tended to utilize a mixture of tax breaks and subsidies, and the balance of funding beyond their own stake has been made available through the pre-selling of rights, supported by a handful of banks and finance houses who discount those contracts or provide gap funding of between 10 and 20 per cent. Gap funding makes up a financing shortfall by providing a loan made against unsold/remaining territories (outside pre-sales and co-producing territories), normally with a minimum of 200 per cent coverage required (e.g. that the total value of the remaining estimates are more than double the amount being lent) and at least two commercial pre-sales in place prior to closing the arrangement. This is designed as a market 'test' on the behalf of the bank. In return, the bank will be in first recoupment position from all available revenues, and all income and sales contracts are assigned to the bank until its risk is recovered. 'Overall, it's a system that has invariably been an expensive and fragmented model, often sub-optimally executed with highly correlated risk for the equity investors aligned to a minimal potential upside in the majority of cases', suggests Beilby.[2]

Traditional bank 'gap' has mutated into 'super-gap,' where instead of 10–15 per cent of the production loan required to complete financing is met, the sum rises to around 25–35 per cent. Super gap, although predicated on the 'last in-first out' positioning, is really a form of high-risk capital investment and accordingly the fees and interest charged reflect that level of risk. When compared to gearing in the finance markets or even the standard house mortgage structure, the concept is not unusual: put down 20–30 per cent equity and borrow the remainder.

Studio risk transference: hedge fund slate investment

There are numerous examples of 'risk transference' and 'exporting risk'[3] that Hollywood in particular has honed down to a fine 'dark art'. The Studios, ever since their inception early in the last century, have consistently searched for external funding to mitigate in particular production cost exposure. From 2005 to 2008, hedge funds and other funds invested heavily in the production slates of the major studios. These funds, including Melrose Investors I ($300m for Paramount) and II, Legendary Pictures (Warner Bros), Marwyn (Entertainment One), Virtual Studios ($260m for Warner Bros), Titan Film Group ($230m for MGM and Lionsgate), Dune Entertainment ($725m for Fox) and Relativity Media (Gun Hill Road I and II, providing $1.3bn for Sony and Universal), have sought to avoid development and overhead risk and to gain from reduced distribution margins and accelerated break-even.

Certain funds also addressed the opportunity in the independent sector in the USA and Europe. Among these are Future Capital Partners/Aramid and Cold Spring Pictures. Investment banks, including Goldman Sachs ($400m funding for Lionsgate Entertainment and owner of Alliance), Royal Bank of Scotland ($350m for New Line Cinema), Morgan Stanley ($150m for Paramount Vantage), Merrill Lynch ($1bn for Summit Entertainment), J. P. Morgan ($225m for Overture) and Goldman Sachs (funding for Canada's Motion Pictures, the UK's Momentum Pictures and Spain's Aurum), have also entered the independent arena. And at least two new funds have been set up to provide advisory as well as investment services, Continental Entertainment (formerly backed by CitiGroup, but now shut down) and Entertainment Advisors (backed with $200m from J. P. Morgan).

The recent hedge fund 'Hollywood era' stems back to 2004, when banks entered the business of film-related structured transactions. Wall Street hedge funds and private equity companies, swamped with capital and surrounded by the availability of cheap debt, began to think that they saw the potential for high returns from the film industry, at the time buoyant in part thanks to high DVD revenue growth aided by excellent ancillary margins. Combined data shows that the hedge fund industry had around $14bn under management by the end of 2006, and the structured film finance elements of that sum broke down as shown in Table 6.2.

It is estimated that more than $14bn of third-party money has accounted for about 30 per cent of the total negative cost of those slates (all film expenses, including

Table 6.2 Structured film finance

Between 2004 and 2009 $14.2bn in capital has been raised for 35 transactions.

The market for structured film financing transactions peaked in 2007:

   13 financings
   US$4.4bn in total capital

Supporting both major studio and independent film product.

As the capital markets began to unravel in 2008, volume receded considerably:

   4 financings
   US$1.1bn in total capital, a 75% decline.

In 2009, one transaction closed – DreamWorks, which is more of a hybrid structure, rather than a pure slate structure.

Several structured finance vehicles are in the process of negotiating take-out ultimate facilities to provide for additional liquidity.

Several vehicles are in the market for independent producers, again these structures are hybrids.

Source: The Salter Group, 'Structured Film Finance', delivered by Patrick Russo at International Film Finance Workshop, Abu Dhabi Film Commission, 28 September 2009.

financing costs, bond fees and contingency reserves, necessary to create filmed product). Some commentators expect that many of these investments will show losses at the junior capital level (not senior debt), although there are some notable exceptions in the Studio structures, some of which have performed extremely well. Patrick Russo, a partner at the Los Angeles based Salter Group, explains that it depends on the specific structure of each deal, and that the independent market in particular has been negatively impacted by multiple influences – including a varied approach, investor oversights on strategy, green lighting, DVD bubble bursting, independent weakness at the theatrical point, and, crucially, 'a shakeout of oversupply of weak performing independent content' since 2004/2005.

What drove the hedge players towards the film industry? Hedge funds need to leverage their investments to achieve their target returns, so slate deals have typically included an element of equity (high risk), an element of mezzanine debt (less at risk) and an element of senior debt (relatively safe). By committing to the entire amount of a slate deal, keeping some of the senior debt itself, and selling the equity and mezzanine tranches to other institutions in the financial market, an arranging bank earns a significant fee for retaining a relatively small amount of debt. Commercial banks such as Dresdner, Société Générale and Deutsche were the main leaders of this pack. The structure was to place senior and mezzanine debt in first and second positions, while junior equity was way back in the recoupment order.

The Monte Carlo 'track' scenarios

The investment notion was predicated along the lines of performance projection rather than qualitative analysis. With the notable exception of Dune Capital (see Table 6.3), most deals were green lit on the back of the so-called Monte Carlo scenario.

Projections, it was argued, could objectively predict downside risk. While this is partially true, suggests Russo, it also shows a range of performance outcomes, while giving

Table 6.3 Dune Capital and Fox

- Dune Entertainment, an affiliate of Dune Capital Management, invested an initial $325m in 28 films at 20th Century Fox.
- Alignment with Fox Studios was undeniably strong. Dune principal Chip Seelig had a direct line to Rupert Murdoch. Seelig gave a speech in October 2006, where he said the two crucial features were agreement over the composition of the slate and Fox's market knowledge.
- But, the important point is that *The Devil Wears Prada* and *Borat* were amongst the early releases. Their success defied the laws of probability.
- It could be argued that investors were really betting on the performance of Fox and its management team as opposed to specific analysis of the slate in question. Fox's annual margins had been between 16% and > 24% since Bill Mechanic assumed the studio's reins in 1993 and nurtured the studio's current leadership before leaving in 2000.

Source: M. Beilby, International Film Finance Workshop, Abu Dhabi Film Commission, 28 September 2009.

guidance to probabilities of loss, magnitude of loss, return characteristics, etc. It is not a predictor of the future, but rather a guide to potential outcomes predicated on the probability that the borrower has enough capital to facilitate his plan and what level of confidence do they have in order to facilitate their plan as well as upside gains, on a given slate of 18 films or more over the life of the investment. Simulation methods model phenomena through analysing key data such as first three-day and first week box office performance, which trigger a set of attached assumptions about future revenue streams from all resulting ancillary media. Just as Wall Street and the City found that new, complex financing structures cannot anticipate changes in the marketplace – instead relying on historic numbers – so too does the Monte Carlo system. Data on drivers of film performance are in constant flux. External and intervening factors over time can trigger considerable differences between original data and its historical assumptions, and the actual release performance of a film within an overall slate deal. According to Beilby, the kinds of influences that alter assumptions include shifts in audience tastes, viewing trends, emerging technologies, competition from other media, and of course, market competition among a crowded release schedule, affected by specific release timings and the success or otherwise of marketing campaigns.

But if one leaves aside the above variables, the key question is whether the Studios and hedge funds were every truly aligned? There is a law of built-in deficiency, whereby if one assumes that the co-financing of movies develops to the point where a studio and an outside investor really do become equal partners, then that is the point that the studio will work out that it does not need that partner anymore, and revert to financing its entire film slate without transferring risk to a third party. Of the early hedge fund slate deals, only the two Dune funds with Fox and Paramount Pictures' first Melrose 1 fund (which included *Mission Impossible III*) covered truly sequential slates. The Studios could not pick and choose, or designate 'opt-out' films. (However, some producers choose selective deals on the grounds that they think they can pick winners better than the Studio.) But overall it can be argued that it was inevitable that some of the slate deals were weighted towards the Studio, and the structured funders were wiped out.

Looking forwards, the closure of tax loopholes, changes in fiscal policy and prospective losses on a number of slate funding deals, taken together with the current

Table 6.4 Elliot Associates and Relativity

- Relativity Capital, an investment partnership between Ryan Kavanaugh's Relativity Media and New York-based hedge fund Elliot Associates, signed a deal in February 2008 with Universal Pictures to co-finance a significant portion of Universal's slate.
- Under the deal, Relativity Media will share in the attributable profits of 45 films through 2011, while Universal will be able to exclude up to two films a year for budget purposes. Relativity can reject up to three films per year.
- Relativity acts as the principal and will retain the mezzanine and equity. Under the deal, Relativity will co-finance approximately 75% of Universal's releases during the term. Relativity Capital underwrote the capital structure of the deal and did not use an outside bank.
- Elliot Associates has over $10bn in assets under management and, before its involvement in film finance, had a reputation for building value through prudence. Elliot's average return as a fund over time is 14%. It has not delivered super profits in good times but has delivered an above average return in lean times.
- This underlines that smart, prudent investors are still prepared to invest in the film business.

Source: M. Beilby, International Film Finance Workshop, Abu Dhabi Film Commission, 28 September 2009.

squeeze in credit markets, means that structured film finance is going to be hard to come by over the coming years. As a consequence, there is likely to be an even greater shortage of investment capital for both the independent and the studio sectors in the near future. On the other hand, some investors have learned from the recent period, and, in the words of Salter Group's Patrick Russo, the 'early stages of smart and new money are positioning to fill the market holes'.[4]

Case study interview: Heather Mansfield, of Mansfield Associates, risk manager to Standard Chartered Bank's entertainment division

The first stage of my work is best described as 'risk analysis'. Each project that crosses my desk has aspects that are immediately apparent from a risk perspective. The script itself may be extremely bad; it may have reputational issues for the financier; or I may personally feel it's objectionable if it were overtly violent or pornographic, for example. But I swiftly move onto technical issues, such as: is the script overlong? Are the content of the script and the size of the budget significantly out of balance? Is it a wildly ambitious subject and yet has a no-name cast? Once past these issues, you work through more standard issues such as a first-time writer, which is absolutely relevant, because somebody can just appear out of a cupboard with a beautiful script. A first-time director, particularly if that person is also the writer is a worry but the fact is that a first-time director can be supported by other significant parties from a hard-nosed line producer to a first-class director of photography to an experienced producer. The first-time producer is a complete no-no, you cannot entrust millions (and it is millions) of whatever currency to someone who has never handled millions before in terms of making a feature film. If one is obliged to deal with a first-time production entity, the only thing you can do is give them the option of what we used to call 'warehousing' in the television industry, which is to come under the wing of a hard-nosed and experienced production entity.

I'm quite often questioned by producers who say 'why do you need to read the script?' My answer is: because if you don't read the script you don't have the slightest idea of what risk it is that you are ultimately managing. And of course it's not just the script, it's that whole balance of director, producer, cast, crew, script and budget. Beyond these elements are what I call the 'hidden waters'. All elements may be perfect for a bank to be involved, but if I am aware of significant background problems or a history of significant dishonesty involving the borrower, then the answer will remain 'no'.

The second stage of my role is 'risk mitigation'. Given that I am considering a risk on behalf of a prospective financier, the key question I ask is how that financier is going to get their money back? Well, obviously, only from the sales and exploitation of the project, and therefore to me the value, prominence and power of the sales agent in the marketplace is just as important as the beauty, value and importance of the project. Things are very seldom linear, but nevertheless, I can often see a project would be a straight 'no', but can be changed and adapted, hence reversing that decision in certain cases. 'If you do this, this and this, then it would work', is the kind of conversation I would have with a producer. And that is particularly the case in the finance plan where the producer may not understand that if you accept a minimum guarantee from a sales agent you cannot also have a bank gap, because they are mutually exclusive in terms of recoupment position. So I might, for example, suggest that a small sales minimum guarantee is placed against a single territory, allowing the Rest of the World to be freed up for the bank to be placed against. Or I will frequently suggest a change of sales agent that is satisfactory to the bank. Ultimately, my role is to be able to sum up very rapidly the value in the balance of the sales estimates, the finance plan and the structure of the finance plan and how it works with what they are asking for. This does actually allow me to say 'no' very quickly or a different route to a 'yes ... if'.

The quality of the sales company rests not just on their reputation, but upon a myriad of additional questions, such as: Are they stable? Are their finances in shape? Have they got cash-flow issues? Is their head of sales about to leave, or have they been poached by somebody else? Market information, often collected at film markets and from various contacts and sources, is primary to my job. Likewise, we need to be appraised of the credit status and willingness of independent distributors around the world to pay on delivery. Banks formally share information about distributors who fail to meet their contractual obligations. And things of course go wrong no matter how much one attempts to mitigate risk. The most dangerous situation for the bank is when a film is undelivered. A bond is taken to guarantee delivery, but in practice, the bank and the bond can part ways when there's a problem. The thing about the bond is that we share information in terms of cost reports right the way through the production. We get what they get. We also get dailies and the cost reports and we do go through them. And, you know, my primary focus is actually on the production accountant. So I always make a point of having a direct relationship with that entity and we have approval over that appointment.

The third key area is risk management itself. It can be as straightforward as simply checking that the cost reports show that everything is on budget and that the progress reports show that everything is on schedule. And that they are timely, and coming in when they are supposed to come in. We also check in with the collection agent, the completion guarantor and the line producer, and just ask: 'everything all right your end?' It can be that simple. Good producers run a very tight ship. And likewise when it comes to the exploitation phase, the sales agent who is timely with their post-market reports, who is punctilious about calling if they have an offer which they wish to discuss.

Film recoupment

The buzz phrase used in reference to film recoupment is the 'waterfall'. Film finance specialist Mike Kelly, prefers to refer to the recoupment process as a 'dammed river'. 'If you stand under a waterfall then you will invariably get wet, whereas you can invest in a film and remain parched', Kelly observes:

> What actually happens is that film revenues flow down tributaries (including theatrical, home entertainment, ancillaries, merchandising, etc.). If they reach the delta, after the dam operators have taken their share (collection agent costs, financing fees and interest, sale company's s&m and commissions, distributor's P&A, sales and distribution fees, etc.) then the delta fills up and the producer(s) and investors are very happy people. Unfortunately that doesn't happen very often.

Figure 6.1 shows a classic recoupment chart, with details of why each player is drawn up in each position. A producer, financier or investor should be able to draw up such a chart from the information available in a legal recoupment order. The pictorial aspect of such a chart is of significant use – as it quickly highlights any conflict of position more obviously than when comparing written clauses in a legal draft.

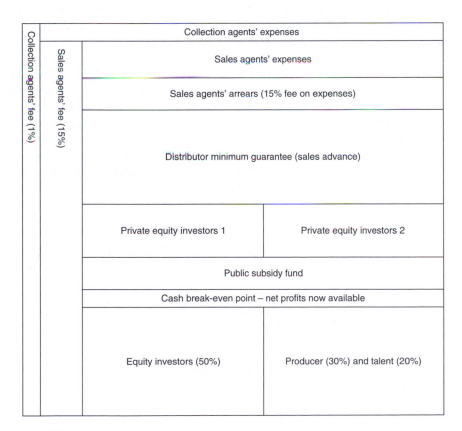

Figure 6.1 Film recoupment.

Case study: The financial packaging of *Confessions of a Dangerous Mind*

Confessions of a Dangerous Mind started life as a Charlie Kaufmann original screenplay, commissioned by Los Angeles based producer Andrew Lazar, who had an overhead and producing deal at Warner Bros. On delivery and reading of the second draft, Warner Bros' chief Alan Horn stated publicly that the Studio would never make the film, as the material – about a game show host who (apparently) moonlighted as a CIA hit man – was deemed far too strong for the Warners' mainstream sensibility. By this stage of development, Warner Bros' had clocked up approximately $1.5m in development and overhead costs against the project.

Lazar and his agent Cassian Elwes at William Morris, had shopped the unpackaged project (meaning that no director or cast was attached) to most of the other Studios. All of them passed, partly due to the unusual and challenging material, but also due to the producer's demands for a $5m fee (some $4m more than his last Studio producer fee, technically called a 'quote').

Renaissance Films, based in the United Kingdom, was introduced to the screenplay by Elwes on a regular trip to Los Angeles at the same time as Bryan Singer (*The Usual Suspects*) became attached to direct. Renaissance, in need of significant international projects that would attract a higher level of buyer than they had previously had contact with, made an offer to finance the film. In order to bring Lazar to the table, Renaissance offered the producer a $2m producer fee, and a generous share of Renaissance's recoupment position as financier and world sales company. The budget quoted by William Morris to Renaissance when it read the screenplay was $25m. Within a four-week period, the project's budget rose from $25m to $30m, in part due to Singer's ambition for the project, and attractive casting attachments, including George Clooney and Drew Barrymore. After considerable delays and a difficult negotiation (where Renaissance learned that Lazar was continuing to try to interest significant independent US players in the project), an 'option to finance' agreement was signed between Lazar and Renaissance, allowing Renaissance 120 days to put the film into principal photography. The contract stated that the production budget had to be no less than $30m.

The financial package

Renaissance proceeded to put together a financial package that involved the following elements:

	Percentage of $30m budget
A German tax fund at $6m inc. costs	20
Foreign pre-sales at $6m inc. discounts	20
Bank gap of $6m inc. costs	20
(but dependent on equity that sat behind its gap or a North American pre-sale to close the film's finance)	
North American pre-sale/partner or equity	40

Total raised in principle prior to re-approaching North America was $18m (60 per cent), although no distributor deals had been signed as all major foreign buyers wanted to know the North American distributor before committing. In addition, the option had not been signed prior to MiFED (the international film and multimedia market) that November, meaning that Renaissance had not been able to introduce the script and package to buyers at that stage.

North American deal

Miramax, one of the leading and most aggressive US independents, responded to the project with enthusiasm, and made an offer of $9m (30 per cent) for North American rights in early January. This would have brought the total raised to $27m (plus financing costs), some $3m less than Renaissance's 'option to finance' agreement for a production budget of $30m with the producer.

What should Renaissance have done to close the film's financing?

1   Accept the offer and work with the producer and Miramax to bring the budget down.
2   As part of (1), attempt to get Warners to place its $1.5m development repayment into the recoupment order, rather than pay it within the cash budget.
3   Sell more foreign territories at a price level that still retained the bank gap level; see (1) above.
4   Find an equity partner prepared to sit behind the bank gap (e.g. the bank would come out in 'first position' from all revenues). Equity would be in 'second position' in the recoupment order.
5   Sell its' 'option to finance' on to Miramax and get out of the film.

What actually happened?

a)   The producer refused point blank to bring the budget down when approached by Renaissance.
b)   Warner Bros' refused to defer their development costs.
c)   Any attempt by Renaissance to sell further foreign territories at a premium price would have depended on: i) closing and announcing the Miramax North American deal, and ii) securing the cast within the lower budget level. Neither proved possible.
d)   Miramax changed its offer. It offered to split the film's financing 50–50, and it would recoup 100 per cent out of North America, and agree to go pari passu with Renaissance in 'foreign' after the bank was out. However, Miramax insisted on 50 per cent of the German tax benefit as part of its 50 per cent cash contribution. Renaissance did not have the financial resources to agree to and close this deal.
e)   After the 50–50 deal collapsed, Miramax agreed to increase its offer from $9m to $11m for North American rights, placing the finance raised at $29m. However, it did not paper this deal, which left the offer worthless as weeks dragged on.

f)   An actors' union strike (Screen Actors Guild) was threatened during the autumn of these negotiations. Renaissance's option to finance (120 days) was under pressure, and the film was not going to be able to enter principal photography prior to the strike's dates. The film collapsed.

g)   It turned out that Miramax's Harvey Weinstein wanted George Clooney to direct the film, not Bryan Singer.

h)   Miramax end up fully financing the picture. Clooney directs.

i)   Renaissance was repaid all its costs, a premium, plus a $250,000 bonus if the film entered net profit. The company was also awarded one executive producer credit.

What should have happened?

1   Renaissance should not have got involved in such an ambitious, difficult, high profile project. The financing was too complex for a company short of resources for a project of this scale despite the potential upside.

2   Once involved, Renaissance was correct to get out in return for costs when such an exit became available. The company was extremely fortunate to be given such an escape route.

7 Co-production and the changing European film audience

> All this talk of how difficult and expensive it is to co-produce is rubbish. The fact is, co-production simply has to be done. Forget whether it costs more. The point is that you won't have a movie unless you do it.
>
> (Cameron McCracken, CEO, Pathe Pictures)

The co-production approach to filmmaking

The strategic importance of partnerships when analysing the collaborative nature of filmmaking can never be overstated in the film business. Co-production (and co-financing) is an approach and strategy that has for historical reasons tended to be enshrined in the post-1960 European method of film financing and production. Film made as a co-production is any type of production that involves more than one producing party in the financing and production process – whether through official channels or unofficial. Co-productions may be made through a partnership, a joint venture or through varying types of co-operation, the most common of which fall under official co-production treaties. During the 1980s and 1990s, co-productions were particularly dominant across Europe, and still remain a vital strategy for continental territories as a means to harness additional finance and distribution potential beyond their national support systems.

Europe's filmmaking experience, in particular during the past three decades, demonstrated that while partners are clearly a necessity for financing many films, two key questions need to be asked: 'How much?' and 'In return for what?' At the crux of this equation lie issues of cultural specificity, national identity and creative integrity: how are these tenets upheld when placed next to a project's financing demands and various partners' different needs? We shall examine later in this chapter Europe's filmmakers' changing, increasingly positive relationship to their audience over the past 10 years. This development in turn suggests that filmmakers, and in particular, producers, have learnt how to mostly avoid the traps of 'Euro-puddings' made to appease each party. The combined skills of focusing on a compelling story and appropriate package alongside an increased ability to navigate the complex 'points' systems that have abounded during the 1980s and 1990s appear to have paid dividends. The evidence for such a statement will become clearer as this chapter develops.

There are two compelling economic drivers that relate directly to co-production: the hard costs of making and delivering a film; and the issue of recoupment of all costs. With notable exceptions, the North American territory has historically been viewed as the only territory in which a producer can recoup their costs from the domestic territory.[1] Hence, in the independent filmmaking industry, there is a pressing need to find partners to raise money, spread risk, and ensure the widest possible distribution of the product. The received wisdom to date (prior to new distribution opportunities) is that the more theatrical the opportunities, even if of a modest scale, the better the potential returns from the film value chain. And the reason why an official co-production is selected is that it allows the film to take advantage of the fact that the production will be treated as a national film by each of the countries involved. This offers an incentive to each producer involved, as it maximizes the value of each national support commitment (e.g. national subsidy/support system) and other financing mechanisms in each territory.

When an independent producer/company enters a co-production it has to execute an official co-production contract which satisfies all the criteria the treaty intends to qualify under. This approach pre-supposes that the producers want to make an 'official' co-production. Any official co-production allows the film to become eligible for support systems under each territory's rules. This may appear to be straightforward, but some of the barriers facing recent efforts to streamline complex bilateral and multilateral agreements are that specific legal intricacies are different for many European territories. Consider in addition that key co-producing territories across the world outside Europe – notably Australia, New Zealand, South Africa, India, Canada, etc. – offer specific arrangements that understandably vary from territory to territory. It is at this point that support from national film bodies and experienced legal advice can help the producer(s) navigate difficult waters. For example, most national funds have experienced production and business affairs advisors; while specialized entertainment legal firms strive to draft documents that are wherever possible compatible, especially as there are certain headings a co-production has to hit.

Co-production – practical headlines

Key co-production questions to address

- Where do the underlying rights lie? E.g. Are they in an SPV? Who is it controlled by?
- Is it a bilateral or multilateral co-production?
- Who is the lead producer (producer deleague)?
- Are the financial percentages being raised from each partner realistic and within the bilateral or multilateral laws that govern the official co-production?
- Are the creative contributions in line approximately with the financial contributions? And are the qualifying nationals working within the framework of the treaty?
- Are the co-producers genuinely independent from each other, and not linked by a common management team?
- Are the general contractural terms agreed?

Applications – the typical three-step procedure:

- 'Provisional' co-production status – granted by the competent authorities on the grounds of an approved agreement between the co-producers.

- The co-production goes ahead, with each producer backed by the National Film benefits in their respective territory.
- On completion of the film, an audit confirms to the competent authorities that the film has adhered to the agreement and rules, and is subsequently granted official co-production status.

The co-financing and multilateral routes available

Financial, rather than strictly controlled creative, co-operation (aligned with points for different nationals etc.), addresses one of the key hitches that has historically blocked many co-productions: namely, reaching detailed agreements on casts, crews, scripts and other specifics. In the past decade a debate has taken place over whether a project is more likely to be accommodated through a 'co-financing' model than a strictly controlled 'co-production' model. Bilateral treaties invariably require that a producer's financial participation be matched by an equivalent artistic and technical participation.

Taking the above logic further, the European Convention on Cinematographic Co-productions (1992) was designed to allow the streamlining of co-productions to reflect more fully the economic realities of film production. Access to Europe's national funds and subsidy systems (both national and pan-European) became more readily available to a wider range of co-produced projects. The convention applies to co-productions where all the producers are nationals of states that have signed the convention. If not, then there must be at least three producers from three states who are providing at least 70 per cent of the production in order to still qualify.

The convention is specifically aimed at multilateral film productions, not television co-productions, and existing bilateral agreements have remained in place. The key difference is that the convention has acted as an enabling umbrella, which has effectively smoothed out the obstructive bilateral problems when a multilateral production can take over. Multilateral co-productions that qualify are able to access national funds in the same way as official bilateral co-productions. In practice, if no bilateral treaty is already in place, the convention may be applied as a bilateral agreement; or, if a bilateral treaty already exists, it will remain applicable. In addition, if the co-production is between producers from more than two states, the convention will apply and will override (where in conflict) any bilateral agreement between any of the states. The rules dictate that any qualifying producer cannot put in less than 10 per cent or more than 70 per cent (compared to the 20 per cent and 80 per cent figures under bilateral contributions).

The convention contains a general provision that each co-producer's technical and artistic contribution should approximately balance its financial contribution. Technically, between 10 per cent and 25 per cent can be purely financial, with no creative or technical input. However, for the film to pass the regulations there has to be a majority co-producer whose technical and artistic contribution satisfies the conditions for the film to be recognized as a national product under that producer's national state rules. Ironically, a 'majority' co-producer may actually amount to as little as a 30 per cent contribution.

A point system still applies. The co-produced work needs to qualify as a 'European cinematographic work'. The definition is reached by a points system, whereby a production needs to score 15 out of 19 points to fully qualify. A breakdown of the system shows that, for example, a director is worth three points, an art director worth one point, and so on. Ironically, a lower score than 15 may still be able to pass, as long as the film 'reflects a European identity'. Each co-producer has to apply for approval from the relevant national authority in their state at least two months prior to principal photography.

Eurimages – the pan-European multilateral approach

Eurimages is the pan-European fund for European multilateral co-productions. It also provides support for documentary, cinema exhibition and distribution marketing, but the focus in this section in on the fund's production support. The fund was established in 1989 by the Council of Europe in Strasbourg and has no direct connection to the MEDIA programme, which is overseen by the European Commission.

Eurimages' member states pay an agreed sum into a central pool, which is then administered by a central selection team. The basic arrangement is in the form of an interest-free loan, repayable from producer's net receipts. A qualifying co-production must involve at least three independent producers from the fund's member states (two are allowed for a documentary, although the production must be aimed for a theatrical release) and be directed by a European filmmaker.

According to a report prepared for the Council of Europe Film Policy Forum by the European Audiovisual Observatory, titled 'The Circulation of European Co-productions and Entirely National Films in Europe, 2001–2007',[2] three main conclusions can potentially be drawn from the benefits of co-productions.

1   European co-productions travel better than their 100 per cent national counterparts, achieving a release in more than twice as many markets as national films.
2   European co-productions attract on average 2.7 times as many admissions as their national peers.
3   Non-national markets are more important for co-productions than for entirely national films in terms of admissions, with non-national admissions accounting for 41 per cent of total admissions to co-productions compared to 15 per cent in the case of entirely national films.

Originally, the majority co-producer could contribute up to 60 per cent of the budget, but this was adjusted to 70 per cent in 1994 to come into line with the European Convention on Cinematographic Co-production. The maximum Eurimages will lend any one co-production is 20 per cent of the budget or a cap of €5.5m. The minority co-producer participation must not be less than 10 per cent of the total production cost. Requests are deemed eligible if principal photography has not commenced, and will not have started before the end of the period of settlement of the application.

In practical terms, any application to Eurimages must have the full support from the film's respective national Eurimages representatives. They in turn must be fully informed of the budget, the creative and practical elements and all details of the partnership. The representatives are then in a position to answer queries when the respective project is discussed at quarterly board meetings; but also in a position to 'champion' the project within a funding structure that has become increasingly competitive over the past decade.

The European market turnaround

Whilst this book generally addresses how the international business 'operates', it is of use to digress and examine the European film market in contrast to where it remained stuck some 10–15 years ago, a task the author was asked to do by the European Film Academy in 2008.

This section is not intended to suggest that co-production strategies are to be cited as the key reason for such developments. Indeed, progress in terms of a connection between filmmakers and the audience appears to be a result of a closer connection between producers and writers and directors, rather than mainly due to financing mechanisms. For example, German filmmaking has witnessed a notable turnaround. This is not only exclusively thanks to the emerging strength of producers, led by the likes of multi-talented Bernd Eichinger, Stefan Arndt and Uli Felsberg, although it is clear that considerable credit lies with them. What is most impressive is the range of examples of *both* culturally and market-driven films that have conquered their domestic market and travelled widely. Not only that, but some of the cultural synergy through links between German and Turkish cinema have resulted in some vibrant films that have also travelled. Look no further than Fatih Akin's *Head On* and more recently *The Edge of Heaven* as exciting examples for a new generation.

On a wider scale, the change across Europe is most marked by domestic films attracting local audiences in a manner that many could only dream of in the mid-1990s. According to the European Audiovisual Observatory, many countries reporting strong growth in admissions in 2006 also registered excellent performances by domestic films. As a result the overall market share for European films in the European Union nearly doubled over this period, reaching nearly 27.6 per cent, compared to a shaky 15 per cent in 1996. Principle contributors to the overall success of European films were French and German productions. French films accounted for 11.1 per cent of total European Union admissions in 2006, reflecting the excellent results for national production on the domestic market. Very strong performances by a number of comedies at the beginning of 2006 helped boost the share of French production within France to an estimated 45 per cent, the highest domestic market share registered since the mid-1980s. Domestic productions also contributed to the revival of the German market, where three local titles figured among the top ten films for 2006 and national market share reached 25.8 per cent, the best score since the Observatory's analysis began in 1991. As a result admissions to German films accounted for 5.1 per cent of total EU admissions, compared to 3.2 per cent in 2005.

The statistics demonstrate that European film has managed to avoid falling face first into an art-house ghetto. However, while there have been improvements, there have also been some setbacks. This author's *A New Dose of Reality: The State of European Cinema*[3] dedicated a chapter to PolyGram Filmed Entertainment, and its strategy to build a European studio. Just one year after the book was published PolyGram had become the largest film producer and distributor in Europe. Its sales – resulting from European and international product as Hollywood-originated packages – amounted to more than €800 million, and amongst its most successful films were *Four Weddings and a Funeral*, *Trainspotting* and *Elizabeth*, three distinctly European productions. The dream was ruined in 1998 when Seagram, the Canadian drinks company, bought PolyGram and in doing so opined that the movie division should be sold off. Former PolyGram president Michael Kuhn has spent considerable time trying to raise EU backing for a 'virtual' European studio with no result to date. His former partner Stewart Till is now embarking on a new international distribution venture, armed with the library, sales and distribution interests after having concluded the purchase of Icon in November 2009. His ambitious plans will be watched with considerable interest.

On the positive side, given where Vivendi and Canal Plus stood back in 2001/2002, when it seemed possible that Studio Canal would be dismembered entirely, France and Europe have much to be thankful for. Under the canny guidance of Frédéric Sichler (who has now moved on), the French powerhouse of cinema gradually reasserted itself to the point of making dynamic acquisitions of key indie distribution companies such as the UK-based Optimum Releasing in 2006, and went on to acquire German distributor Kinovelt in 2008.

Such aggression to acquire European territorial distributors needs to be placed in perspective. According to *Screen Digest*, there has been a massive growth in competitiveness within the theatrical distribution marketplace in Europe – specifically regarding the average number of films released into cinemas on a weekly basis. Across the Continent as a whole, numbers grew by an average of nearly 40 per cent from 1995 to 2005. This also reflects the higher levels of films available at the production level to be picked up. There were 3,329 films produced in the world in 1995 (around 500 of those from the then smaller European Union). This had grown to 4,603 by 2005, (of which around 862 films came from the European Union) all of which are searching for a place in the market. Add the rising production levels to the concentration levels in the exhibition sector in many European territories, and it is no wonder the independent distribution sector is hugely more competitive than a decade ago.

For all its inherent and current problems, the European film project finds itself in a stronger place than 15 years ago. That there has emerged a strong range of directors, producers, writers and vibrant filmmaking companies is unquestionable. Many are clearly focused on reaching audiences in a manner that sharply contrasts with the dark days of the 1980s and early 1990s. Self-knowledge has resulted in a greater level of reality.

Case study: Zentropa

Over the past 15 years, Danish-based Zentropa has built a considerable international reputation as a producer and international sales platform for high quality, distinctive specialized films. Today, the company has a turnover of more than €30m, and is the largest film production company in Scandinavia. In February 2008, Scandinavian major Nordisk Film and TV acquired 50 per cent of Zentropa, buying shares from the 50 per cent co-owners Lars von Trier and Peter Aalbaek Jensen, and 110 employees, directors and creative talent that had been given the opportunity to acquire 50 per cent of the company's shares in 2006. The deal was designed to provide more capital to Zentropa as it aims to step up its international production levels.

Zentropa is an enigma. It strives to make films that are non-genre, highly individual, and its recruitment policy is to hire women over men as producers, and generally avoid graduates from the highly acclaimed Danish National Film School (although many still make their path to the company at some point or other). Despite having an internationally heralded sales operation, Trust, (now Trust-Nordisk), no projects that are green lit ever have assessment from marketing, sales and distribution departments. The producer is solely responsible for the film's commercial success, in balance to the amount that the production company invests.

Zentropa is the company that initiated the Dogme movement (Dogme 95), a vibrant approach that redefined aspects of filmmaking technique and style. The minimalist, reality-based approach, dismissed by the French critics but widely applauded around the world, helped brand and place Danish filmmakers on the international map in an inspired manner.

More than 100 films have been produced or co-produced under the Zentropa label, and key films, including company co-founder Lars von Trier's *Breaking the Waves* and *Dancer in the Dark*, Lone Sherfig's *Italian for Beginners*, Susanne Bier's *Open Hearts*, *Brothers* and *After the Wedding*, Annette K. Olesen's *Minor Mishaps* and *In Your Hands* and Per Fly's *Draben*, are some of the highlights of the Zentropa catalogue. Creatively, the company strives openly to avoid following genre films. In contrast, it actively supports filmmakers that are striving for artistic quality – films that are notably different from the mainstream, preferably both in content and in the way that they are made.

Each producer (around ten senior ones work on a fixed salary rather than a share in each of their films)[4] is given an open book – meaning that there is no target number of films they have to produce over a year or fixed period. The producer is empowered to green light his/her own films under the Zentropa system, but strict attention is paid to the level of investment by the company compared to the film's ultimate earnings. Some have a staff of four–five people, and the numbers vary as at least one or two are fired each year. Many producers now senior in the company are women, and most started as 20-year-old trainees rather than emerging from the Danish National Film School. (Meta Louise Foldager, von Trier's producer, and Sisse Graum Jorgensen, Susanne Bier's producer, for example, never attended any film school and started at Zentopa as trainees.) Foreign producers are encouraged to join the company, but are forced to learn Danish within four months or they are let go. Trainees work for no pay for their initial six months, and are then drilled into the Zentropa ethos over a further 30-month period before being hooked up with their own directors.

Directors are hired on a film-by-film basis, and have no longer-term contract. However, long-serving directors were offered part of the company's shares in 2006, and their loyalty is taken very seriously by Aalbaek Jensen. He takes the view that it can take a director two to three films before they are capable of making a really successful film. However, new directors can find the company tough – as Zentropa sets very exacting deadlines and demands that the directors have their next project lined up prior to completion of their first one.

Since 1998, Zentropa has also controlled and built a film studio a few kilometres outside Copenhagen, Filmbyen at Avedore. The studios are set in a previous military barrack compound, and encompass a group of experienced (around ten) and new producers (around 20–25 at any one time), post-production facilities and a host of production equipment that has helped Zentropa keep both producers and directors within its unorthodox family/studio system. A Danish producer explained: 'The great thing about working at Zentropa is when they say yes, it means your film is genuinely green lit. There aren't many companies in Europe, let alone Scandinavia, that can do that.'

Zentropa was set up by writer/director von Trier and Peter Aalbaek Jensen, and they divided the company along artistic and management lines. Von Trier is able to make the films he chooses; Aalbaek Jensen runs the company how he wants to. Initially, they invested in film equipment and paid bills by producing commercials.

Their first film *Europa* (*Zentropa*) was not successful, and Aalbaek Jensen is open about the fact that for a number of years he was paying back a bank loan while trying to turn the company around. In addition, both owners recognized that their 'top down management' approach in the early years was not working. Instead, Zentropa gradually evolved into a 'flatter' environment, where the troika of the screenwriter, director and producer were enshrined as the filmmaking team, and the producer in particular was placed at the centre of the filmmaking process.

Zentropa currently produces around five features a year, and co-produces a further five. It has built a strong network of European partners – some formally owned by the company, others deliberately loose associations that allow it to take full advantage of co-production rules in the European Union. Trollhattan AB, a Swedish company, has invested heavily in Zentropa's productions, and the company established Zentropa International in Berlin and Cologne. The company has experimented with North America co-development and co-financing partnerships, but Aalbaek Jensen and von Trier's determination that the producer, director and writer are able to control the film clashed heavily with the US tendency to insist that financiers not only have but share, and sometimes insist on, their creative viewpoints.[5]

However, Aalbaek Jensen notes that the key turning point for the company was von Trier's *The Kingdom* (1994–1996), which was made in order to assist raising the finance for *Breaking the Waves*. The TV mini-series helped von Trier develop his relationship and skills with actors, and some of the stylistic elements, including hand-held cameras, simple lighting and jump cuts, helped pave the way to Dogme 95. Crucially, *The Kingdom* sold in a 4-hour version to more than 30 territories around the world, making von Trier a more bankable and internationally acclaimed director despite the unorthodox and risk-taking tenor of the extended drama.

Film case study: *Breaking the Waves*

Zentropa's cinematic and financing breakthrough arrived with *Breaking the Waves*. An extremely complex multilateral, multi-partner project, the film remains one of the most illuminating case studies for European co-productions despite being financed more than a decade ago. The film presents one of the most difficult co-financing challenges within the EU system, with Zentropa as lead producer, supported by four additional co-producers, and 23 co-financing partners.

The screenplay's development was supported by the Danish Film Institute and the European Script Fund (the MEDIA precursor to the current Development Support system). It took more than three years from inception to principal photography, and four drafts. Two were written by co-writers, Peter Asmussen and David Pirie, but the final draft was distinctly von Trier's. Initial budget projections were for a film that would cost $6m. When Vibeke Windelov joined the company as a senior producer to partner with von Trier and Aalbaek Jensen, the work she carried out on the schedule and budget placed the film at $7.5m. The location was initially the Outer Hebrides in Northern Scotland. That placed the budget at Windelov's $7.5m, but von Trier then suggested that he could shoot the relevant scenes as back-projection, bringing costs down considerably. Hence a budget of $6m was introduced to the cornerstone Scandinavian funders.

After more screenplay work, it became clear that von Trier was not going to work on a back-projection schedule, so the budget went straight back up to $7.5m. After considerable work, Zentropa got the Danish Film Institute to move from $700,000 to $2.5m towards the film's budget. The producers then brought on a Swedish co-producer, a Norwegian co-producer, and made an application to the pan-Nordic fund (the Nordic Film and TV Fund). Each Scandinavian co-producer brought in its national subsidy body; and the Swedish producer also brought in the public Swedish broadcaster and a Swedish pay-TV channel. Once these financiers were in place, co-producers in Finland and Iceland were also brought into the film's finance partnership.

By February 1994 the producers had a commitment from all five Nordic territories to support the film, even if no further funds could be raised and the budget was to be lowered to $5m. A small film crew went to the Outer Hebrides in Scotland for 4 weeks in May/June to shoot the panoramas of the film. (The panoramas were to form the chapter pictures in the film, which were digitally elaborated after being filmed.) At the time of this initial shooting, which Aalbaek Jensen explains was a way of ensuring that his financiers were and remained committed, no key cast had been attached:

> Despite the cash flow problems these early shoot days cost us, the shoot really helped make the project real. And we'd spent so much money on these four weeks that it was now very hard for any investor to pull out.

Further money was raised from Eurimages. Originally, when the application was made the film seemed to be a purely Scandinavia co-production. Eurimages, however, decided to support the project on the grounds that Denmark, Sweden and Norway are small film-producing territories. Later, demonstrating considerable flexibility, Eurimages accepted the introduction of two European principal co-producing partners, France and Germany, necessitating a different co-production structure to the one initially supported.

Germany and France, especially following the success of *The Kingdom*, were the logical territories to expand the co-production. However, both territories proved resistant to the script, and they only joined the production post the panoramas being shot. The United Kingdom, despite the film being shot in Scotland in the English language, proved either resistant to the script, or in the case of the then European Co-production Fund, too tough a recoupment position for Zentropa to accept. Unlike the genuinely soft positions taken by the Scandinavian funds, the United Kingdom's national funds (British Screen Finance, followed by the UK Film Council) have continued to take an active recoupment position when investing.

La Sept Cinema/ARTE, the French broadcaster, became interested in the project mainly on the back of *The Kingdom*'s success, which the group had co-produced. The contribution from ARTE was both in the form of a pre-sale and a co-production commitment, but the channel eventually agreed to recoup their investment from the French producer's share, making their position much softer than any UK offer. However, for the French co-production to work, certain budget spends had to be moved to France. According to Windelov, the co-production with France raised the actual budget by around $150,000.

Initially the producers had been negotiating with the Dutch distributor of *The Kingdom* for the rights to distribute *Breaking the Waves*. However, they turned out to be keen on formally co-producing the film and succeeded in raising money from the Dutch Film Fund, Dutch public TV and a Dutch TV fund designed to support co-productions, called the COBO Fund. This commitment was made post the start of principal photography.

Approaches by the lead producers to key territorial distributors had been made (supported by Philippe Bober, a highly specialized and experienced producer and boutique sales executive). German, Italian and UK distributors of *The Kingdom* had been keen to pre-buy *Breaking the Waves* – and the French producer had been able to pre-sell the film to French pay-TV operator Canal Plus. German broadcaster ZDF made its money available for the production, but Zentropa's producers remained wary of pre-selling other territories, as it felt that the cost of discounting 80 per cent of each advance was prohibitive. However, the producers still faced the problem of how to discount into cash enough of the film's budget to pay for the production and competition of the film. The national funders assisted by paying nearly all of their respective shares of the budget upfront. In addition, a local Danish bank lent the production $450,000, and the French co-producers discounted ARTE's and Canal Plus' agreements.

During 1994, Helena Bonham Carter had been attached to play the lead role. However, her agents later informed the producers that she wanted to pull out, and was replaced by a then unknown actress, Emily Watson. This placed pressure on the film's pre-sale value and directly impacted on the North American value of the film, despite Watson ultimately turning out to be an inspired choice by von Trier.

Aalbaek Jensen also remained cautious about appointing an international sales agent. He took the view (prior to forming Trust), that sales companies charged a high fee, and therefore were best avoided. It was only when the film was in post-production, shortly prior to the premiere at Cannes, that an agreement was made with Christa Zaredi's sales operation (in February 1996). A minimum guarantee (MG) was paid upfront for the rights outside the producing and co-producing territories. The MG helped with cash-flowing the film's completion until the receipts of all the financing from final instalments, pre-sales and distributors were paid up. Strategically, given that *Breaking the Waves* was selected to participate in the official competition at the 1996 Cannes Film Festival, it became vital for the producers to work with an experienced international sales agent.

Breaking the Waves had gone into (full) principal photography on 7 August 1995, and had wrapped by October 19 after an 11-week shoot. The film played in Official Competition at the 1996 Cannes Film Festival where von Trier was awarded the Grand Prix.

The Financiers

Danish Film Institute, Danmarks Radio/TV, Swedish Film Institute, Sveriges Television, Norwegian Film Institute, Finish Film Foundation, Icelandic Film Corporation, OY, YLE, TV1, Nordic Film and TV Fund, Dutch Film Fund, VPRO/COBO Fund, Eurimages, Media Investment Club, La Sept Cinema/ARTE, Canal Plus, Lucky Red, TV1000, Villealfa, ZDF, October Films, Zentropa Entertainments Aps (Denmark), Trust Film SvAB (Sweden), Liberator Production Sarl (France), Argus Film Producktie (The Netherlands), Northern Lights A/S (Norway).

8 Exhibition and the changing cinema experience

> Who the hell wants to hear actors talk? They're silent the way they should be!
>
> (H. M. Warner, 1927)

> Digital technology doesn't mean everybody is going to retreat in to their bedroom and watch 'content' on their phone. The movie business is, at its heart, one of the most opportunistic businesses the world has ever seen, and out of the threats and opportunities presented by digital technology, the latter will predominate.
>
> (Karsten Grummitt, managing director of Dodona Research)

Exhibition's role in the film value chain

In Neal Gabler's controversial book *An Empire of Their Own: How the Jews Invented Hollywood*,[1] the film historian cites the vaudeville experience as a key catalyst that propelled 'live entertainment' from floorboards to, ultimately, the moving picture-going business. That shared experience, collectively witnessed, together, under the one roof and within the dark, helped cross linguistic, social and cultural boundaries and paved the way to the importance of the exhibition sector as we know it today.

It is still called 'theatrical', which to newcomers may seem a confusing term, but its roots go all the way back to the 'theatre' experience – a shared sanctuary for entertainment – that Gabler and other historians have written so eloquently about over the past century. And that emotionally charged experience remains as critically defining of the movie-going act as carried out through the visiting of theatres to watch films as it ever has been.

Historically, even in the peak years of the 1980s and 1990s, levels of cinema-going attendance in the USA were well below the levels of the 1940s and 1950s. The abrupt drop in attendance during the 1950s and 1960s was deemed a result of competition from the arrival of new visual entertainment media – most notably television. And by the 1980s and 1990s, cinema exhibitors also faced new challenges from video rentals, cable television and ultimately the sharper delivery tool of Digital Versatile Disc (DVD). Between 1980 and 1995 VCR-owning households in the USA had grown at an average yearly rate of nearly 30 per cent. Yet despite the proliferation of alternative entertainment, including film at a later stage of the window sequence, the exhibition sector stood up to the onslaught with resilience. Whilst the building and proliferation of multiplex cinemas had an important role in the market, multiple-screened cinema theatres only go a limited way to explaining the retained strength of the theatrical market.

Combined market studies have indicated that there were four major factors that determined whether movie-goers decided to go and see a movie: a) the quality of the film itself; b) the location of the theatre; c) the starting time of the screening; and d) the overall quality of the cinema. Whilst developing technology assisted the cinema-going experience, such as Dolby sound systems and for ardent movie-goers the size of the screen, research has not indicated that these developments made crucial differences in terms of exhibitors' performance. Neither has ticket price or customer brand loyalty.[2]

And we are yet to see if the re-emergence of 3-D will add value to the actual business returns. Some argue that 3-D has a distinctive, unique experience, but much will depend on the suitability and playability of the product designed for the 3-D experience. On the one hand, leading distributors are attracted to 3-D's technical rebuttal of piracy, and the further elevation of the theatrical 'shared experience'. However, some filmmakers and executives are uneasy about 3-D's re-arrival. Whilst the technical wizardry clearly rewards clearly headlined genres, such as action, sci-fi and horror, how relevant 3-D will be to drama, or how the audience might relate to more sensitive, emotional material in this medium remains up for debate.

The most important factor was, and still is, the quality of the film that the audience selects to see. Therefore, all exhibitor companies place great emphasis on their selection of films that they licensed and booked for screening. Just as a distributor has to take a commercial view on the 'package' – including the story, script, director, actors and genre – so too does an exhibitor. In addition, an exhibitor has to consider the specific timing of the film in question. Is it the right weekend? What is the film competing with? Should the film be programmed for a holiday period, or a specific season? What the growth of multiplex cinemas in the 1990s allowed was for theatre operators to offer a wider selection of product and reduce some of the pressure for picking 'hits' when licensing. On the other hand, certain operators played so safe that the new market was observed by some critics as 'flat' and regressive. When 20-screen multiplexes in New York City, for example, were playing the first *Batman* film on 19 of their screens in the film's first weekend, no wonder observers questioned the homogenizing effect of the multiple screen era.

As we have seen in Chapter 2: The Film Value Chain, film distributors (including major studios and independents) make revenues through the selling or licensing of their film product for exploitation through a range of windows, including free-TV, pay-TV, video rental, sell-thru video (retail) and cinema releases in theatres. Major studios estimate that only on average around 20 per cent of film revenue (NB just revenue, not 'profits' as the general media constantly mix up) is derived from the theatrical release. Less than 50 per cent of that revenue now comes from North American releases; while more than 40 per cent is derived from video and around 30 per cent from all formats of television sales. However, a film's value through each of the ancillary windows is, critically, first determined by its, a) release and b) performance, at the theatrical stage. It is this leading economic 'bar setting' that makes the exhibition sector so interesting and important, despite the sector often feeling somewhat divorced from the mix of imperatives that drive the other sectors of the film industry.

Terms of trade

The standard arrangement between a distributor and an exhibitor is called a film licensing agreement. This governs what is called a 'film rental fee' that is paid by the theatre owner to the distributor in return for screening their film. Negotiations normally take place at least three months before a film opens (and in many cases earlier, especially concerning tent pole studio fare). The structure of the film rental fee is normally governed by the greater of two amounts, which are calculated under the following formulas:

a) The gross receipts formula. The distributor will receive a specific percentage of box office receipts, with that percentage dropping over a period of time. For a new film, the percentage is normally 60–70 per cent in the first week and then declining gradually to around 30 per cent after 4–7 weeks.
b) The adjusted gross receipts formula (also known as the 90/10 clause). This arrangement allows the distributor to receive 90 per cent of the box office receipts after a deduction for the cinema's expenses (aka the house allowance – which is negotiated on a distributor/exhibitor basis for each cinema in question).

From a film booker's perspective (working on behalf of the cinema or chain), their role will be to consider the different available titles being released in a specific week (or month/period), so that they can programme or counter-programme effectively. They will then set about negotiating a deal with their counterpart at the distribution company that addresses the following points:

- the film rental
- the number of screens
- the total seating capacity
- the number of show times (very important for long-running films)
- the duration of the overall run.

The most significant aspect is the film rental agreement. Of the two examples above, the adjusted gross receipts deal (b) is the most typical when dealing with studio/major distributors' product. The key to the 90/10 deal and its precise calculation is the specific theatre's pre-negotiated house allowance figure.[3] The exhibitor and the distributor examine a range of facts when it comes to their determining the house allowance. These include the quality of the theatre, number of screens and number of seats. The house allowance figure is then taken into account when calculating the final payment: e.g. it is subtracted from the films' 'gross' for the week and the remaining sum is multiplied by 90 per cent to calculate the 90/10 film rental owed to the distributor. If the 90/10 rental is larger than the film rental worked out through the 'floor' percentage for the same gross then the exhibitor will pay the 90/10 rental. If the floor percentage provides a larger film rental, then the exhibitor will pay through the floor calculation method.

Table 8.1 provides a simple example of how the above formulas, when applied and compared in a specific week at one theatre, are calculated. The example assumes box office receipts of $12,000, a gross receipts percentage of 60 per cent and a house 'nut' of $5,000 (The 'nut' is the overhead – normally including payroll, rental on theatre property, maintenance, insurance, utilities, and standard advertising.)

In Table 8.1, the exhibitor would pay the distributor the greater of the calculated amounts, i.e. $7,200. It is important to note that there have typically been exceptions to the normal practice. In a process known as a 'settlement' the formal agreement was subject to a renegotiation if the set terms meant that the exhibitor would not make a reasonable profit on the deal. Normally, this kind of renegotiation would not take place unless an exhibitor had lost out to more than one film from the same studio.

Table 8.1 Cinema gross and adjusted gross deals

	Gross receipts	Adjusted gross receipts
Box-office receipts	$12,000	$12,000
Gross receipts	60%	
House 'nut'/allowance		–$5,000
Subtotal	$7,200	$7,000
90% Adjustment		–$700
Payment to distributor	$7,200	$6,300

Source: G. Verter and A.M. McGahan, 'Coming Soon: A Theatre Near You', Harvard Business School, 24 September 1998.

Exhibitors would also sometimes be required to pay a non-refundable advance rental fee in order to secure a film licence – normally a 'hot' film that the studio could use to negotiate such a hard-line position.

When dealing with 'speciality' or independent films (even if produced or acquired by Studio speciality divisions), exhibitors play a critical role in the exposure these films require if they are to work on the theatrical circuit. Exhibitors track the upcoming market through festivals, trade reviews, business word of mouth, and will contact a distributor directly when they have found out about an interesting/appropriate title. Normally, the distributor will contact the exhibitor and arrange for them to screen a film and consider booking it in one or more of their theatres. A typical example of a US exhibitor booking a foreign language film involved minimum terms and a minimum playing time, and called for a split of 90/10 above the house nut. A minimum floor for the first week was set at 70 per cent, the second week at 60 per cent, third at 50 per cent, fourth at 40 per cent and all remaining weeks at 35 per cent.

The floor protects the distributor if the film does not work; while the 90/10 split also protects against the downside. So, for example, a distributor may negotiate the following deal:

a) Minimum terms and minimum playing time.
b) Split of 90/10 above the house allowance, with minimum floor for first week at 70 per cent, second week at 60 per cent, third week at 50 per cent, fourth week at 40 per cent and all subsequent weeks at 35 per cent.
c) For example: theatre week one has $40,000 gross on a 90/10 deal, with a 60 per cent floor and a house 'nut'? of $5,000.
d) Start with $40,000 as the gross, subtract $5,000 (house 'nut'). Then split remaining $35,000 for the distributor.
e) How does that compare with the $60,000 'floor' figure? Sixty per cent of $40,000 is $24,000.
f) Since a new film rental of $31,000 (the distributor's share) is about 78 per cent of $40,000 or about 18 per cent higher than the floor, the 90/10 split will govern, with the theatre paying a higher percentage to the distributor than a straight 60 per cent gross.

Exhibition economics

Cinema owners have traditionally made most of their money from theatre admissions and from what the business terms 'concession' sales. Concessions include all drinks, sweets, popcorn and other foods sold on site. Specialized cinema owners have deliberately introduced licensed bars and higher-end food to cater for a different clientele. Overall, theatre operation costs and film rentals are the main costs that have to be met. Remaining income is derived from theatre advertising (commercials shown prior to trailers), foyer games and the rental of theatres for business, group or special event meetings. These make up the miscellaneous income streamlines below.

Income

For a multiplex cinema (owned or leased), against the theatre gross of 100 per cent:

	Percentage
Box office receipts	72
Concession sales	26.5
Miscellaneous (theatre ads, etc.)	1.5

The above numbers are for a typical hypothetical 16-screen US multiplex as outlined by Redstone.[4] From the total theatrical gross, the largest cost to be deducted is the film rental (the share of box office income that is to be returned to the distributor). The film rental is only calculated as a percentage of box office revenue, and does not include other income streams.

Items that are listed after film rental include rent (if paid), payroll, cost of goods, utilities, taxes, licences, insurance, maintenance and repairs, payroll taxes and employment/social benefits, services and supplies, miscellaneous (such as travel and promotion), and advertising. Each item below is listed as percentages of 'total theatre gross'. Hence, 'theatre-level cash flow' is, according to Redstone, in effect, 'multiplex revenue after all costs are deducted, When corporate overhead costs are then deducted, we achieve a "net cash flow" or profit margin of 15 per cent before depreciation, taxes or debt servicing for his hypothetical model.'

Costs

Against the theatre gross of 100 per cent:

	Percentage
Film rental (to distributor)	35
Rent or cost of money	15
Payroll	12
Cost of goods	4.25
Utilities	3
Taxes, licences, insurance	2.5
Repairs, maintenance	2
Payroll tax and benefits	2
Supplies and services	2
Miscellaneous	1.5
Advertising	0.75
Theatre-level cash flow	20
Less overhead	5
Net cash flow	15

A typical profit level ranges from 15 to 45 per cent depending on whether the theatre/ circuit is owned or leased. However, it is important to recognize that 'rental' figures vary considerably from territory to territory. For example, even strong independent distributors in the United Kingdom only get a 30 per cent rental figure from exhibitors. Some rental figures from smaller UK distributors are as low as 23–25 per cent. In the next section of this chapter and the case interview, we shall see how the economics of the above, standard approach, are already altering the way the exhibition sector is, and crucially, will be operating over the coming decade.

Digitalizing the exhibition experience

There has been a generally held assumption that the digital age will bring huge change to the movie industry's primary window – the release of films at the cinema. There are a multitude of factors in play, including the potential reinvention of content, alternative programming, the specific kinds of films that could become available, alternative and highly flexible, targeted programming, non-feature film material such as live performance and sports events, new ways of presenting film material and groundbreaking technical experience devices including, most importantly, 3-D viewing.

Broken down more categorically, the key element to focus on is the stage termed 'digital cinema'. This is the term used to describe distribution and projection of films in a digital format without the need for physical film prints. This development allows distributors considerable flexibility, and major cost savings. By way of example, if all cinemas were to operate with digital projectors overnight, actual movie prints would become obsolete.

The average cost of a print varies depending on the relationship between the buyer and supplier, but generally one print is deemed to cost around $2,000 (or generally £1,500 in the UK market). Specifically, the Boston Consulting Group estimated that annual savings would amount to around $2.5bn globally – with $1bn of savings annually in the USA alone. Approximately 80 per cent of the benefit would accrue to distributors, and 20 per cent to exhibitors, and a further $1.5bn of savings would be made in the international market.[5]

'For the past 15 years, digital has been on the horizon, but it's always been two years off. Now it's here', explained Tim Richards, CEO of Vue Entertainment.[6] Generally, film has not allowed cinemas to screen that many films in any given period, due to the physical size of the product. The physical task of casting prints, handling them in canisters and moving them around the network of theatres, is an industrially heavyweight job. Now, thanks to new technology, through a simple 19-inch monitor with ten different rows on it, Vue has the ability to cater for a market in a much more specific, 'perfect way'; explains Richards:

> Our programming ability and potential to reach specific audiences is now phenomenal, and the picture quality in digital has clearly surpassed analogue. I wish the consumer would pay more for it, but they are starting to appreciate that it's a cutting edge technology of the industry.

Richards, who is an entrepreneur who co-owns his company Vue Entertainment, is the first to acknowledge some of the teething problems they encountered when the company opened a major site in Hull. There is nothing worse than having hundreds of people in a dark room watching a screen that suddenly goes blank. But Vue has persevered and conquered its technical teething problems and is now very much at the forefront of new theatrical pioneering.

Many exhibition executives suggest that the key to the new digital exhibition technology is all about programming. A blockbuster release, such as *Spiderman*, was able to be show at 15-minute start intervals in Surrey, over an opening weekend, leading to groundbreaking audience figures. But by the same flexible token, Odeon and UCI Cinemas CEO Rupert Gavin points out that come Monday, the taste, appetite and profile of the audience will change, and the flexibility of digital programming allows the theatrical exhibitor to change with it.

To summarize, the advantages of digital exhibition technology for producers, and in particular distributors, are aplenty. They include economic cost savings such as in the release costs through savings in prints and advertising. The new technology also can be utilized to enhance the customer experience, and potentially increase the ticket price – notably when alternative, enhanced and flexible programming is achieved. However, the challenge has been to shift across to digital projectors (on average a cost of $100,000–$150,000 per screen, see the case interview below). Another issue has been the shift in control from the distributor to the exhibitor in terms of the management of the allocation of movies to screens. And organizing standards has been a significant challenge, which once again the USA has accomplished with more cohesion and speed than Europe or the Rest of the World.

It is not this book's role to track the initial testing phases of the digital roll-out across the world's screen base. Organizations such as Screen Digest and Dodona Research offer excellent in-depth analysis, statistics and constant updating and tracking. But the case interview that follows provides a detailed insight into the surprisingly positive results when public policy, harnessed with a commercial partner, can 'bend' and encourage the market to move forwards.

Case interview: Howard Kaidaish, managing director of Arts Alliance Media

In 2005 the UK Film Council selected Arts Alliance Media (AAM) to equip the Digital Screen Network (DSN), a network of 250 digital cinemas across the United Kingdom, at a cost of around €20m. The intention was to promote the screening of independent films in the United Kingdom. By 2006 AAM had completed the installation of 50 screens in the centre of London and Manchester, to JPEG 2000 standard. The second stage of the project, adding a further 190 or so screens, was completed by early 2008. Arts Alliance Media's MD Howard Kaidaish spoke to the author at the start of 2008 about his digital cinema roll-out experience:[7]

The UK Film Council had decided in the early 1990s that it wanted to promote more specialized contact on the screen, and encourage people to experiment and have access to a wider variety of cinema. In essence it wanted to change the cinema-going culture, giving audiences more access to European film, local film, and movies with more challenging scripts etc. What the market calls specialized films. Now, *Broke Back Mountain* for example is considered a specialized film. It was made by Focus, which is owned by Universal, which is owned by General Electric – so it's not exactly an 'independent' film, but it's a gay cowboy movie and there aren't that many gay cowboy movies ever since Montgomery Clift died. So the challenge was how to widen the market to allow more of that kind of product to be screened.

Digital was seen as the solution. The deal was that if the cinemas agreed to play more specialized content, they would be offered this new digital projector, which was mostly paid for, but in return the cinema had to benchmark what they currently played in terms of specialized content and then 'bid' how much more they would increase it by in return for the digital support. A bunch of cinemas all bid. The UK Film Council (UKFC) figured out which ones it was going to give the equipment to based on who bid the most and who would deliver. At the same point they were doing the auction, it realized that it needed a company to manage the initiative, install the equipment, offer delivery services and negotiate with film and sound companies such as Technicolor, Dolby, etc. AAM won the contract.

I think we were successful in winning the UKFC contract because our model offered flexibility in terms of pricing and in a way 'quotas' – so some cinemas could pay more for the equipment but commit to a lower threshold, while others could commit to higher levels for more contribution. Thomas Hoeg [the entrepreneur backing AAM] actually owns City Screen, which is one of the largest independent art house cinema chains in Europe, and we were already doing a lot of work with the network to experiment and install digital cinema equipment, including a lot of festivals and trial runs. We'd done fifty or more set ups, which was probably more than anybody else had done at that time, especially in Europe. So we knew how to do it; so where the power of solution was rolled in for the demo purposes, it was actually rolled in, the projector was rolled in and there was an umbilical cord that came out of the projector, and it was a box we would install at the cinema that would attach to the lights and the curtains and everything else, and you'd just plug the umbilical cord in; you plug the power in and away you go. It had a real simplicity to it that made it much more attractive.

The thing that slowed the implementation of the scheme down most was the process of getting the cinemas ready. They had to prepare – and do things like change their power system. Getting that schedule to work was an internal management problem. Ironically, the little guys would just do it, but the bigger guys had to go through a process, and there were probably different layers of management who had to decide what and whatever. There were some server issues but we managed to get round them without too much delay. Overall it's been remarkably smooth.

The UK Film Council project has grown, because the body paid for it, and we're glad that's all been able to happen. However, if you want to convert many more cinemas, it's a quite expensive proposition. Each cinema costs around one hundred thousand dollars to digitally convert. When you talk to cinema owners they say: 'We don't make any money, we're all starving, we're ready to shut down any minute', so they've always been hesitant to invest in the equipment. Conversely, for the studios, there are big bags of money to be saved, once you convert from celluloid to digital. A celluloid print comes in big heavy cans. What I do, when I have these people in my office, is say: 'Look at this', and one person can barely lift the cans for just one film. So, imagine sending out a digital file, when the cost is twelve or fifteen hundred dollars per print, verses two hundred dollars, so that means there's a thousand dollars to be saved every time a digital print is sent, verses a celluloid print. One financial analysis estimates that there's a billion dollars a year to be saved in a post-digital world, so it's that billion dollars a year that the studios want to unlock. How do they do that? Well, you've got one group of people that are going to save a lot of money, and you've got another group of people that are going to have to spend the money, that's how our business all of a sudden popped up, as we became the third-party integrator who goes in the middle and says 'Ok, we'll take some of the money from you guys and we'll buy the equipment, and we'll take a little bit of money from you guys and we'll pay for the whole thing' and so on. The mechanism that's kind of come to pass is what they call a virtual print fee motto, when the virtual print fee is the one that represents the eight hundred dollars or thousand dollars in savings, and we say: 'Look, Mr Studio, you're going to save this money every time that a digital print is sent, and you give us some of that for a period of time', and once the equipment is paid off everyone goes home happy. So, that's the business model that emerged.

Part 2

Users and the changing digital market

9 Users, consumer behaviour and market research

> No picture can be considered a success unless it appeals to the matinee trade. When you've got a picture women want to see, the men will have to go along. But a woman can always keep a man away from a picture than only attracts him.
>
> (Irving Thalberg)

> The images come first, and with images, like music, the primary reaction is emotional ... .
>
> (Richard Brooks, director, *In Cold Blood*)

Time, space and the marketplace

When examining the overall operating environment that media exists within, time and space are key defining factors. Together they are referred to as 'marginal utility'. Time is fixed, as there are only 24 hours a day available within which the public can select and consume product, or simply spend time doing an activity that does not involve the purchase of any product or monetary outlay. One of the economic variants that media analysts focus on is how cultures and economies vary from territory to territory, and within different sociological demographic groups. Specifically, people and communities that spend relatively less time working in turn create more available leisure time. Higher levels of working hours, by contrast, are assumed to create less leisure time. By calculating the marginal utility of leisure versus marginal cost of foregone income from working, market analysts can take an initial step towards understanding media market parameters.

The next issue to consider is the heavy competition within the available leisure place. Films are launched into an intensely competitive marketplace. As a cost-per-unit, Studio films for example are one of the most expensive media in the world to produce and to market to the audience.[1] And yet, of the 51 hours per week each American adult spends on leisure, movies and video take up less than 2 per cent of that time.

We shall examine the increasing competition from other forms of entertainment later in this chapter, but film destined for a theatrical release presents certain distinct challenges in itself. Unlike other consumer products, which can be tested in limited markets and then refined and repositioned before full theatrical launch, films are not able to be relaunched (with certain extraordinary or outstanding back-catalogue exceptions).[2] In the USA and leading international territories, every weekend is an 'opening' weekend, with new pictures facing competition from existing ones and new rivals; allowing audiences a relatively wide choice of what they can choose to see on any given weekend, albeit limited by the homogeneity of Hollywood-style 'opening' fare.

Successful commercial results depend on a Studio or major film's launch during this all-important opening weekend. By contrast, smaller independent films generally struggle to find appropriate screens and cinemas, and rely on critics, press coverage and, crucially, the key common success factor, word of mouth. For both sectors, the theatrical release affects all other revenue streams and ancillary markets.

What elements help attract a given audience to a film? Key motivators for the audience to buy a cinema ticket include:

- the awareness/visibility of the film
- the 'want to see'/level of desire/aspiration
- word of mouth (personal recommendation from peers)
- digital word of mouth (social networking, Internet forums/message boards and Twitter, for example).

The corresponding challenges presented to the industry include:

- an effort to meet end-user demand and appetite
- expanding and heightening the overall cinema-going experience
- demand for detailed audience research, and trends in leisure time
- an upward pressure on film production and marketing costs.

Market research

Given the above factors, market research is therefore of critical use to both Studios and independent film distributors and producers. It can provide information on: a) the market before the film is released; and b) the outcome once an audience has seen the film.

Marketability

This provides information about consumers that enables creative, advertising and marketing materials to be planned and executed to maximum effect. What and why is the audience attracted to (ultimately why would they buy a ticket)? How can this be optimized? How can the research be utilized to maximum effect?

Playability

This concentrates on consumer feedback specifically focused on how a film satisfies (or otherwise) its audience, and the likelihood of broad word of mouth and playability that can be gauged through both initial test screenings but also in exit polls.

The key methodological tools available include qualitative research and quantitative methods. Qualitative research can be used for early stage concept/creative development work and to explore how best to position the film, as well as to get a deeper understanding of trends in the marketplace.

Quantitative research can provide information on how strong, effective and persuasive the materials may be. Materials in question normally include trailers, TV commercial adverts and posters. Other quantitative research will focus on competitive testing and tracking studies. One of the key tools that can be used to determine both playability and marketability are recruited audience screenings. The intention is to replicate as closely as possible the cinema-goer's typical experience. These screenings are deliberately held in regular cinemas at regular times of the day; in suburban or provincial locations – in an effort to avoid heavily urban audiences, which have a higher percentage of 'avids' and cinephiles. The market research aspect of the screening is not revealed until after the film.

Audiences are selected according to demographics, films seen and their interest in the film concept being presented to them. Examples of perceived target audiences may be fans of the main stars or cast, genre fans, older females, franchise followers, younger teens, highbrow audiences, etc.

Test screenings normally fall into two key categories:

- Production screenings – sometimes a smaller audience, often more qualitative in nature, with more focus on the story, editing and elements that can still be refined.
- Marketing screenings – always a larger sample size (in other words conducted in large auditoriums) aimed at assessing overall appeal and across demographics, key strengths to build and focus on, and potential for word of mouth.

A vital lead finding tops the market screening process: How does the film play to an audience of cinema-goers interested in seeing that sort of film? Once that is established, the next key finding is whether the film has the potential to break out beyond that audience into a broader audience. It will only achieve that wider result if word of mouth is likely to take place. What will people say about the film? How will they describe the film? Will they recommend it, and how strongly? Word of mouth is one of the most important market phenomena that cannot be bought, no matter how much money is spent on a film's budget or its marketing launch. Strong test screening results are not a guarantee of box office success – they simply serve as a guide to the 'playability' of the film. A large number of other factors are all brought to bear on how a film performs when it is released.

Other market research tools include *opening weekend exit surveys*. These provide information on who went to see the movie; the audience's satisfaction and hence the film's potential for strong word of mouth; key media draws – what worked, what didn't; and how the film might play in later ancillary markets. Studios tend to use opening weekend exit surveys, combined with box office takings, to strategize their marketing and advertising strategy for the remaining length of the theatrical release, and to refine the DVD release.

Tracking films prior to their release is a market research tool used extensively by the studios. Tracking occurs on an ongoing basis, with data and reports being sent out to Studios/distributors at regular intervals throughout the week. This kind of information helps to establish the level of interest and awareness in a film about to be released, in release or some weeks/months prior to its release. Tracking information helps studios and distributors to strategize their release dates; their advertising spend (aka 'media buys'), theatre bookings and overall allocation of marketing budget and spend.

Understanding cinema audiences and consumer behaviour

The blockbuster approach

Each year the Hollywood Studios release around five titles that are intended to become *event movies*. Event movies are also known in the business as '*tent pole*' films around which the Studio's other pictures are slotted. They are high budget films (now sometimes more than $200m in budget size), and are produced by Studios with the intention of becoming mass-appeal vehicles with 360 per cent business models. They are supported by huge marketing spend and intense strategic planning.

Examples from the past decade include the following kinds of hit films or major franchises: *Lord of the Rings*, *Harry Potter*, a Pixar film, a Batman film, a Bond film, a Jerry Bruckheimer production, etc. And Summit Entertainment's Twilight franchise proves that it is not just the big six that can create such commercial franchises. The Studio's demographic target for event movies focuses initially on the 16–24-year-old market, and then it strategically attempts to broaden out to a wider audience. Parental Guidance and PG-13 films, for example, accounted for 85 per cent of the 2006 top 20 movies in the USA.[3] Today's market dictates that the anticipated box office needs to exceed $200m at the domestic box office in order to join this club – a considerable inflation on the equivalent $100m plus entry-ticket during the 1990s.

When we consider that of the $9.49bn taken at the US box office in 2006, that year's five leading movies grossed collectively $1.338bn (when some 607 films were released),[4] it is clear that the drive to achieve mega-hits is intense. The same pressure applies to the world market, which reached a box office all-time high in 2006 with $25.82bn. Just five films grossed collectively $2.237bn – almost 10 per cent of the worldwide total box office.[5]

The industry has applied the traditional 20/80 model (where 20 per cent of goods take 80 per cent of the market) to theatrical box office take. Known as 'Murphy's law', after the celebrated *Variety* statistical journalist Art Murphy, it states that 20 per cent of the films released in any given year take 80 per cent of the box office. However, given the above domestic and worldwide statistics, the trend has become polarized to the extreme.[6]

The independent approach

Bringing an independent film into the marketplace is now arguably a harder task than finding the finance and resources to produce and complete it. The traditional system for distributing independent films has been in a critical condition for the past decade; although certain industry professionals are confident that as traditional distribution paths have become more dangerous, promising new ones are opening up.

Peter Broderick, an independent film business consultant argues:

> As the costs of marketing and distribution rose, studios increased their dominance over theatrical distribution. Distribution advances paid to distribute independent films declined, along with the willingness of distributors to take risks on

independent features without stars or other pre-sold elements. And when such films found distribution, their fate was often determined by the size of the audience in their first weekend in the theatres. Unless a substantial crowd appeared, their theatrical life was usually short, undercutting their ancillary possibilities. While every year a handful of independent features succeed in distribution, these are aberrations that belie the fate of the hundreds of films that find little or no distribution.[7]

Independent movie-going audiences present a host of different challenges compared to the Studio roll-out of tent pole and larger budget film releases. The standard target audience for independent films is normally 30-plus, although students (18–25) present an important demographic for specialist films. University towns, for example, provide strong opportunities for target programming aimed at students. One of the best US examples includes Boston/Cambridge (with Boston University, MIT and Harvard within the catchment area).

The 30-plus audiences are generally harder to reach through advertising and marketing and, crucially, have considerably less leisure time available. Typical barriers to theatre-going for this age group include having young children, both partners working, one or both working later hours, the prohibitive cost of childcare, etc. Unlike Studio mainstream releases, independent films are not just competing with other leisure activities per se, but are competing against major lifestyle barriers to physically attending the cinema.

On the one hand the above barriers only go to serve the importance of market research, including production and marketing test screenings, even more strongly. On the other hand, many independent films are made at a fraction of the cost of Studio tent poles, leaving little funding available for this kind of test at the production stage.

Specialist independent distributors also tend to be working to a different economy of scale; hence their marketing research tends to be centred on festival screenings, inherited marketing information and materials from the sales company they acquired the film from, and their experience and gut instinct. Detailed market research is a luxury this sector rarely can afford.[8]

Segmentation analysis: How does the cinema industry (e.g. theatrical) deal with different audiences?

Classification exists in nearly all territories, and generally tends to rely on an age-related scheme, which awards film certification. The categories set by the British Board Film Classification (BBFC) in the United Kingdom, for example, are shown in Table 9.1.

The classification categories roughly translate to the following four audience groups:

- children (5–12 years old)
- family groups
- teenagers/young couples/students
- adults.

Table 9.1 Classification ratings

U	Suitable for all children below 12
PG	Parental Guidance – some scenes need adult to be present
12 and 12a	Suitable for 12 years and older
15	Suitable for 15 years and older
18	Adults only
R18	Restricted to licensed cinemas and sex shops

Source: British Board Film Classification.

Table 9.2 All Industry Marketing Committee's categories for audiences

AIM's *lifestyle* categories include:

* teens (to 16 years of age)
* teens/singles/couples (to 25 years of age)
* young families
* older families.

AIM's *attitude* categories are:

* film enthusiasts/avids
* social ('if nothing else to do ... ')
* reluctant
* non-attenders.

Source: All Industry Marketing Committee.

The above categories are broad, and the industry has attempted to define them more closely. The All Industry Marketing Committee, AIM,[9] has categorized audiences into two groups: by 'lifestyle' and by 'attitude' (Table 9.2).

The AIM is also concerned with the physical difference between urban and rural barriers to cinema attendance. Urban theatres tend to be within easy reach; offer a wide choice of films and screens, and offer a range of other entertainment activities either pre or post the film at close hand; but a trip will still demand a baby sitter for a family with young children. Rurally located theatres require the audience to travel – normally by car – to reach the cinema; may not run a multiplex or multiple-screen cinema, therefore limiting choice; will need to provide or offer food nearby to help attract customers; and shares the baby sitting issue with urban screens.

Cinemas face a considerable challenge in expanding their audience base. Some of the tools they use include the effort, over the past decade, to make them places for social meetings and activity beyond just screening films; offering regulars family tickets, loyalty cards, and subscription schemes; and promoting lifestyle combinations such as attached clubs and restaurants.

Establishing a theatre's catchment area

One way of understanding the challenge facing cinema operators is to consider what a cinema manager or exhibition site developer needs to consider when building a site. The industry as a whole tends to focus on the success or otherwise of film product, but the physical and sociological culture surrounding where and how the audience sees films is vital to understanding the market as a whole.

The numbers of screens per person – known as 'screen supply' – is a key starting point for any exhibitor. Currently there are nearly 19,000 people per screen in the United Kingdom; down from 1995 when there were nearly 30,000 people per screen. When compared to the USA, which is supplied at approximately 7,500 people per screen, the United Kingdom has a strategically steady ratio, where as the USA is significantly over-screened.

The planning of a cinema development involves estimating the catchment area that the new enterprise will serve, and from which it attracts customers. Associated issues include the drive time boundary (most people use cars outside major cities, and often inside urban areas); including travel radius; quality of roads, and utility and time of public transport.

The key factors to consider re strategy and position of a theatre include:

- scale of the cinema (10–20 screen multiplex? two screen independent?)
- scale and number of competitors
- quality and range of other leisure activities
- scale and quality of public transport services
- car parking facilities
- age and lifestyle profile of the target audience
- surrounding geography (are there many smaller villages/towns; or is the cinema really remote, e.g. in an isolated town not surrounded by population clusters)
- future town planning and upcoming changes in surrounding population need to be checked.

All of the above requires research, projections and a clear screening strategy. And all of the above is changing due to the near arrival of digital cinema.

Demographic and lifestyle data (United Kingdom)

There are a range of sources where data are available. These include: local authorities; national statistics; commercial companies (Experian, etc.); and CACI Ltd. CACI Ltd runs ACORN – a geo-demographic system that classifies neighbourhoods into descending subsections of statistics, including for example: 6 categories, 17 groups, 54 types, etc. Each category includes patterns of consumer, economic and lifestyle behaviour. Additional sources of information include Mintel, British Market Research Bureau (which works for the UK cinema advertising industry), the UK Film Council, whose website has a wide range of information and research, and the Arts Council.

All the above information can be analysed and adapted to understand audience patterns, which in turn can be used strategically to establish a site and target audience for a cinema. There are certain limitations to the impact of this kind of demographic research. Individual films can vary widely re their attraction to different audience types. Specialist audiences have very different profiles when compared to multiplexers. They tend to have higher education qualifications and work in professional careers. Teen audiences rarely attend specialist film screenings.

Audience development

Much has been written about the importance of the cinema-going experience: the size and scale of faces larger than life; spectacles that do not exist in real life but take extraordinary form on the big screen; the emotional, visual, listening senses all stimulated in a dark auditorium surrounded by other people. The 'shared experience' of the cinema theatre has been likened to the telling of stories around camp fires way back before the days of mass media and global communication technology.

Two key elements will drive audience development. The first driver still relies on the quality of the product. But quality does not necessarily mean large, big budget films packed with stars; or the third or so film in a proven franchise that historically took huge numbers in its opening weekends but is now tired despite being previously tested. The 20/80 law dictates that many blockbuster films fail to recoup their overall production and marketing spend even at the end of their full ancillary run. Break-out specialist films, in particular those that cross over from a niche audience to a wider appeal, can be highly popular and profitable.

The second driver is the inexorable advance of technology. Digital distribution, digital sound, picture quality and general viewing conditions are under constant development. Given that the theatrical experience is entirely different to watching a film at home, developments to enhance the cinema-going experience are critical to its sustainability. The selection process and physical commitment are different; and the power of being able to do other things at the same time as semi-watch a film – turn off, pause, and start again – are not part of the cinema-going experience.

Mass broadband penetration is driving change throughout all media industries. In the entertainment sector, video-on-demand, downloading to own, net and cell phone marketing, blogging, video up-loading, etc., are all helping drive significant change. These new delivery and information platforms are, in turn, making new demands on audience research experts.

The role of digital leisure substitutes

Annual UK cinema attendances, after a steady rise throughout the 1990s, stopped expanding in 2002, and by 2005 had fallen by 11 million to 165 million.[10] The plateau in cinema attendances was, for the first time, mirrored by a slump in DVD/video sales, which fell back in 2005. Traditionally, weakness in cinema-going has been laid at the door of a strong DVD/video market (which rose between 1996 and 2004), but according to a recent UK Film Council paper written by economist Hasan Bakhshi,[11] recent research raised 'the possibility that some third, common factor is responsible for the muted cinema and DVD/video audiences'.

In the report's summary, Bakhshi points out that the fall in cinema attendance by the 25–44 age group is particularly marked, and that there is some evidence that the fall in DVD/video use is concentrated in the 15–24 year olds. Rather than assuming a demographic explanation, the plateau has coincided with a 'rapid rise in the availability of online entertainment and multi-channel TV, both of which may be substitutes for cinema and DVD/videos'. According to available expenditure and time use surveys, it is reasonable to suggest that there has been substitution away from DVD/video into Internet use, which is 'likely to have been particularly strong amongst 15–24 year-olds'. And it is these same younger consumers that have been heavy users of new digital technologies.

Bakhshi goes on to stress the need for further research in three key areas, including analysis in international patterns in cinema-going, DVD/video audiences and digital technology consumption patterns, but the initial conclusions are yet another warning to all filmmakers how difficult it is to achieve a slice of the pie.

10 Traditional film marketing

> What a distributor thinks of your story matters. What's the concept, the 'catch'? Is there something there that they can play with, market, and help reach people with?
>
> (Jake Eberts, producer, Allied Filmmakers)
>
> Don't outspend your revenues, but don't under spend your potential.
> (Rob Friedman, Co-Chairman and CEO, Summit Entertainment)

The scope of film marketing

Historically, early films were driven by publicity generated around stars, normally while a film was being shot. The two key marketable elements were stars and the picture title, and every effort was made by the Studios to get those names and titles into the press. Later, the long release patterns – sometimes months – of the 1960s and 1970s allowed film titles to build a following (via word of mouth) without the urgent pressures of a make-or-break opening weekend. Today, given the competitive pressures of the entertainment mass market discussed in the previous chapter, marketing presents an all-encompassing and ever-present challenge at every stage, starting with a film's inception and all the way along its journey towards finding an audience. Marketing in the film business has historically suffered from a tendency to be approached and viewed from a tightly drawn and narrow perspective. The standard, traditional assumption is that marketing stands for a set of elements created and executed by a department at a certain stage of a film's life – most often restricted to the theatrical release.

Whilst later sections of this chapter will focus on the strategies and tools specific to film product, many of the issues and techniques are relevant to wider business strategies. Issues of how to sell, place, brand and differentiate a product should start all the way back at the inception of an idea. These challenges might, for example, include the initiation of a company; the start of a brand; the impetus behind a film-making team; the placing of a product by a sales company into the international distribution market; and the positioning of all associated media materials and spend, not just at the theatrical stage, but during the video/net download, pay-TV, free-TV and even library re-packaging stage. And certain films will demand associated merchandising and/or music spin offs that all help create awareness of the product. In summary, marketing is a key and ever-present element of any strategy concerning the film exploitation process.

How can we best define marketing as it mainly relates to the film business? Marketing offers a range of communication tools and strategies that connect product with buyers (aka distributors) and audiences. Each film is different, and hence each film requires a different specific marketing strategy. The initial starting point – such as a book, short story or newspaper article – can often offer or suggest a critical concept that can then be refined and built around. If a screenplay is based on an original idea rather than on source material, it may still have a key defining element that can be used as a marketing 'hook'.

The specific *genre* of a film – if it definitely fits into one – is a strong starting point. Concepts that communicate clearly and simply what a film is about – meaning the *type* of film the audience can expect to see – are enshrined in a key photographic image, a logline, a title, a poster, a teaser trailer, a trailer, and so on. Often defining concepts are there to be found in the source material, but they can sometimes be in danger of being overlooked if the filmmaking process has typically become divided and disjointed between departments or different companies.

Each element of the creative package, including the director, the writer(s), the lead cast (and sometimes even departments such as photography or music), presents important marketing opportunities. Naturally leading movie stars bring a different set of hooks, awareness (and pressures of expectation) in contrast to unknown leads – but the impact of festival and prize-giving awards and press 'discoveries' should offer significant opportunities to capitalize on.

Marketing plans and successful execution sometimes fail due to poor internal communication between the filmmaking team, financiers and distributor(s). It is essential for producers, executives and specialist marketers to agree on a plan, and organize meetings so that ideas are properly explored and examples are circulated in a timely manner. Communicating to a buyer further up the value chain or to the audience end-user effectively requires excellent communication between the originators and exploiters of the product.

A marketing plan will be mapped out over a timeline, but its strategic utility is how effectively it gauges opportunities and entry points into targeted and specific areas of the overall market. These are known as 'platforms' (not to be confused with 'platform releases') and by breaking down the overall market into different segments, the shape and scope of a plan can become apparent, and weaknesses addressed before the wrong message or emphasis has jeopardized the film's value.

The Studio perspective: Hutch Parker, former vice chairman, 20th Century Fox, chair of Regency Pictures

Marketing is the force that has had the most comprehensive impact in shaping all of our lives who are involved in making movies. The increasing need to achieve a level of mass marketing for Friday night openings is influencing what movies get made, with whom, and how. Movies are getting dated in advance of being made, and that push to get a certain release window is influencing the way the picture is executed. The competition for audiences has gotten more fierce, and that final push represented in marketing has become the final battleground for one film to differentiate itself from another, ultimately making that final connection with the audience.

We've seen marketing dollars increase radically. Your television marketing campaign, which is obviously your most expensive component, is something you have to do just to get on the playing field. Now the scramble is for alternative ways to reach the audience, and kind of 'event-ize' these movies in their minds courtesy of whatever other means necessary. What it's reflective of is that it's harder and harder to get the message across, and get it heard in the midst of the number of movies that are being released. The sophistication that's evolved in the marketing of movies is such that people are seeking out new and different ways to augment the movie campaigns. That includes promotional partners, [and] groundbreaking techniques on the Internet. It's gotten to the point where one of the first things you shoot on a movie is stuff that you will use in your marketing materials.

As the Internet evolves [and becomes a more viable] content platform, it's further enhancing the amount of competition for people's attention when you look at how they're spending their leisure time. Particularly with the next generation, the challenge – 'How do we get these messages across?' – will continue to be fierce. And it will continue to impact. It's going to be increasingly difficult for studios to make and fund pictures that they don't have a clear idea how to sell. And what that will mean is seeing franchises and sequels. We're seeing it already: a preponderance of titles that had some level of pre-awareness before they came to the screen. ... That's all reflective of how crucially important marketing has become as part of our process. Creative-based decisions now have to take into account much more marketing-based decisions, and not just domestically, but globally.

The player value chain

Conceptually it is useful to consider the filmmaking process – all the way from inception to final delivery to an audience, as a 'chain' (in the same way that we use the film value chain to analyse the different stages of inception, production and delivery). Each key player plays the role of a link in that chain. Key 'links' include the producer, the writer, the director, the financier(s), the sales company, the key distributors in major territories, the exhibitors controlling access to cinemas, and so forth. Between these links, facilitators, advisors and specialists all play a role. They include agents, lawyers, managers, accountants, designers and specialist marketers, publicists, etc.

All of these players need to 'pitch' or 'sell' a product or their own services/skills at various stages in the film business process, whether it's the 'idea' for a story (producer to writer, or writer to producer), the project to a favoured director, the package to financiers, or a distributor screening a film to an exhibitor, etc. What each player is really doing is marketing themselves and their product to each other. A weakness in the links – or critically, a break in the chain – will mean that the product either stalls or ultimately fails.

Long before a film has to be presented to an audience it will have gone through a highly exacting process of being pitched from one sector of the business to another, in an effort to maintain momentum. The ability to 'pitch' an idea, material, or an overall package forms one of the key roles and skills required in a film producer. However, the demand for strong presentational and intercommunication skills is high among all areas and sectors of the film business. Early mistakes and sloppy presentations lead to films normally never being financed and shot, let alone meeting their intended or otherwise audience.

Business-to-business marketing

Most industries operate on a number of different levels or platforms. The buying and selling of product is often done more than once during the process of bringing the final 'goods to market' and it is often referred to as 'business-to-business' activity. The film industry operates on a number of levels, all of which require different practitioners and customers to position themselves and 'pitch up to the next level'.

A simplified player value chain is outlined below, with notes on who markets to whom:

The screenwriter

First, a screenwriter markets themselves through the quality of their ideas, work and track record. Second, established writers have agents, who control access to talent and are responsible for shaping careers and finding appropriate work for their clients. Producers – in particular creatively driven producers who generate their own ideas and material – are extremely important for writers to be championed by. Directors also play a role in the work and marketing of writers. Established directors may chose to work with a writer on a long-term, multi-project basis; or recommend a writer to other filmmakers. To operate effectively, a writer must be able to: a) write treatments/outlines as well as full screenplays; b) verbally communicate their views, concepts and work; and, c) understand where their work is targeted in terms of the overall market.

The producer

Self-reliance is critical to a producer's market value. They need to be able to market themselves, generate their own ideas, have an ability to raise finance, attract talent (including writers, directors and actors), and be strong project managers. During their contact with the rest of the player value chain, they are constantly selling their ability to produce. Producers have allies – such as a lawyer (and sometimes agents, especially in Hollywood) – to guide and help them. That relationship is also an important part of a producer's positioning and marketing, as they will be judged by the quality of their advisors.

The director

If a director is also a writer (in particular an 'auteur' voice) then they arguably will have the potential advantage of being more 'visible' to producers and other financiers. Their work and 'vision' is already partly committed once they have produced their own screenplay. Otherwise, a director's bank of work is important. Agents do play an important role in the Hollywood/English-language market sector. However, a director will have to sell themselves when they are: a) a first-timer; b) coming off a poor or mediocre film; c) changing direction or genre; d) trying to direct their own script for the first time; or e) working at a new budget level, in particular a higher one.

The distributor

An independent distributor faces two ways: towards producers, studios and sales agents in order to acquire product; and towards exhibitors, and all the ancillary distribution outlets in order to reach an audience/end-user. Their brand, specialist knowledge and ability to market and book appropriate to their market are all noted by sellers, but often a distributor will have to stress their strengths and skills beyond just price in order to compete for hot product. Their relationship to exhibitors will depend on their strength in the market and their supply of upcoming product, but they will have nurtured and spent considerable energies on positioning and branding their operation.

Film marketing to the theatrical audience

Much has been written by academics and by industry practitioners about the significant changes in the exhibition landscape, in particular in the USA, which in turn has radically changed the way films are released over the past decade. The rise of the multiplex and its impact on cinema-going was analysed in Chapter 8, but for any producer and distributor, the following questions are important to consider:

1 What kind of film are you launching? Can it be presented as a genre film? What is the target audience if it is a specialized film?
2 Who's most likely to want to see it? (E.g. what is the demographic of the core audience?)
3 How are you going to reach that demographic? (What kind of release is appropriate? Wide? Platform?)
4 Is there a unique selling point (USP) hook (e.g. a major star in small film; a real life story hook)?
5 What tools are you going to use?
6 What tools have you already got (normally via the shoot and the sales company) and are they still applicable?
7 What tools are you going to create?
8 What test screenings have been done?
9 Are you holding marketing test screenings?
10 What is the level of the 'prints and advertising' (P&A) budget to be spent by the distributor? (See below.)
11 How did the exhibitors respond to the screening? What pattern of booking do you want, and what are you expecting in reality?
12 What are the best release dates/programming/counter-programming issues?
13 How are you going to handle the press?
14 Do you need to think of ways to make your film critic proof?

The above list is by no means exhaustive, but it provides an indication of the level of practical, strategic, creative and execution-dependent demands on the distributor as they launch a film to the theatrical audience. A key part of the planning for a theatrical release is the level of the P&A budget. Ironically, this term will soon be outdated as physical prints will soon be replaced by digital distribution (see Chapter 12). Each distributor puts together a P&A budget for the initial theatrical release of a film. It is this exposure, in addition to that from the press and by word of mouth generated by the release that 'legitimizes' the film, and helps create further value down the value chain. A poorly planned P&A budget can lead to too many, or too few screens booked (and prints struck), not only damaging the strategy but wasting considerable financial resources. An advertising campaign that does not reach the specific film's target audience may not only waste considerable sums of money, but garner poor word of mouth through the wrong audience seeing the film in its first few days. A media spend (the 'A' part of P&A) will need to be checked carefully. Too much emphasis on television spots may not be beneficial to a film's market – or no spend in this area may be equally damaging, depending on the product and the distributors' plans in terms of video and so on.

Screen International and *Variety* box office charts each week publish within their statistical information the number of screens each film is playing on and whether it has changed week-on-week. The important number is the film's screen-average in addition to its overall three-day or seven-day total. The screen average is an important indicator of a successful release. For large blockbusters, a screen average of around $4,000–$6,000 represents a strong showing for releases of more than 3,000 screens. For small, independent fare, the number may be much higher per site over just one, two or double-figure numbers of screens. These averages can be up to more than $20,000 per screen and sometimes much more.

The best organized and experienced distributors have a detailed plan for each of their films' release, informed by previous P&A campaigns, similar profiled product, and strong tools.

The poster

As with photographs in papers and in cinemas (windows, etc.), the poster may be the first visual element a member of the public sees of the film being marketed. It is very important and presents an opportunity to place a film.

Great posters can reveal the 'feel' of a film, and guide the audience's expectation without trying to say or achieve too much. Some directors such as Spanish auteur Pedro Almodovar – whose company prepares his marketing material – capture their brand and work through colours. His posters are always distinctive, as are the stills selected for the press.

Most Hollywood posters and US indie posters handed across to 'foreign' are unsuitable for many territories. But the photos delivered are also poor.

Key issues to consider when building a poster campaign include:

1   Who is your key target audience, and is your image appropriate?
2   Clear images, which are not trying to tell too much but are attention catching, work best if available or able to be created.
3   A clear title is important, as the image must appear in much smaller ads in newspapers.
4   How good was the set photography, or do you have to start again or take prints from the negative?
5   Colours are very important. They often run in keeping with genre. Bright loud colours denote comedy. Dark blue/black denote thriller and sometimes horror. Red can mean love/romance. These are not hard rules, but worth being aware of.
6   Quotes – often very useful from festivals/early reviews.
7   Updating: new quotes, prizes of 'biggest indie hit in UK this year' etc.
8   A poster is always limited: it can only say so much.

The trailer

The trailer is a key tool designed and used to encourage an audience to 'want to see' a film. Very strong trailers can attract word of mouth even before a film's release. The trailer is a more targeted tool, and can be more powerful than a poster, given that it is using the film medium – images, sound, fast cutting, music, voice over, dialogue from the film (and sometimes deliberately not), etc. A good trailer can offer a powerful combination, and can be utterly off-putting if poorly executed.

There are three main trailer groups (in addition to a promo made by a sales company or producer for showing to buyers only). These include the theatrical trailer that normally runs from around 2–3 minutes; the teaser-trailer, that runs at around 1–1.5 minutes, and TV spots, which can be 5, 15 and sometimes 30 seconds.

Key issues to consider when building a trailer campaign include:

1   The positioning of the trailer – what other film(s) is it playing with? What type of cinemas, screens?
2   Positioning of the TV spot/teaser – what programmes, what time, what audience demographic?
3   What information is being communicated – Genre? Characters? Style? Narrative – but not whole story? Emotion – probably the most important?
4   Holding attention – is the information conveyed in a compelling manner?
5   Does it drag, feel long, and is it intelligible?
6   Is it too fast to follow, too visual to the point of disengaging the audience?
7   If two stars are the leads, are we clear who is the protagonist … ?
8   How large does the film feel? Is it a major blockbuster?
9   How emotionally affecting and intimate does it feel, if that is appropriate?
10   Is the music working? (And crucially, has it been cleared?)
11   How does the trailer test? (E.g. with colleagues, etc.)

Case study: *The Mother*

The following case study examines business-to-business marketing, sales and promotion prior to the consumer release.

The background

The Mother was an original screenplay written by Hanif Kureishi, which the author initially wrote for Stephen Frears to direct. The film never happened. Only when Duncan Heath at ICM put Stephen Evans, MD of Renaissance Films, and a list of filmmakers including Kureishi, director Roger Michell and producer Kevin Loader together, did the screenplay have an opportunity to be packaged and ultimately financed and produced. The writer-director-producer team was reunited, following their successful partnership on *The Buddah of Suburbia*, an adaptation of Kureishi's acclaimed novel.

The screenplay was a sharply drawn, family-focused drama with a significant twist: the 'mother' loses her elderly husband of many years during the first act, only to take up an affair with her daughter's errant boyfriend. By the third act the family – including the daughter – find out what's been happening behind closed doors.

Renaissance Films picked up the project in 2000, and then, with the support of ICM and Michell and Loader's Free Range Films, brought BBC Films in to be the lead financier on the £1.6m film. Renaissance Films retained the world sales rights outside the United Kingdom, which BBC Films controlled.

Despite the pedigree of the filmmaking package, *The Mother* was a testing read from a distributor's perspective. The film had an edgy and challenging perspective on families, sexuality and emotional trust. Michell – who had experienced commercial success with films ranging from *Notting Hill* to *Changing Lanes*, was determined not be lured into typically 'commercial' casting choices, opting for theatre and television veteran Anne Reid over other suggestions, such as Dame Judi Dench. The boyfriend attracted up and coming actor Daniel Craig, not yet known as James Bond; while other roles were filled by strong UK actors including Stephen Mackintosh (*Lock Stock and Two Smoking Barrels*). However, none of the actors were of significant value to distributors.

Pre-selling The Mother

Renaissance and BBC Films were aware that for the film to work, it required a carefully staged marketing plan to distributors over a series of film markets that were to include Cannes 2002, the former MIFED (November 2002), and ultimately a first-half 2003 festival that would launch the film to the world market. At Cannes 2002, a simple, typographical concept poster with the title and the names of the filmmakers was designed in green, with deliberately no images run at that stage. BBC Films was credited as the financier, meaning that the film was, in the eyes of distributors, very likely to go into production.

When Sony Pictures Classics, run by Michael Barker and Tom Bernard, heard of the re-teaming of Kureishi, Michell and Loader, they showed considerable interest in the project. SPC had previously handled *Buddah of Suburbia*. A screenplay was sent after Cannes 2002, which Barker responded positively towards.

SPC was very keen to pre-buy the film for what Barker calls his 'standard' $300,000 advance. This sum was $200,000 lower than Renaissance's 'Take' sales estimate, but the sales company stressed to BBC Films that with North American distribution secured, a commitment that is very valuable to foreign independent buyers, the film would attract further cornerstone distributors prior to its completion. SPC was keen to build awareness of the film at an early stage, and set up a website for the film with quotes, images and information about the film and the filmmakers. Most importantly, the deal was able to be announced prior to the MIFED market in Milan, attracting considerable attention from specialist buyers.

By the time the Milan market took place, the film was being edited. Producer Kevin Loader and Renaissance convinced Michell to allow a couple of clips to be shown (lasting just a few minutes, with no grading and no music), including one of the sexually intimate scenes between Craig and Reid. Tele-Munchen came in with an offer for German-speaking rights of $220,000, just $30,000 lower than the take price, which was accepted by Renaissance and BBC Films. A couple of smaller territories, including the Benelux countries, also pre-bought the film. Strategically, this meant that the film had some strong specialized commitments before any of those buyers had actually seen the completed film.

The festival challenge

The next step in terms of positioning was to find a launch pad for the film at a key festival in the first half of 2003. Despite the pedigree of the filmmaking team, *The*

Mother was rejected by all sections of the Berlin Film Festival, to the surprise of the sales team and financiers. Renaissance's marketing team decided to try to convince the Cannes section, Director's Fortnight, to support the film. After deliberations, Director's Fortnight offered *The Mother* the opening film slot. All other Cannes slots had also rejected the film, so Director's Fortnight was the last slot for a premiere launch.

As soon as the film was accepted by Cannes, Renaissance organized a screening of the film in Paris. The strategy for sales companies when a film has a slot at Cannes is to find a French distribution partner prior to the festival. This allows press and festival marketing costs to be shared, but most importantly it enables the French distributor to organize and take best advantage of the attention a film attracts with the world press during the festival. Philippe Helman, MD of UGC PH, offered $125,000 for the film, and once again, the deal was able to be announced prior to the festival premiere, further attracting buyer interest. During this period Michael Barker saw the film in New York, and rang Finney to give him his reaction: 'Angus ... I've seen the movie ... it's spectacularly un-commercial.'

The opening slot in Director's Fortnight was a good place for the film to be premiered. From a sales perspective, it allowed the film to be reviewed early and subsequently screened to buyers in the first half of the market. This in turn allowed for sales to be closed during the second half of the two-week festival. If a film screens very late in the festival, it can be hard to impossible for a sales company to take advantage of the market and close out un-sold territories.

The film was supported strongly by the makers and talent. Michell, Kureishi, Craig and Reid all came to Cannes for the premiere, and then dedicated two full days to give press, television and radio interviews. Kureishi in particular was popular, opining about American foreign policy mistakes during the festival press conference, and attracting significant press attention due to his literary fame as much as his film work. A modest party was held at Renaissance's garden offices, attended by more than 150 guests. Despite divided reviews, the film picked up good festival word of mouth, and a steady flow of specialized distributors visited Renaissance's offices over the first week of Cannes.

By the end of the market, a significant number of territories had been sold, including Italy (Lucky Red), Spain (Vertigo), Scandinavia (CCV), Australia and New Zealand (Dendy), most of Eastern Europe and South Korea (Dong Soong). BBC Films had also found a UK distribution partner in Momentum. It should be noted, however, that due to the tricky subject matter, the film failed to be sold to Japan, and outside South Korea, no other Asian territories bought the film. Japanese male buyers explained that an affair between such an old woman with a young man would 'never happen in Japan'; while Japanese female buyers stated that 'affairs of this nature do happen, but no one talks about them'.

What was notable was that no two distributors went head-to-head for the film during Cannes. The pattern of sales was exclusively governed by appropriate and committed distributors, which in turn meant that final sales figures were modest rather than strong for *The Mother*. On the final weekend of the festival, the film went on to receive the Prix Europa, winning distribution support across the European Union from the MEDIA programme.

11 Digital production

> Show me the budget, and I'll show you the movie.
>
> (Jean-Luc Goddard)
>
> It is now possible to make a film for hardly any money at all ... [yet] so often, people fall back on excuses to not make a film – possibly because filmmaking, suddenly being let loose and having complete freedom to create 90 minutes of visually storytelling, is still a very daunting idea.
>
> (Mike Figgis, filmmaker)[1]

Singing all the way to production

'One day some little fat girl in Ohio is going to be the new Mozart',[2] opined Francis Ford Coppola on the set of a big budget feature whose size was threatening to engulf it, *Apocalypse Now*. Coppola then was talking of the possibilities new developments in 8 mm and VHS cameras gave to aspiring filmmakers. Little could Coppola have imagined how, in a generation, the conversation would shift completely to digital technology, both in cameras and methods of production, as the Trojan horse that would finally open the doors of the movie business and (to shift metaphors slightly) finally lower the substantial barrier cost imposes on new filmmakers.

To an increasing extent, the little fat girl has now started singing. The number of films produced on low and micro budgets has been growing exponentially from the turn of the twenty-first century onwards.[3] This growth has of course been fuelled by the arrival of digital technology that promises new opportunities for such films. This chapter explores, in part, some of the technical developments that are actively changing the means of film production (though the author warns that such changes are constant and quickly outdated); and goes on to discuss the implications for filmmakers and how the relationships between 'old' and 'new' and 'production' and 'finance' can benefit from sharing knowledge, creating alignments and by all sectors being forced to take a very hard look at how they can go about their work with more 'discipline'. Badly made films can find a seriously committed audience, while fabulous-looking, technical masterpieces can fail dismally at the box office. And crucially, just because a filmmaker 'can' – thanks to the advent of digital economics – does not answer 'what', 'why' or, crucially, 'who for?'

The future is RED

Historically and even right up to the mid-2000s, the main cost barrier for filmmakers was the cost of buying or, far more typically, renting state-of-the-art camera equipment. The industry standard 35mm stock has offered a visual resolution of approximately 4,000 lines, or '4K' in filmmaking language. The promise over the past decade has been that digital cameras would continue to lower in price and increase in quality and offer a cheaper alternative to shooting on physical film. High-definition cameras were expected to replace film over the past decade, but filmmakers remained deeply resistant to them.

Technically, most digital video cameras utilize prisms to split incoming light by colour, and send it to three separate sensors, which in turn has the effect of softening the images. While footage is sharpened, halos and exaggerated edges are introduced. But what filmmakers really objected to was that when the small sensors placed too much of the picture into focus, the footage took on a 'canned' look. Cinematographers in particular took umbrage to the fact that what was in front of the lens and some 20 or 30 feet away looked sharp, creating a flat image similar to that found in art or painting. The ability to guide the viewer's eye by selectively blurring focal planes is, according to producer and director Pierre de Lespinois, a favourite 'storytelling tool',[4] and filmmakers resented losing that creative control.

So to take on the challenge of celluloid, any truly competitive new digital camera needed to be built around an image sensor identical in size and shape to a single frame of 35mm motion picture film. It would also have to accommodate the top of the range lenses used for these cameras and be able to give cinematographers a free hand to choose focal length, focus, aperture and all the variables that gave them the options in the storytelling styles they were used to.

The first attempts at digital cinematography to gain wide acceptance were after the introduction by Sony of CCD technology in the late 1990s and the further introduction of HDCAM recorders. The first movies to be widely advertised as having used digital filmmaking technology were the three *Star Wars* prequels, released starting in 1999, the second of which used Sony's HDW-F900 for the entirety of its shoot.

In the meantime, formats like Mini-DV (released 1995) had revolutionized the consumer camera market and made these devices increasingly competitive in regards to image quality – two tiers had developed: high-end digital cameras designed for major big budget productions, and improving consumer cameras which, in conjunction with new editing software programmes, gave budding filmmakers a peek at the basics of movie-making. But there was still no bridge between the two, which would allow independent filmmakers access to cameras fit for the big screen. And then along came the RED camera.

Case study: the RED camera

The RED camera is a good example of the potential of digital technology to disrupt the old barriers to entry in the film industry. Founded by Oakley billionaire Jim Jannard, the RED Digital Cinema Company spent five years or so in the research and development of perfecting a digital camera that would approximate as much as possible the look and feel of 35mm. Taking into account the myriad of high-definition shortcomings, much of the technical work focused on perfecting a sensor that could stand up to 35mm comparison. Today, the RED One records moving images in a startling 4,096 lines of horizontal resolution and 2,304 of vertical. For comparison, high-definition films such the *Star Wars* prequels and *Sin City* are at 1,920 by 1,080, set at the same resolution as HDTV.

Filmmakers such as Peter Jackson and Steven Soderbergh have used the company's first product, the RED One, the latter for his two films on the life of revolutionary Che Guevara. In reference to the problems of electronic and microphonic barriers often associated with highly digitalized equipment, director Soderbergh explained: 'We beat the shit out of the Reds on the *Che* films, and they never skipped a beat'.[5] Upcoming features to be shot in RED will include the 2009 Lionsgate release *Game*.

In early 2008 the company announced the launch of RED Scarlet. It retails at less than £10,000 ($17,500) for its basic package without lenses – making high-resolution filmmaking far more widely accessible than ever before. Filmmakers can afford to buy rather than rent, and when compared to the standard $25,000 for four weeks rental on a Panasonic 35mm camera, the future looks RED. As Jannard points out: 'There's talent on the streets, kids with ideas who have stories to tell and never have a chance. Up to now, they've been limited to tools that confine their stories to You Tube.'[6] Not any longer.

Of course, image resolution is not everything. The RED still cannot compete with high-end digital cameras in other aspects, such as colour or luminance information gathering, but for its price it is a highly competitive product. It signals the shortening gap between consumer and professional cameras.

Who's shooting on what?

Looking at recent releases (See Table 11.1) it is interesting to note the wider scope of digital cinematography, encompassing both blockbuster-sized budgets and of course smaller, low- to micro-budget films.

The changes that count

Is digital significantly cheaper? The answer depends on which sector of the market you are examining, and overcoming the way that the industry relates to film budgets per se. Big budget productions, which make up such an important part of the marketplace do not see their budgets affected by use of digital cameras in a major, groundbreaking way. Savings are at most in the tens of thousands. And some of the filmmakers in Table 11.1 have deliberately mixed different stock and technical equipment for heightened effects rather than due to any budget considerations.

What about independent, small- or micro-budget productions? On one level, an initial assessment of direct cost savings (leaving aside RED for a moment) is not necessarily asking the right question. The level of ambition, scale, scope and 'size' of the film (including numbers of pages to be shot, and set-ups to be covered) still effectively determine the level of costs required to capture the material. It is here that the experienced director can be very instructive in getting below the surface of the filmmaking process.

Mike Figgis points out in his excellent book[7] that a filmmaker who starts with an ambition to shoot at a specific location on 35mm, will find himself/herself locked into a budget that in turn informs both producers and financiers that the film will automatically require around £500,000 simply because the overheads (accommodation,

Table 11.1 Recent camera system choices

Film	Year	Cinematographer	Camera/system
Avatar	2009	Mauro Fiore	Fusion
Naan Kadavul Tamil	2009	Arthur Wilson	RED One
Slumdog Millionaire[a]	2008	Anthony Dod Mantle	Silicon Imaging SI-2K
Apocalypto	2006	Dean Semler	Panavision Genesis
Che: Part One	2008	Steven Soderbergh	RED One
Balls of Fury	2007	Thomas E. Ackerman	Panavision Genesis
Before the Devil Knows…	2007	Ron Fortunato	Panavision Genesis
Chemical Wedding	2008	Brian Herlihy	Thomson Viper
Click	2006	Dean Semler	Panavision Genesis
Cloverfield	2008	Michael Bonvillian	Sony HDCAM/cinealta[b]
Collateral	2004	Dion Beebe	Thomson Viper[c]
The Curious Case of…	2008	Claudio Miranda	Thomson Viper
Deception	2008	Dante Spinotti	Panavision Genesis
Flyboys	2006	Henry Braham	Panavision Genesis
Gamer	2009	Ekkehart Pollack	RED One
Get Smart	2008	Dean Semler	Panavision Genesis
Che: Part Two	2008	Steven Soderbergh	RED One
I Now Pronounce You…	2007	Dean Semler	Panavision Genesis
The Informant	2009	Steven Soderbergh	RED One
Inland Empire	2006	David Lynch	Sony DSR-PD150
Jumper	2008	Barry Peterson	RED One
Knowing	2008	Simon Duggan	RED One
Miami Vice	2006	Dion Beebe	Thomson Viper
Next	2007	David Tattersall	Panavision Genesis
Once (film)	2006	Tim Fleming	Sony HVR-Z1
Planet Terror	2007	Robert Rodriguez	Panavision Genesis *Rachel*
Getting Married	2008	Jonathan Demme	Sony HDCAM/cinealta
Reign Over Me	2007	Russ Alsobrook	Panavision Genesis
Sin City	2005	Robert Rodriguez	Sony HDCAM/cinealta
Speed Racer	2008	David Tattersall	Sony HDCAM/cinealta

Source: Various, E. Triana

Notes
This table is by no means a complete list. Some of these films were going for what audiences would consider a 'cheaper' look due to their subject matter. Others were very effects heavy, so that post-production had as much to bear on the look of the film as what was shot in camera.
a First digitally photographed film to win 'Academy Award for Best Cinematography', doing so in 2009. Shot on multiple formats, including 35mm and digital stills.
b Segments, other shots include the Panasonic HVX-200, as well as the Thomson Viper.
c Only for exterior night scenes.

transportation, etc.) and equipment are set in stone. On the other hand, Figgis points out, the filmmaker can be in a situation where he/she can say to financiers,

> 'How much money do you think you can give me? I can make you a really erotic thriller, but just let me know how much I can have to spend.' And if they say a certain amount, you say 'Okay, for that much I could shoot on 35mm for four days, or on Super-16 for ten days. If I went handheld, I could maybe get even more time. If I went on DV-Cam or mini-high-definition camera – if I don't carry too much equipment – that's maybe a month of shooting.'

It's a big mistake to overload the expectation of the film in advance by writing a script that is inflexible and highly ambitious visually, in terms of location and look and equipment. That may well mean the film will never get made. On the other hand, if you concentrate on what is the *point* of the film – and if the script has a certain amount of tolerance built into it – you can then negotiate with yourself based on the reality that there is only so much money available.

Figgis concludes his point by stressing the need for 'new film' to make a strong marriage between the reality of the cheap, lightweight equipment and budget. 'Budget can no longer legitimately be used as an excuse not to make a film.'

Since Figgis's book, an important caveat to costs has emerged: digital production is currently much cheaper if you are making an 'out to film' (i.e. if one needs to print the digital copy on 35mm film for exhibition). But the cost structure is completely different. Whereas with film all the costs were effectively upfront, in digital the possibility exists to shoot the film in a high-definition format like HDCAM first then decide whether a transfer to film is worth it, or if there is enough interest within the industry for a transfer. Digital technology therefore allows more flexibility for producers to choose between the direct to DVD or television and film exhibition businesses, rather than cementing them to one specific route at the start. Currently the main strategic advantage could be argued to lie in the 'cost structure' rather than in simple direct budget savings.

However, it seems inevitable that the promise of lower costs will be realized. Digital cameras that were once at the forefront of technology like the Canon XL1S (used to shoot *28 Days Later*) are now at consumer prices. Although lenses will continue to be expensive to manufacture and to buy or rent, the need for film stock should eventually disappear. Shooting films will not cost zero, but will be significantly cheaper. Another important saving will be in terms of process – in the world of film, a director of photography (DOP) had to trust his film stock and lighting to give him what he wanted. With digital cameras it is much easier to set them up to get them to give you what you want, to test the image, and to go back and tweak, before shooting gets underway. It does not require a DOP to trust his instincts, as corrections can be made on site. Digital cameras are also lighter and more flexible than their film counterparts, although the difference here has often been exaggerated, as commentators confuse consumer with high-end digital cameras.

The image debate

But does digital match the quality of image of film? This is a complicated question as it relies on subjective perceptions as much as on objective measurements. For example, it has long been able for cameras going back to the VHS days to shoot at a higher frame rate than the 24 fps used for film. In theory a higher frame rate is 'better' since when we open our eyes we do not see the world as a set of flickering images, but as a continuous take. However, audiences have so long been used to the 'flickering images' style of cinema (initially developed out of necessity) that modern productions shot on digital drop the frame rate (a practice called de-interlacing) in order to fit to that aesthetic. Technically, a lower frame rate should be considered 'worse' but aesthetically it is what we are used to and enjoy as audiences.

Another similar issue arises with black colours in an image. Traditionally film cameras have been very bad at handling poorly lit areas (hence all the lights on a set) leading to deep black colours, and strong contrast between lit and non-lit areas. However, this has become a defining aesthetic of cinema – for example, see how it was used to great effect in *The Godfather* by cinematographer Gordon Willis. With digital cameras better at capturing information it is ironically no longer a problem, but one DOPs are trying to unsolve, as audiences have become accustomed to associating deep blacks with 'the cinema look'. By contrast, digital cameras are poor at handling overexposed areas of too much light, leading to the classic problem of a completely white sky, or other areas of deep white colour. This has now become associated with a cheap, video look and is a constant headache for those using digital cameras.

So have digital cameras matched the look of film? With high-end digital cameras, to this writer's eyes (which is of course an important caveat), most certainly. A film such as Mel Gibson's *Apocalypto*, shot on the high-end digital professional Viper camera, is indistinguishable from other titles shot on film, with the exception perhaps of some moments of very fast movement where the image has a 'progressive feel'. However, the camera used for *Apocalypto* and high-end digital cameras that rival film are still not competitive in terms of pricing. Cheaper digital cameras, that use formats such as HDCAM, are getting better and better in terms of the image quality they provide. It should certainly not be long before they overtake 16mm, if it cannot be said they have already, as the format of choice for low budget filmmaking. It is notable that recently Sony gave their CineAlta brand (used to signify the cameras that are film-worthy in their range) to the PMW-EX1, which at £4,000 retail at its launch is getting not far off the prices of consumer cameras.

Post-production

Artificially separating production from post-production is unhelpful. Many DOPs have complained about the lack of discipline that digital shooting creates, as directors do endless takes and there is less respect for set-ups and camera changes. Often, these mistakes dictate the hidden costs of digital production. (Again, Figgis is excellent in his advice on these pitfalls.) At their worst they result in a 'fix it in post' attitude that puts a lot of pressure on the post-production end. This stage of 'post' has become increasingly expensive for films overall. Will attitudes change as directors become more used to digital technology and learn the value of greater discipline and preparation? Extensive storyboarding, the logging all shots religiously, and making sure that all cameras are set at the same colour balances (constantly), are crucial if the post is not to become either wasteful or create a logjam of material incapable of being edited into a coherent film.

If filmmakers are serious about avoiding the above pitfalls, Figgis advises that you should be thinking about the post-production stage during the shooting stage. By applying a disciplined level of shot and camera restrictions, 'then it will not only be possible for a great idea to emerge, but you'll also have the space to make it work. In that kind of Spartan environment you find there is *room* for the new idea.'

Consumer editing software is as complicated as professional versions (technology for Avid having been developed for Lucasfilm), and certainly much more advanced than those used only a couple of decades ago. It is now possible to do digital sound, and blue and green screen effects easily at home.

In conclusion, ultimately the major step-change will come when digital projectors are far more widespread and filmmakers do not have to convert their digital images to a film print. Then there will begin to be a major separation in costs between film and digital.

The UK low- and micro-budget film sector

The future of the UK film industry is increasingly being split into high-budget productions built with international partners, and the low- and micro-budget film sector. Between 2002 and 2007, close to 450 films of budgets under £1m were produced in the United Kingdom according to Northern Alliance's report for the UK Film Council[8] (June 2008). Funded mostly by private investors, these projects cost around £18.5m, and only 18 per cent were released theatrically in the United Kingdom and 16 per cent were released theatrically in foreign territories. Some 49 per cent were sold or distributed in the DVD/video format. Around 50 per cent of this sector's films secure an international showcase of some kind, but only half of these in turn are handled by conventional sales companies. Based on Northern Alliance's extensive research of the sector, the report estimated that together with UK distribution, the 450 or so films generated net revenues of around £5–6m for their investors and/or makers.

However, with support from public and regional agencies, there has been an increasing investment and organization in the low-budget sector that points to its importance as a focus for R&D of directing, producing and writing talent. And, as a vehicle for promoting new talent, the advantages of micro filmmaking are numerous. The discipline of very tight budgets fit neatly into the Figgis school of filmmaking, and force teams to make difficult choices and develop a clear strategy that ultimately necessitates their ability to get a film 'structured' and 'in balance' if it is to achieve a life beyond the shoot and post. For example, Film London' Microwave scheme, backed by BBC Films, Skillset, the UK Film Council and the London Development Agency, managed to achieve considerable UK distribution and international sales appetite for its first two £100,000 films, *Shifty* and *Mum & Dad* and its latest two. Such schemes underline the fact that, once made, a film can transcend its perceived production 'value' and become commercially appealing beyond its micro roots.

Overall, there is no clear film-by-film business model for one-off micro-budget films. Key questions that remain to be answered include: What is the audience expectation and demand for films in this budget range? And how are these audiences best reached in the digital age? Or put another way – how is the relationship between audience/consumer and the filmmaker best forged in the digital age? Which leads us to new forms of digital distribution, discussed in the next chapter.

12 Digital distribution

> The VCR is to the American film producer and the American public as the Boston strangler is to the woman home alone ...
>
> (Jack Valenti, late head of the
> Motion Picture Association of America)
>
> Digital distribution is becoming the next iteration home video. We all know that the days of recouping with an upfront MG aren't really here anymore.
>
> (Matt Dentler, Cinetic Rights Management CEO)

The current state of home entertainment

An assessment of the state of digital production, with the advent of affordable digital camera equipment and state-of-the-art living room editing software, augurs well for the advancement of digital filmmaking. However, turn to the challenge of distribution, and the landscape becomes more confused and complex. It is arguably tougher to bring an independent film to the market with success than it is to actually make one. The traditional structure and system for distributing independent films is encountering a period of growing tension. There is rising pressure on the sales/territorial distributor relationship in the value chain, alongside escalating costs of marketing and distribution that has enable the Hollywood Studios to dominate theatrical distribution. Advances paid to acquire and distribute non-Studio films have now dwindled to near extinction. Without pre-saleable elements such as stars, top directors or proven genre credentials (e.g. mainstream sequels), distributors have grown increasingly shy of paying advances. The narrow, intensely competitive theatrical window has also worked against the smaller, niche film that has struggled to find its audience in the first three weeks, let alone first three days.

The long-existing approach of attempting to 'sell' films (which normally means 'licence') or minimum guarantees (i.e. advances against rights) in return for significant cash advances that in turn contribute towards repayment of the negative cost of the film or (in exceptional cases), take the film past break-even and into profit, is set for considerable change. Even prior to the changing economics of film acquisitions, however, independent filmmakers often found in return for cash, experience, relations with exhibitors and the wider marketplace, the sales and distribution axis also presented considerable problems and barriers to success.

Specifically, problems with the standard producer/distributor relationship that often arise are as follows:

A loss of independence

The producer becomes entirely dependent on the distributor. Any change of the company's financial fortunes, or commitment to your specific product, can kill the distributor's ability (or enthusiasm) to carry out the sales and/or distribution strategy. The producer and financier are also dependent on the distributor's financial reporting and accurate/fair accounting.

A lack of control

Rights deals have tended to be for 10–15 years in Western Europe (and now 20 for German speaking, etc.), and often from 25 years to perpetuity in North America. The distributor, albeit in consultation with the producer and financiers, will have overwhelming control over the strategy, marketing and execution of all avenues of exploitation of the film.

Compromising video and ancillary opportunities

The distributor has control over what happens to all ancillary rights, from DVD, VOD, cable, satellite, and broadcast television rights and beyond. DVD has become the key, most profitable window since 1997.[1] Often, relationships (e.g. output deals) and corporate structures dictate which company or division handles ancillary rights, and they may not be the right or best company for your particular film.

Revenue leakages and losses

It is a fact that a distributor can make considerable distribution fees, and have their expenses repaid, without monies being returned to the filmmakers/financiers. Distributors are normally paid fees off the top, and then have their expenses and (if any) advance paid back.

Terms that favour distributors

All revenue streams and expenses are cross-collateralized, maximizing the distributor's chances of recouping, and minimizing the likelihood of the film going into 'overages' – meaning revenues being shared with the producer/financier. Even the standard terms for theatrical have changed over the past decade, with costs-off-the-top, then a 50–50 split, being replaced by a 35 per cent distribution fee, with expenses and advance coming out of the producer's share.

Self-distribution

Before examining the opportunities and barriers to digital distribution, there are interesting steps open to filmmakers by which they can take more control over the process of exploitation, and, in certain cases, overcome some of the above barriers.

Splitting up rights, where some rights are licensed to third parties and others are exploited by the filmmakers, can work well. Decisions can be made without the dependence of an initial heavy outlay of prints and advertising; while direct marketing (direct video sales) of DVD sales (in particular through the Internet) has proven to be a profitable source of revenues that completely alters the standard 'royalty' system that exists between the producer and distributor in standard contracts.

Filmmakers can often target, aim and reach their core audience more successfully than the normal distribution operation can, especially if they have been researching and making additional material for that intended audience, and have built up a data base of contacts. In an argument made forcefully by experienced film industry consultant Peter Broderick,[2] returns to filmmakers from direct online sales are higher than those made from retail sales. A typical 15 per cent royalty on a £10 retail price and a £5 wholesale price would leave the filmmaker receiving 75p per DVD sale. However, if the DVDs could be purchased from the video distributor for, say, £3 a unit, then the profit per sale could be as much as £7 (not including credit card charges), rather than 75p. Even if the royalty was 25 per cent, yielding £1.25 a sale, and the cost of the DVD purchased from the distributor was £4, the profit is still far more from direct sales (NB numbers have been changed from $ to £ examples). And as Broderick points out, there are no accounting or cash-flow delays.

Other examples point to the importance of web streaming, supported, for example, by well-placed Google Ad Sense plugs, which in turn also generate DVD sales. Messianic fervour often accompanies experiments that have worked: Digital distribution 'is the difference between being able to pay the rent and not being able to pay the rent', explained filmmaker Seth Caplan, whose *In Search of a Midnight Kiss* was heralded creatively, released theatrically by IFC in North America and won a Spirit Award.[3] But it was not *Kiss* that made Caplan money. Instead, it was a 30-minute, 2-D animated featurette titled *Flatland: The Movie* based on Edwin Abbot's cult novella about mathematics and dimensions that went into profit. Going online in the autumn of 2006, the 30-minute direct digital distribution campaign generated twice as much profit as *Kiss*.

'When it comes to indie films,' says Caplan, 'the drains are clogged. And what's been clogging them are these middlemen, these layers of sales agents and distributors, which soak up every cent of profitability. You just don't have that with digital.' That sounds attractive, but the challenge of actually getting the film to its intended market without the aid of a sales company and network of distributors remains a significant challenge.

New technologies and Internet piracy

The rise of websites like ZML.Com, which offers nearly 2,000 films for download to personal computers, iPods and other hand-held devices, or for users to burn to DVD, are forcing the digital distribution issue. ZML is inviting, simple to use and competitively priced. The catch is that it is a pirate website, and it 'looks like a fabulous legal website', in the words of a Studio executive.[4] Users have been voting with their mouses. Controlling web activity is the antithesis to controlling audience access to product through the structured window system of releasing across different platforms on different timetables.

The new world is one where content is often created and accessed through open platforms, rather than proprietary, DRM-dictated systems. These apparently polarized positions are raising considerable questions about new business techniques re the future of film distribution across all platforms. Before delving further, it's worth clarifying terminology. Video-on-demand is widely used in the industry but it can include an analogue form of delivery such as Netflix sending the DVD in the mail based on online demand. Digital distribution can include distribution to digitally enabled cinemas, and online distribution (OLD) is a useful catchall for films reaching users through the Internet.[5]

Bit-Torrent and other Peer-to-Peer (P2P) file sharing systems have aided the illegal circulation of film product throughout the net. Indeed, practitioners refer to 'file sharing' as 'file nicking'. One overriding problem, however, is that the choice of what is legally available remains less impressive and slick, especially when compared to the likes of ZML's masterful pirate day trips. This is not to suggest that piracy is 'right' and the incumbent are 'wrong' – but there are a range of strategies and tipping points required before the Studios and the leading independent distributors realize that the old game is up. The 'old' game, in North America alone, marks a business model where DVD brings in nearly $24bn a year (although spending is dropping by 3 per cent a year), next to less than $10bn at the box office. So any damage to the DVD window creates fear and hostility in the risk-adverse Studio ecology. And understandably, the distraction of new formats, including Blu-Ray and HD DVD, are, in the longer run, irrelevant to the future of film distribution. The only growth area is the net, but the Studios are not servicing it proficiently to date.

There are technological hurdles still remaining, before digital distribution really breaks through and changes the entire landscape of film circulation. Downloading a film still takes around 30–40 minutes on average in the USA, and films in high definition take around two hours or more to download. However, standard downloading in South Korea and Japan has now been reduced to around 5 minutes, so the technology exists and is catching up. Other barriers include the fact that most people want to watch films on television sets, rather than personal computers – especially if they have wide 'home theatre' screens or wall projectors. Connectors between PCs and TV sets have not expanded widely due to significant operational 'un-user-friendliness' – meaning they are hard to install and use. Apple is changing some of these barriers, and new 'link' technology is on its way, to solve the bottleneck.

The last barrier, which is formidable but is gradually being tackled, is the lack of common standards across devices and websites. Download rights tend to utilize and sell different usage rights, a problem described as 'a format war on steroids'. Apple and Microsoft are not proving easy for the Studios to co-opt in their efforts to create a standardized electronic film product that was called Open Market.

Fresh eyes: understanding the rate of change

One of the overriding and unhelpful tendencies in the film business – not aided by 'Hollywood versus independent' binary perspectives, and trade commentators' instinct for chasing conflict – is to assess change in starkly oppositional terms: 'change is the new indie dynamic' next to 'luddite Studio hegemonies', or 'cultural crisis' next to inevitable 'corporate triumph', are typical, simplistic examples. In a groundbreaking research paper by Stuart Cunningham, Jon Silver and John McDonnell, Queensland

University of Technology, on 'Rates of Change: Online Distribution as Disruptive Technology in the Film Industry' (presented by Cunningham as a keynote address at the University of Oregon),[6] the authors look at an aspect of the challenges to business models that have served established media industries for decades: the eruption of digital distribution into the film industry in recent years. The study is of such value that this next section refers in a detailed box extract to the authors' research, findings and arguments, and it is highly recommended as 'cutting edge' academic work for all practitioners, teachers and students interested in the new digital horizon and how to examine and understand it.

Online distribution as disruptive technology in the film industry

Instead of having to decide whether disruptive technology, for example, is good or bad, Cunningham, Silver and McDonnell ask: How do we study the *process* of change and the question of the *rate* of change? As an indicator of change and possible innovation, are there genuinely new players disrupting the established oligopoly and, if so, with what effect? Is there evidence of disruption to, and innovation in, business models? Has there been cultural change as, again, evidence of innovation? Finally, outside mainstream Hollywood, where are the new opportunities and the new players?

The film sector was selected as the focus of this work as it has been the most stable of the main media content industries over the long term and, relatively speaking, the least affected to date in terms of digital technology undermining the market power of the major corporations that dominate the industry. The authors studied 220-plus websites of digital distribution enterprises – focusing on sites that offer film distribution or film with other screen content and technology or software that facilitated content delivery. This corpus included both legal and illegal websites and a small number of websites that are now defunct. Content across the total sample of 220-plus sites ranged from sites offering professional movies on demand (both Hollywood and independent films); to world cinema content aggregators; to sites offering user generated content in short and/or long form; social networking sites providing user uploaded video content and some with original web series; manufacturers of media players, set-top boxes linking Internet movie delivery to television sets and games consoles that offer video-on-demand including movies; and finally video-on-demand portals on video search engines.

Online video-on-demand first emerged in 1997 but a decade later remains a relatively small but rapidly growing market the authors estimate (for the USA/Canada only) at about US$1.9bn compared to theatrical (US$10bn) and home video (US$20 billion). The authors point out that since the first online films became available for download many have fallen: pioneers iFilm, Atom Films, Pop.com and CinemaNow either failed or were absorbed by larger companies after failing to establish sustainable business models. The second wave of expected market leaders emerged in 2001 with the backing of six of Hollywood's Majors – Movielink and Moviebeam. However both websites were sold in 2006 after failing to establish themselves as dominant players. A third wave is now building led by Apple iTunes, which rapidly emerged as the leading movie download site, Amazon, Veoh, Hulu, Netflix and Blockbuster (which acquired Movielink) and some others. The authors' research indicates that 2008 may have become a consolidation point in terms of shaping the digital distribution future of the industry as a limited number of workable business models gathered momentum.

The research indicates that, when compared to the impact of P2P on the music industry and the blogosphere and online classified advertising on newspapers, change in film has been slower and has had less disruptive influence, so far.

Three categories of profitable business models have emerged. The authors' analysis clustered each of the major commercial websites reviewed into one of three broad business model categories based on advertising, sales or subscriptions. *Advertising* supported sites that enable visitors to watch movies and TV programmes free – this is the commercial free-to-air TV model migrated to the Web (the most successful online site is Hulu); *sales* sites that offer e-customers the option of renting and/or buying individual movies or TV programmes as paid downloads (Apple iTunes is the leader among sales sites); *subscription* sites provide the opportunity for their subscribed customer base to rent or buy movies or TV programmes – typically this is done on a pay-per-view basis; while others provide a value add-on in the form of free streaming movies or TV programmes to their subscribers who pay a monthly fee to receive physical DVDs shipped to their home (e.g. Netflix). Three (and two partial cross-overs) of the top ten employ rent/buy (Amazon, iTunes, Blockbuster); Fancast and Vuze rent as well as show some free with ads.

Blockbuster and Netflix are really virtual versions of a video store and so is Amazon. iTunes is similar but it is more like its music model because of its ultra-thin margins – Apple is trying to sell devices and using movies and music as the attractive content loss-leader to get people to but iPods, iTouch, iPhones and Apple TVs. Netflix differs because until now it has let its large subscriber base that rent DVDs online and get them at home to access its online content via streaming free to subscribers. There is now some media speculation that Netflix will set up a premium service enabling anyone to stream a rental movie on a pay-per-view basis, not just their subscribers.

Six of the top ten sites in Cunningham, Silver and McDonnell's list do free movies with ads (Hulu, Veoh, Fancast, Joost, Vuze, Crackle). One of the top ten have free OLD to subscribers who rent DVDs (Netflix). As the authors have argued, iTunes and Hulu seem anecdotally to have had the most impact – they lead in downloads and streams.

The third wave market leaders in the online VOD sector – Hulu (free streaming with paid ads) and Apple iTunes (paid downloads) have succeeded because their Hollywood content (movies and TV) has rapidly attracted a critical mass of customers now that the technology diffusion preconditions are being met. But there is a key differentiator and new element introduced by the forced entry of the IT-innovation model. Hulu is classically content-driven, while iTunes employs a device-led strategy, i.e. consumers must own an iPod, Apple TV, iPhone or other compatible media device to be able to access content at iTunes. The rapid success of Apple iTunes must be emphasized: since it began offering movies and TV shows as paid downloads in 2006, it has dominated the paid-for online video download market and was selling 50,000 or movies globally daily in 2008. This is a spectacular disruption and a great threat to standard business models because this is selling premium or near-to-premium content 'at close to break-even with a view to profit from hardware device sales (iPod)'.

Meanwhile, Hollywood looks to have 'bet the farm' on an ad-supported business model for VOD online with Hulu. The meteoric rise of Hulu in 2008 appears to have been a game-changer with powerful players within the US film and TV industries having clearly decided that the familiar 'content is king' catchphrase still applies and that Hollywood can prevail in cyberspace.

To that point, the Majors must have had a sense of déjà vu. Apple was once again succeeding in making money (despite widespread piracy) by offering a cheap price point for movie and TV downloads, just as it had done previously in the music industry with iTunes selling individual music tracks at 99 cents each that resulted in iTunes becoming the 'Wal-Mart' of online music sales. History was repeating itself. Apple proved that paid downloads can work at the right price; the problem for Hollywood was that the Majors resented the super-thin margins offered by iTunes while Apple made huge profits from iPod sales. It is fair to say that the paid download model is not an option for Hollywood because it is foreign to its business culture. Therefore the only other logical option for Hollywood was the commercial television model of free content model supported by paid advertising that the Majors have lived with for half a century and understand well.

But, just as significantly disruptive has been the impact of user-generated content (UGC). There is now co-evolution between the commercial/professional and household/consumer/pro-am sectors. In 2008, as market leader YouTube looked over its shoulder at the incredibly rapid rise of Hulu, it responded by committing to high-definition video downloads; introduced 16:9 aspect ratios and negotiated deals with Hollywood Studios (MGM, Lionsgate) for high-end content like *The Magnificent Seven* to be placed on its site, supported by paid advertising.

Cunningham makes the following points in his summary: There has been significant *convergence* of different elements of the communications and content fields. The coming together of what we have called the IT-innovation culture and the mass media content culture, a mainstream theme of the past few decades, has a new twist: in the case of Hulu, it is now the IT-innovation model at the service of the mass media content model, and in competition with the purer IT-innovation model represented by Apple.

There is significant *co-evolution* of the market and non-market sectors. This is clear in what YouTube/Google is doing to position itself to meet threatened litigation as well as the innovation challenges of a commercialized OLD field. But the degree to which the non-market sector and UGC is being integrated into a leading and innovative business model is clearest in the case of Amazon – that is, if Amazon fully exploits the potential value of createspace and withoutabox, together with imdb.com.

But there is also the question of those enterprises to which Cunningham gave least attention – Rest of the World and independent film – and how substantively they may provide new affordances for non-Hollywood product and distribution that will also be a key indicator of how 'creative' this current disruption of Hollywood's established practices are.

Making money? Yes and no ...

All the above barriers that are making the Studio oligopoly struggle to embrace digital distribution are less apparent in the independent film world. Arguably, the Internet is lowering barriers to new and pioneering filmmakers, but also enabling key components and players in the indie value chain to reconsider and recalibrate their strategies. The leading digital and e-commerce portals, including Amazon, Hulu, iTunes and YouTube, have all established movie download businesses.

Certain films have found success through these channels, but the argument that follows is that the producers have not managed to monetize their investment. 'The problem with streaming is you need millions of views for what's essentially a niche product', explains Bob Alexander, president of IndiePix, a US-based virtual studio. 'What streaming can do, however, is provide the visibility and platform to lead to transaction-based sales.'[7] So, streaming is fine but all it really leads to is more DVD sales, but what if the DVD market is in decline? Perhaps the most dynamic model is Netflix Inc., which passed 10 million subscribers in February 2009, and has witnessed an exponential rise in customer subscriptions recently. Apart from receiving DVDs through the mail subscription system – which was the company's initial distribution business model launched in 1999 – subscribers can stream content over the net and watch on computer and television. The key to future change and growth is focused on the rental share that is on the up. The customer value proposition is becoming more attractive. Why? Because to the user (or customer if buying/paying) the online cost works out about 50 per cent lower than the DVD cost of rental, with no late fee and far more choice.

Reepel's law

In an informal paper put forward at Cass's MBA module, 'Understanding the Film Business',[8] media finance expert Mike Kelly cited Reepel's law as an interesting perspective on Internet disruption. Kelly pointed out that Reepel's law states that technological development tends to favour incumbents not new entrants.

> Reepel drafted his thesis when films were still silent and he likely never had the film industry in mind when he proposed his law, but, a century of celluloid later, it seems to fit well.

> The film industry has been challenged by technological developments before; by the introduction of sound and then colour, the development of terrestrial TV, home entertainment, satellite and cable and now by the Internet. Arguably though, it reached its nadir not as a result of those technological developments, but when it lost sight of the source of all film value; its theatrical root.

Kelly pointed out that the arrival of the Internet as a means of distribution of film may just be the latest background music to the industry's equivalent of musical chairs. When the music stops it is as likely as it has ever been that the same figures will be sat in the same positions. He cited that the Centre National de la Cinematographie (CNC) has already observed that in France those who use VOD services are also those who go most frequently to the cinema and buy the greatest number of DVDs. 'One can therefore consider that this growth in VOD consumption will continue more to complement rather than to substitute other methods of audiovisual consumption. From Reepel's point of view, this may be beginning to look familiar.'

However Kelly adds:

> In the absence of a secure way to monetize more openness there will be no market led transformative behaviour, most established rights holders will continue to be

conservative, and the gap between what consumers want from the Internet (any film, free, any time) and what the market will provide will continue. Illegal suppliers will fill the gap.

The overall effect of the Internet has been to disrupt a secure, dependable and steady flow of income in favour of revenue streams that, apart from an uncertain trickle, tend to flow underground. Because of the associated shift in the culture of consumption, rights holders will have to work harder and smarter with the new technology. In particular, the Internet represents an opportunity or threat for those marketing film, and a challenge for those who protect its value, technically or via the courts.

But, for those incumbents who can use the technology to refresh their existing business model, especially those who can employ a revised marketing mix to launch films made with the potential of the Internet as a promotional tool in mind, Kelly argues that their prospects could be very promising.

Help at hand: how to approach digitial distribution

There are specific ways that the independent business – including producers, old-style distributors and digitally focused rights companies – can organize themselves in relation to digital opportunities. Some of the most relevant pointers with regards to distribution planning were set up by NESTA's (National Endowment for Science, Technology and the Arts) Take 12 programme – 'Digital Innovation in Film':[9]

- Encoding and digitizing is becoming a commoditized activity, but many producers give away potential revenue in return for digitization costs. It is possible to digitize and encode for low per-film costs. Crucial is the need to use common standards.
- The video-on-demand deals need careful consideration. 'Closed' TV-based VOD services such as Filmflex are currently attracting more revenues that 'open' ones.
- Try to keep deals non-exclusive or for short exclusive periods, allowing you to experiment. Also try to aim to sell content to as many platforms as possible.
- Consider partnering with providers such as Sky and Virgin Media. Why? Because both platforms offer easy to use VOD services. Also think about partnering with other VOD services as well, such as Joost, Babelgum, Blinkbox and YouTube. They are all free and generate buzz and demonstrate demand. Paid services such as Jaman can deliver modest revenues, but do not do exclusive deals with such services to the exclusion of TV companies and closed platforms.
- Experiment with self-distribution. This will help build profile, garner attention and assist in the funding of your next project. Commercial success, however, remains some way off.
- Mobile phone opportunities are important to consider. However, content needs to work appropriately in this format. Screen and format size and the way users engage with phones can be limiting. Entertainment is only one of four main user categories, which also include personalization, information services and user-generated content.

- Mobile content has to be easy to find and priced competitively. Video content is currently a niche market and content owners' share of revenue is still low. Network operators are effectively the gatekeepers in this arena and you need to navigate them to get deals done.
- Collaborate with other rights holders and pool catalogues where possible, as it will help build scale.

13 Film marketing through the Internet

> Tell us some good stories and capture our interest. Don't talk to us like you've forgotten how to speak. Don't make us feel small, remind us to be larger. Get a little of that human touch ...
>
> (Chris Locke, *The Cluetrain Manifesto*)

The start of a revolution

Just prior to *The Cluetrain Manifesto*'s publication in the spring of 1999, along came a micro-movie called *The Blair Witch Project*. *Cluetrain* (www.cluetrain.org) had argued that the future of the Internet and therefore the majority of all future business was rooted in conversations. Top-down marketing was over. Two-way dialogue was the only way to go. *The Blair Witch Project*'s marketing campaign, however, managed to go far further than just a two-way, company-to-customer dynamic. Indeed, the impact of its pioneering viral campaign benchmarked the film much higher than either the filmmakers or its distributor Artisan Entertainment ever imagined when acquired at Sundance in January 1999 for $1.1m. Made for approximately $50,000 and grossing more than $100m at the US theatrical box office alone, the low-to-no-budget shocker-horror film was the movie industry's first mainstream Internet marketing success. It left the major Studios' shoehorning of the Internet as a secondary, supplementary marketing tool standing still in the water.

On 1 April 1999 Artisan relaunched *The Blair Witch Project* website with a host of new material, including material presented as out-takes from 'discovered' film footage, police reports, the 'back story' on missing film students, and a mythological history of the Blair Witch legend. Instead of premiering trailers on the TV or in theatres, Artisan trailered on the 'Ain't It Cool News' website, and send out *The Blair Witch Project* screensavers to more than 2,000 journalists.

Fiction and fact were deliberately mixed and blurred across the web campaign; which in turn spurred unofficial offspring websites, parodies and new narratives emanating from an ever-expanding fan base. Even the offended citizens of Burkittsville, Maryland, created a page to detract from the film's authenticity (sic), further fanning the flames of debate across usernet groups, online chat rooms and web boards. While Artisan spent around $1.5m on the Web promotion, (from an overall campaign costing $20m), the viral spiralling was worth exponentially more than the cash injected. Replication of the 'passing off' strategy that mixes fiction with fact has, however, proved a tough Holy Grail search over the past decade. The best examples are those that crept up from nowhere, with 'barely a whisper … '. That was how *Cloverfield* came to pass nearly eight years after the *Witch*.

The macro and the micro impact

The relationship between the Internet and film from a marketing perspective can be viewed at a micro level, encompassing interactive media and its impact on audiences through social networking, widgets, applications, podcasting, etc. It can also be analysed at a macro level, whereby film marketing encompasses a meeting point of social, economic, creative, technological and structural dynamics which reflect both the industry's changing architecture and its 'reflexive' relationship to the consumer – taking 'interactive' to its full level. In an MSc dissertation essay, Michael Franklin usefully pointed to the numerous gaps in this field, including those between academic theory and hard research;[1] and the surprising reluctance by both the Studios and mainstream distributors to fully embrace the Internet's potential both as a targeting tool and a wider 'space' to explore their relationships with audiences/consumers in full.

Before fully testing his thesis, Franklin sets out the landscape that governs new interactive digital media, pointing out that the impact of the Internet in film has been both as a marketing tool and a new mode of consumption. Peppers and Rogers[2] argue that digital marketing represents a complete transformation of the marketing paradigm, from a 'one-to-many' broadcast relationship (controlled by gatekeepers), to limitless one-to-one relationships. Others (Deighton), point out that marketing as a profession, and the associated theories and science it draws upon, are heavily determined by the tools at its disposal. 'The marketing toolkit is clearly experiencing massive innovation, suggesting the discipline is under pressure to reshape. The Internet's interactive abilities allow mass marketing concepts to become customized and responsive to the individual: promising a new marketing paradigm.'[3]

What makes online marketing so revolutionary? The key factors are its interactivity and its scalability. As Franklin declares, the Web is not simply a vehicle for adverts, nor just a step-up in 'addressable media'. The interactive multimedia platform

> offers opportunities for advertising, selling, service delivery, production, distribution and market research that are inseparable and complementary. Digital technology has reduced conversation costs to zero, providing limitless any-to-any communication that is a dramatic contrast to the historically dominant one-to-many broadcast model. … Any-to-any communication operates on a global scale and affords limitless possibility for both information and value transfer between consumers and businesses in any combination.
>
> (Franklin, p. 24)

But the additional factor that enhances the phenomenon is timing. The major online marketing draw is 'being able to reach an audience, communicate with them, establish a two-way relationship with them well before the film comes out', explains Russell Scott, CEO of Jetset Studios, a leading US online marketing agency. 'Online, there's an unprecedented chance for the filmmaker to reach an audience and let them interact with a brand that doesn't exist yet, well before one-sheets and any kind of trailer appears.'[4]

We know now that the producer/distributor can generate messages to the consumer, which in turn can provide feedback (both specific and generic), which in turn the producer can respond to. Hence, to borrow Soros's 'reflexive' theory about financial markets, a circular dynamic is in existence. Unlike financial circuits, the marketing dynamic has a considerably more positive aspect in terms of fine tuning the message and respecting the audience. Opportunities to foster relationships, build intimacy and loyalty, and most importantly, construct consumer communities, which in turn may generate and build upon 'fan' bases, are far flung from standardized twentieth century 'push' advertising techniques.

Much has been written about online marketing since the advent of *Blair Witch*'s marketing project. When a Web campaign becomes so hot that it 'buzzes', it can create news itself and self-perpetuate awareness, word of mouth and 'word of mouse' far beyond the core target fan base. But since *Blair Witch*, the emergence of YouTube, MySpace and other platforms, costs have risen exponentially[5] if Studios and mainstream distributors go the 'old' approach and simply buy out 'pages' in an effort to dominate headlines. Such thinking goes against the grain of the viral world.

The viral approach to marketing

'Viral marketing' and 'viral advertising' descriptions refer to marketing techniques that use pre-existing social networks to produce increases in brand or product awareness. Viral marketing achieves this through self-replication, (not to be confused with the spread of computer and pathological viruses), where the effect is carried by an 'ideavirus' in which the medium of the virus *is* the product (Seth Godin, 'Unleashing the Ideavirus'[6]). Viral promotions may take the form of video clips, interactive flash games, advergames, images, or text messages, etc. Viral marketing is a marketing phenomenon that facilitates and encourages people to pass along a marketing message voluntarily – hence mirroring the peer-to-peer recommendation system of word of mouth. However, Godin and other commentators suggest that word of mouth dies out over a given period, whereas a successful 'ideavirus' can grow exponentially.

Why? 'Because something amplifies the recommendation to a far larger audience.' That could be TV or other forms of media (a good review in the *New York Times* that amplifies the message of one reviewer to many readers) or it could be the Web (a site like planetfeedback.com amplifies the message of the single user). Marketing research shows (generally) that a satisfied customer tells an average of three people about a product or service he/she likes, and more than ten people about a product or service which he/she did not like. Viral marketing is based on this natural human behaviour of sharing, disseminating and interacting.

The goal of marketers interested in creating successful viral marketing programmes is to identify individuals with high social networking potential (SNP) and create viral messages that appeal to this segment of the population and have a high probability of being passed along. The term is also sometimes used pejoratively to refer to stealth marketing campaigns – the use of varied kinds of astroturfing both online and offline to create the impression of spontaneous word of mouth enthusiasm. Of course, not all films lend themselves neatly to stealth-based campaigns, but the link between two-way traffic flow and user-generated content allows for a wide diaspora of ideas, gossip and 'buzz' to be disseminated. And traditional marketing materials also have their role in this landscape. Teasers, trailers, artwork, production notes, progress reports, stills, exclusive interviews, talent snippets all play a role – but crucially in a way that allows the consumer and the emerging community to control and/or adapt the material and concepts, bucking the traditional 'push' strategy.

Observers have noted that 'virals' have their limitations. While 42 Entertainment's campaign for *The Dark Knight* worked to considerable acclaim and viral effect, the same company was hired by Sony to build an alternative reality game for *The International*, but the fan base remained completely unmoved and the campaign was a dud. Without diving into the detail, the viral spiral that catapulted *Snakes on a Plane* into a headline news story nevertheless remained just that – and the viral buzz ultimately generated just modest box office and predictable ancillary revenues. Peter Sciretta (/Film: Blogging the Reel World, 25 February 2009) concluded that virals

> only work in two arenas: 1) With a project hidden in mystery that fans are eager to uncover (i.e. *Cloverfield*); or 2) A highly anticipated property that has a year or more runway to develop a connection with its audience.

And quantifying 'value' has altered: measurements of success used to tend towards the 'how many members became friends with the film's profile'; whereas the viral approach only really takes off when users distribute applications and generate and send on original content.

For those interested in viral marketing beyond just film, David Meerman Scott has written extensively and draws on a wide range of creative media and digital executive experience.[7] Ultimately, any attempt to create a viral campaign needs a very clear, focused strategy, and to understand the odds: either it's right, or it would have been better not to try at all.

Key elements to consider include the following:

1   Try to create or do something unexpected. This may sound obvious, but copycat campaigns or promotions that stick to hard-core selling do not work in this arena. 'Man bites dog' works. 'Dog bites man … .' Well. Exactly.
2   Create emotions – a reaction or at least a feeling. Strong ideas, extreme opinions accompanied by dedication, passion and commitment are important to generate. Extremes mean exactly that: love/hate, happy/furious, clever/stupid, etc. Neutral does not work. Extreme emotive and emotional binary approaches have been proven to work best.
3   Sharing: create the opportunity to download and send on. Viral could be called 'sharing' – which in turn means making it easy to download content in easy formats and easily embedded in the content on their won sites; with simple links, and sites/networks that publish, and allow bookmarking to be added.
4   Avoid advertising or hard-sell promotions. Stories work far better than corporate messages or brands.
5   Once caught, get other people to make the sequel (or the prequel, or the spin-off).
6   Connect with your audience: allow comments and feedback. Include the negative or you will be found out to be manipulating the space.
7   Non-exclusivity: never restrict access. The Studios could do with learning this one. Do not insist on registration; membership; to download additional/special software, to enter 'unlock' codes or demand anything to be done to get the right links.[8]

The independent opportunity

The success or otherwise of networking platforms in promoting films remains to an extent governed by scale and marketing spend. However, the independent film business has much more to gain than the Studios from exploring all avenues offered by the digital network. The focus on the loss-leader opening weekend theatrical window instantly places independent fare at a disadvantage. Mature, mixed-sex audiences (rather than predominantly young males) respond more slowly to word of mouth, and their availability is much more constrained. Sometimes weeks go by before a typical couple with children get the opportunity to make it to the cinema – long after the film of their initial choice has played.

Independent cinema circuits and their audiences tend to suffer from the crowded marketplace and intense competition each weekend. In the United Kingdom alone, some 12 films are being released each Friday. So will smaller indie fare continue to depend on the theatrical window to make any sense of the increasingly pressurized business model? Perhaps not, given the digital exhibition changes and restructuring film value chain.

Case study: Cloverfield

Webpage blog: Harry Knowles AICN:

> For the last week, the internets have been busy trying to figure out just what the film was all about. They had been provided with clues on two websites. ... Could the mystery monster be a giant squid or maybe even the legendary Cthulhu? Godzilla it is not.
>
> The film comes out, you guessed it, on 1-18-08. That's only six months of non-stop rumours and speculation.

Update 1: J. J. Abrams sent this message to Harry Knowles of Ain't It Cool News:

> Dear Sir, Thanks for your support of our little movie. I can't wait to talk to you more about it – of course, knowing you, by the time we talk you'll know more than I will.
>
> Regarding the online stuff you posted: yeah, we're doing some fun stuff on the web. But, obviously, if the movie doesn't kick some massive ASS, who gives a rat's about what's online? So as you can imagine, we're focussing mostly on THAT. For what it's worth, the only site of ours that people have even FOUND is the 1-18-08.com site. The others (like the Ethan Haas sites) have nothing to do with us.
>
> Stay cool the rest of the summer – and thanks per usual for AICN! JJ

It has been claimed by some bloggers/cinema-goers that 'to understand *Cloverfield*, you really had to know/check out all the viral information on the net'. If that was the case, those who only imbibed the Paramount Hollywood release marketing strategy might have missed much of the hidden texture of *Cloverfield*. Or was the theatrical audience actually limited predominantly to viral addicts only? The film serves as a useful case study that demonstrates both a far-reaching web campaign that spiralled into viral, alongside a more traditional marketing roll-out. According to the website Movie Marketing Madness (The Tale of Two *Cloverfield* Campaigns – was it actually successful?), *Cloverfield* had two distinct types of marketing campaigns: one was the classic standard – aiming to get to the target audience, and made up of the 'traditional elements of a movie marketing push. The intent has clearly been to sell the movie to a particular audience using, as most campaigns do, clips and other material from the movie in order to build interest and enthusiasm.'

The other was based on interactivity and an alternate reality game (ARG), broader in audience scope if narrower in the methods of getting to that audience. 'This branch of the campaign has happened parallel to the mainstream campaign, occasionally coming close to but never quite joining that other push. This one has been designed to be more interactive, engaging and interesting to the online audience.' Of course, the traditional campaign's 'official' website and online campaign was forced to be specifically muted and understated, in order not to detract from the more radical, 'unofficial' campaign.

The first campaign

Like most films, *Cloverfield* had a carefully timed release pattern for its trailers and TV spots. Two elements, however, separated its mainstream campaign from most others:

- No title was initially released or even given to the film.
- Audiences that wanted to know more about the film had to initially go online.

The first trailer was released in 17 July 2007 in front of the largest blockbuster of the year, *Transformers*. It only provided the release date (18 January 2008) and not the title of the film. The website mentioned in this teaser added to the mystery, it being www.180108.com rather than the typical website with a poster of the film. This strategy was enshrined from the start of the film's planning: Paramount had green lit the film in total secrecy, and the production was kept under wraps as much as possible.

Therefore the normally well-informed sites such as AintitCool, Chud and ComingSoon were caught completely by surprise – which only assisted in boosting the buzz of the film. Audiences who saw the trailer during *Transformers* emerged from the cinemas and set about trying to find the new movie, untitled in the trailer. Or as the official site put it by January 2008:

> Five young New Yorkers throw their friend a going-away party the night that a monster the size of a skyscaper descends upon the city. Told from the point of view of their video camera, the film is a document of their attempt to survive the most surreal, horrifying event of their lives.

But that description was later. All the audience then knew was that there was a party and an invasion of New York by something 'capable of decapitating the Statue of Liberty'.

The strategy was carefully gauged towards the film's core audience, who would be mainly attracted to the film's producer, J. J. Abrams (*Alias*, *Lost*, and most recently *Star Trek*). In his earlier shows, Abrams had tied up and led and misled his audiences across wild goose chases on the Internet, and his followers were already broken in for a mystery ride when encountering his projects. The first website contained simply a Polaroid photo of one of the main characters at a party with almost no information. To get more clues, visitors had to keep coming back to the site. Photos would be added, sometimes related to the film, and others would be deliberately cryptic, such as a chef holding up his creation. Trackers worked out that if you 'flipped' the photos, further clues were on the other side. And each photo was time stamped, allowing the visitor to see when it was taken. Shortly after, a teaser poster was released. No title was on this image, and only a photo of the headless Statue of Liberty looking over New York was apparent.

The main campaign was put on hold at this point, and not restarted until November 2007. A more conventional trailer was placed prior to the release of *Beowulf*. Although the general premise and style of the movie was more transparent, audiences were still teased about what kind of monster was at work. The film was also finally given a name, albeit a codename: Cloverfield. Television spots were soon to be released and Paramount could not afford to confuse the general audience by this stage.

A more traditional website was launched: www.cloverfield.com. It contained a poster, brief synopsis, and a widget that showed 5 minutes of the film and a commentary by producer J. J. Abrams that was easy to access on any hardware, underlining the rule of full accessibility. A competition was attached to the widget, which was based on who could get further viewers to download it off their website (tracked by a code), and in turn significantly assisted in word of mouth and word of mouse.

The run up to the film's release in early January 2008 was typically conventional, with 15 different TV spots in major markets and wide press attention. The film had (deliberately) no known cast or director, so the campaign and coverage naturally gravitated towards J. J. Abrams and the web hype to date.

The second campaign

The second campaign was exclusively online based, and continued throughout the fall to the time the film was released and was online ARG based. It consisted of a series of websites that created a story that added to but was ultimately separate to the main film. The first website was www.slusho.com. Slusho was a fictional brand that had first appeared in Abrams' series *Alias*. It was leaked onto the Internet as part of the film's plot shortly after the first teaser trailer. The website was set up as just another corporate website, detailing the facts and figures of major drinks company Slusho, and its interest in entering the American drinks market. Regular visitors to the site, however, noticed that 'hackers' would sometimes manage to deface the site and write comments critical of the company's activities in farming an undersea component. A plot of corporate malpractice and cover up was initiated.

In the film itself, the monster was awoken from the sea by undersea mining, so the Slusho website served as a vaguely related prequel to the plot of the film. Another of the film's websites, http://jamieandteddy.com/ gave the story of one of the couples at the opening party, including a video diary with a similar mystery story component. There was also a MySpace website for the film's main character, where other fictional characters left their best wishes on their impending trip to Japan.

Were the campaigns a success?

Cloverfield had one of the biggest January weekends in film history, taking $40m during the weekend opening in a traditionally hard box office month. The film's campaigns appeared to have created significant hype and buzz to overcome the January blip. The film's actual production budget was between $25m and $30m, which was significantly lower than most films capable of such an opening three days.

The Movie Marketing Madness website[9] went on to point out the following salient themes about the dual approach to *Cloverfield*'s campaigns:

1   Marketing costs did not follow the trend of the film's budget, and were actually quite high, despite the strong online element. The *Los Angeles Times* estimated them as being 'significantly higher than the overall film's budget', which would place it at least at the industry average of $35m (for 2008). The success of the *Cloverfield* campaign was as much due to Paramount's studio muscle as to an independent approach to marketing – and the opening release was in more than 3,400 theatres.
2   The film's success was limited to a strong first weekend. *Cloverfield* had a near 70 per cent drop off on the second weekend. Ultimately, the film's performance did not meet early industry expectations that it would be the first film of the year to $100m, as it ended up at $80m.
3   The poor second week might have been due to bad word of mouth, but given the strong reviews, it appears most probably that the film exhausted its core audience in the first weekend and never broke across to the wider public.
4   The film's audience in the first weekend was heavily skewed toward the profile of its core fans. It was 65 per cent male and 55 per cent under 25.
5   The film performed better internationally, where the campaign had been more traditional and had a much lower Internet component.
6   *Cloverfield* was, however, a huge home entertainment success. A sequel is being considered, although some of the Internet tools used first time round will not be so readily available second time coming.

Lessons to be learnt from the *Cloverfield* campaign are likely to be the following:

1   Internet campaigns are a good idea with a young audience and to get your core fans involved. But it is a challenge to expand from there to a wider audience, just as specialist films find it hard to deliberately target and chase a 'cross-over' audience.
2   Marketing costs will not be zero in the Internet age, but a film company can create considerable hype and awareness for a no-name project through investing online.
3   A strongly thought-out online marketing campaign will invariably need to be supported by a solid traditional media campaign. In the case of *Cloverfield*, both fed off each other without cancelling each other out. Paramount, to its credit, was willing to take risks to help develop new strategies in marketing a film with few recognizable elements – with the notable exception of the enigmatic J. J. Abrams and his smart team at Bad Robot Productions.

Part 3

Business and management strategies

14 Business strategy

> The banks couldn't afford me. That's why I had to be in business for myself.
>
> (Sam Goldwyn)

Business planning for film enterprises

Whether you are in the film business or any business, the fact is that at least nine out of ten new business ventures fail. Most new businesses fail not due to poor business plans, but because their owners are underprepared for the business they have chosen to be in. This chapter departs from film-specific material and explores the key business demands required to run an operation effectively.

Many entrants and even experienced business people shy away from writing a business plan. Excuses run from 'not enough time' to 'we all know that the business plan is far from what actually happens … ' to a basic lack of understanding about what a business plan can achieve for your company going forwards. There are some key questions that have to be answered when embarking on the discipline of a plan:

1 Can I make money investing my time, energy and cash in this business (what's the risk versus reward)?
2 Do I like and understand the business I am investing my time and money in?
3 Do I trust the people I am investing with?

The areas a business plan forces you to address are: a) fund-raising, if required; or initial sunk costs and cash-flow management if you are not looking to raise third-party capital; b) a road map, which acts as a benchmark to your subsequent progress; and c) a document that promotes accountability and ultimately, if enshrined in a Shareholders' Agreement, a legally binding document that dictates key business parameters of practice.

Taking the arguments further, a business plan allows both yourself, and your team and potential investors, to test your concept properly. Ultimately, any investors are interested in one key ultimatum that bests all others: how much cash does your idea generate, and how fast does it flow? Next to those cash flows, both an entrepreneur and/or an investor will look at the costs – both sunk and running overheads, the revenue being generated, and the timing of those revenue returns.

The utility of capital in business

Before we explore business planning further, it is important to examine typical uses of capital, as applied to any business, rather than just film. There are two main sources of capital for a limited company: share capital and loan capital. Share capital is normally raised by selling shares in a company to investors who wish to own a piece of that company. The shareholders are the owners of the company, though they do not normally take part in the day-to-day management of the business. Shareholders receive rewards from their investment in two different ways: a) they may receive regular dividends, if the company is profitable, and directors can afford and decide to pay out dividends; and b) they may benefit from a gain in the value of their shares.

Loan capital is provided by organizations and individuals who lend money to businesses in return for the payment of interest, and often a premium. Loan interest is payable whether the company is in profit or loss, while dividends are only payable at the election of the directors.

Capital is employed in two key areas: fixed assets and current assets. Any expenditure on fixed assets is termed capital expenditure, and consists of expenditure on items, which the business will retain and utilize in the business for a number of years. Examples of fixed (or sometimes called 'non-current') assets are buildings, land and office equipment.

Fixed assets normally lose value over time, either because they become redundant or wear out. The term 'depreciation' is used to describe the accounting process for this loss of value, which is estimated on an ongoing basis by accountants. Intangible fixed (non-current) assets – which are particularly important in film – include assets such as acquired licences. These also, over a period of time, reduce to a zero value, as the licence period expires. The 'using up' of the value acquired in the buying of such rights is termed 'amortization'.

Current assets are those assets that are constantly changing. They usually consist of stock, debtors (receivables) and cash balances. Stock is items held for ultimate sale to a customer. Items of an inventory on which work has started but which are not ready for sale are called a work in progress. Debtors (or receivables) are amounts owed to the business by customers who have been granted time to pay for goods or services sold to them. Given that there is always a possibility that certain customers may not pay, accounts must contain a provision for debts that may ultimately not be met.

Creditors (also termed accounts payable or payables) are the suppliers who have provided credit to the business for goods and services supplied, but who have not yet been paid. They, therefore, are a further source of finance, and can often help to provide a 'financial buffer' to allow a business to obtain resources and begin to process or sell them before any cash is spent. If a business turns over very fast, it may even be able to sell goods or services, collect payment, all prior to any creditor demands payment.

Working capital, which is usually referred to as 'net current assets', is the term granted to part of the capital invested in a business that is continually moving. This is essentially the capital, which is working to generate cash for the business: raw material is obtained on credit and converted into finished goods, which are sold to customers on credit. When the customers pay, the cash can be used to pay creditors, who then supply further raw materials to be invested in the working capital cycle.

The term given to creditors and other types of short-term debts such as short-term loans, bank overdrafts, etc., is 'short-term liabilities'. These creditors provide a buffer for current assets and so help to reduce the level of money necessary for working capital. When current liabilities exceed current assets, the working capital is a negative figure – and is referred to as 'net current liabilities'.

Once a business has started to generate profits, there is a further source of finance available to it: reserves or accumulated retained profits. Directors may decide to pay out or distribute profits as dividends to the shareholders. However, if they decide not to, or to withhold some of the profit, then this profit can continue to act as an important source of finance for the business – also called 'retained earnings'. Such access to additional finance can help acquisitions of new companies, diversification, or rapid expansion in existing activities.

The relative proportion of loan capital to share capital in a business is referred to as the 'level of gearing' (or leverage) in the business. If a business has a large level of loan capital (shown on the balance sheet under non-current liabilities) compared to share capital, then it is viewed as highly geared or highly leveraged. By contrast, if a business has a small amount of loan capital compared to share capital, then it is low-geared or has low leverage. If revenues start to fall and a company is highly geared, then managers will need to move very fast to ensure there is enough cash in the company to continue to trade. Shareholders are also directly affected by changes in revenue in a highly geared company. If profits fall, then earnings per share will reduce faster in a more highly geared company; if profits rise, then they will grow faster.

Business plan approaches

It may appear simplistic to ask a range of questions at the onset of any business plan, but a careful analysis of 'who?', 'what?', 'when?', 'why?', 'where?', with, in addition, 'how?' and 'how much?', goes a long way to producing general background notes before starting to compile and flesh out the template of a business plan.

The 'who' is important because investors, speculators and financiers tend to follow people who demonstrate experience, education, a track record and the ability to communicate their business concept with exceptional skill and simplicity. The 'what' (and the 'why') is normally the concept that enshrines a business and, most importantly, the investment opportunity; the 'when' describes not only the inception but also the timing of anticipated investment and exit; and the 'where' explains if the business is a national, pan-territorial or global business, and under what legal and regulatory environment/territory it is going to trade.

A business plan is an intersection of:

a) everything inside the business (costs, product, services, people,); and
b) everything outside the business (competition, market trends, political/regulation changes and forces, technology development, etc).

Most inexperienced managers/entrepreneurs looking for investment spend too long on their own business, and do not pay enough attention or provide enough analysis on the overall market they are seeking to exploit. The ability to describe your product or service in relation to the wider market and the industry or kind of business it exists within is nearly always underestimated.

Essential business plan elements

A well-organized business plan will normally incorporate the following sections (business strategy, marketing strategy and financials), and within each section will be included the following main headings:

a) The business strategy

- Opportunity
- organization and operations
- legal structure
- business model
- operating procedures
- management
- board (as far as it has been structured)
- personnel
- risk management
- strengths and weaknesses
- core competencies and challenges
- track record and historical data on past performance
- location of business
- product offering – meaning the investment offering
- records and insurance.

The difference between a start-up company that cannot show previous trading records, growth and competence and a company re-financing or looking to expand is significant. Many equity and venture capital investors are wary of start-ups, especially in the film business. They are aware of the previously analysed issues surrounding the sensitivity of timing of creating cash flows and the problems often associated with no additional income streams from existing ancillary rights (e.g. library exploitation). The risk management section is particularly important to include in a film production, sales or distribution plan, as it goes to the heart of an investor's understandable concerns about security and management and operational controls.

b) The marketing strategy

- Industry and market trends
- target market(s)
- strategy to exploit target market(s)
- distribution of product
- key customers/buyers, and secondary customers/buyers
- competition
- relationships
- branding
- advertising
- pricing.

This section is where you analyse the wider market, and the 'positioning' of your business in relation to the overall business you are entering or re-financing within. Rival or similar companies are important to research. Even private companies have to submit accounts that are available on request, and can provide illuminating trading evidence.

c) The financials

- Use of funds
- start-up budget (one time deal costs including advisor fees)
- income statement (profit & loss account)
- cash-flow statement
- balance sheet
- cash-flow forecast
- profit and loss forecast
- sales revenue forecast
- capital spending plan
- budget
- break-even analysis
- sensitivity testing (if appropriate in initial business plan offering).

Assumptions

All of the above data projections rely on a set of assumptions. In the film business, for example, the assumptions would include size of budgets, number of films, size of projected fees, level of commissions, sales and marketing budgets, P&A budgets, size of minimum guarantees paid, timing of product flow, etc. The assumptions would also need to take into account expansion of the company and its rising cost base (management and staff costs, overhead, etc.). The assumptions will be analysed intently by any investor or prospective manager looking for an interest in the proposal.

Time period run-out

Most prospective investors expect to see a five-year plan. While some investors may then ask you to run a longer plan, all are aware that estimating performance after the five-year point becomes a decreasingly accurate exercise. Those investors looking for a faster exit that five years will still expect to see a five-year plan submitted.

The key three financial statements

Each business has to prepare three financial statements for its annual accounts. As such, these statements also have to be prepared for any business plan submission. They are:

- the profit and loss account (income statement)
- the balance sheet
- the cash-flow statement.

The *profit and loss account* is a financial statement that shows the profit or loss earned by the business in a particular accounting period. The sales turnover is shown at the top of the statement, from which is deducted only those costs which have been incurred in achieving that turnover.

Hence, expenditure that has been incurred but which relates to a future accounting period (e.g. prepayment) must not be included in the costs to be matched against the revenue. It also means that any expenditure which has not yet been paid for but for which a liability was incurred in the accounting period (known as an accrual) should be charged against the revenue, even though the cash has not yet left the business. An income statement, in summary, tells you if you are making money.

The *balance sheet* is a statement that shows the financial position of a business at the end of the accounting period. It tends to be referred to as a 'snapshot' of the business on this particular day or moment. The balance sheet is made up of two parts, the totals of which will always be equal. One part shows where the money was invested at the date of the balance sheet; for example, how much was invested in fixed assets and how much in working capital (current assets less current liabilities). The other part demonstrates the sources from which the capital was obtained to finance these assets. The two parts (use of finance/sources of finance) have to balance. While other presentations are sometimes used, ultimately the balance sheet shows what assets the business owns, and what it owes (e.g. liabilities) at the year end. When interpreting a balance sheet, it is important to remember that a balance sheet only shows the position of the business on one particular day. This may be entirely different on another day, and not representative of the typical trading position of the business overall. But the balance sheet does tell you what the business is worth at the end of the period.

The *cash-flow statement* shows where the money in the business has come from, how it is used, and where it goes. A good way of looking at what a cash-flow statement can tell you is: 'where did the money move?' The importance of the cash flow in managing a company on a day-to-day basis is critical. The cash-flow statement shows you the amount of cash available for the business (including, for example, sales revenues, interest income, any sales of long-term assets, liabilities, such as loans, which are still cash into the business, equity drawdowns (owner investments, venture capital, etc.); the cash that leaves the business (including, for example, start-up costs, inventory purchases/rights); controllable expenses (advertising, packaging etc.); fixed expenses (rent, utilities, insurance); long-term purchase assets; liabilities (e.g. paying back loans); and owner equity (money taken out by you or investors). With this information a manager will have a sense of the moving target of cash required to run the company.

Capital expenditure and revenue (operating) expenditure

Revenue (operating) expenditure is that which is incurred on the day-to-day running expenses of the business. For example, it would include rates, rent, salaries, electricity, phones, etc. Revenue expenditure is also referred to as operating expenditure. Capital expenditure is that which is incurred by the purchasing of or adding to the value of fixed (non-current) assets. It is important to remember that it is only the revenue (operating) expenditure that is charged in total against revenue for the period (allowing for accruals and prepayments).

Capital expenditure is not charged against revenue in the profit and loss account as it is incurred, otherwise those accounting periods in which a fixed (non-current) asset happens to be purchased will show a comparatively low profit. Also, subsequent accounting periods that benefit from the use of a fixed asset will not receive any charge in the profit and loss account, because the whole charge was made in the year of purchase.

To get over this problem, the accountant makes a charge of depreciation (or amortization in the case of an intangible fixed asset such as software or a film distribution library) in the income statement of each accounting period that benefits from the use of the asset. In this way the original cost of the asset, less any projected final value, is shared out as fairly as possible over its life.

Gross profit is the difference between the sales turnover and the cost of the goods or services that were actually sold. Administrative and other operating expenses are then deducted from the gross profit to arrive at the operating profit, which is the profit before interest and taxation.

Once the net interest costs and taxation costs have been deducted from the operating profit, any remaining profit is available for appropriation by the directors. If any dividend is to be paid it will be deducted from this figure and the remaining balance will be transferred to reserves.

Sensitive areas

Investors pay particular attention to the *overhead* of any company they are looking to become involved with. The management and staff salaries will be analysed very carefully; as will the fixed and running costs. Management looking to take too much out of the business in salary, while also expecting to share (normally through share holdings) in the upside of any success and profits, will normally be negotiated into a compromise that focuses their reward being primarily tied to the overall success of the business rather than them being heavily remunerated through a contracted position.

Common mistakes in assumptions, in particular in film business plans, include the underestimation of costs and income streams, and a slower product flow than anticipated. By contrast, overall cash generation and timing are overestimated. Optimism is normally counteracted by sensitivity testing, whereby an investor re-runs a business plan's financials, but adjusts the timing of key product, and/or the success of 'hits', in an effort to gain a more realistic picture of what might happen when a business is slower or less successful than the one being estimated in the pitch document. It is a worthwhile exercise for the entrepreneur/manager to also run out sensitivity tests prior to key meetings with investors, in an effort to be prepared and have answers for major fluxes in fortune, and some idea of how they would attempt to counteract such difficulties.

All business plans are best served by a clear statement of the offering (and projected internal rate of return on behalf of an investment, known as the IRR) at the front of the document. This normally is clearly stated within an executive summary, which essentially provides the 'highlights' of the plan.

Other typical omissions include the prospective exits available to investors. Does the entrepreneur/manager anticipate a private sale, an initial public offering (IPO), a trade sale? Lastly, a health warning is required for any plan going out to investors, and an FSA registration for those going out to more than 49 sophisticated investors.

15 Entrepreneurs and investors in the film industry

> From deep caverns he will come who will make all the peoples of the world toil and sweat, with great trouble, labour, and anxiety, so that they may have his help.
>
> (Leonardo Da Vinci, of gold and the money made from it)[1]

Film investor definitions

We have already established central issues around the economics of the independent film business that make it a high-risk business, based on a 'failure' model; albeit it is often pitched as a 'hit-driven' business. Unlike the stocks and shares of the FTSE-100, for example, the returns on which can be approximated and modelled, the returns to investors in individual films – in particular independent films without one world distributor – are wildly difficult to predict. Overall, there is a fractional minority – beyond Pareto's 80:20 power law that actually return financial benefits. That stated, film investment and film culture – with associated artistic, national and supra-national creative voices – cannot be shackled together at the heel.

Ironically, mega-hit potential within a very high-risk business is not an automatic problem for investors. The risk of holding alternative assets in the form of a portfolio of perceived 'risky' investments is smaller than the sum of the risks of holding each investment individually. This enshrines the principal of diversification and portfolio management. The problem lies in the fact that at present, the gatekeepers who control distribution and are closest to the top of the income stream are the most cash-rich centres for investment: they essentially act as portfolio managers. Smaller, fragmented entities – such as development and production companies in the independent film market – do not offer the same spread of risk and are too far away from the key cash flows of the business.

Film industry investments are viewed in the commercial sector as 'alternative' investments. Investors are seeking 'uncorrelated assets' which, in theory, reduce the risk inherent in traditional, lower margin portfolios. However, film-interested investors arrive from a range of sources, including:

- private equity (hard to find);
- angels (more common in the film production business);
- venture capital funds (starting to become more interested in film, but tend to be specialized rather than highly 'spread' investment vehicles);

- hedge fund managers (which have recently experimented again in Hollywood);
- tax-orientated investors (normally not at risk, although often state and regional rules state they need to be seen as at-risk investors to qualify);
- highly successful entrepreneurs that utilize cash and assets from previous businesses success, and strive to build up portfolios and both invest and start up new business strands.

Definitions of entrepreneurship in the film industry

Before breaking down the opportunities that the film business presents to an entrepreneur, it is useful to assess the generic qualities an entrepreneur requires if they are going to launch their own business operation.

The personality profile of an entrepreneur tends to follow a pattern, and include character traits that an individual will tend to demonstrate, such as: being results driven and often impatient; a strong need to achieve, and highly goal motivated; competitive, but able to learn from mistakes; a strong sense of self-responsibility, and a belief that they can control their own destiny; the capacity to choose and build a management team and delegate day-to-day operations where appropriate; a calculated risk-taker; an open mind towards innovation and new concepts; a talent at spotting opportunities and gaps in a market; a creative as well as a business mind, with the ability to trust their own instincts; an acceptance of uncertainty and financial insecurity; and finally, the ability to either move on from, or fold an operation and start again. Critically, many entrepreneurs do not make strong day-to-day managers of companies. That is neither their area of skill nor their motivating goal in business.

Entrepreneurs tend to be instinctive business people who can identify a concept and raise money from investors or a bank or use their own money to launch that concept and test it against a market. Their starting point is normally the combination of a concept and an opportunity or perceived gap in a market. The typical tools they utilize include the ability to spot an idea and opening; the skill of pitching an idea in person; the ability to put together a business plan (see later in this chapter); and the ability to build a team and select managers that can implement his/her vision.

Interestingly, some of the most instinctively talented entrepreneurs in the independent film business have steered away from film development and production. Those business-minded producers who have built assets and integrated companies have normally emerged as significant filmmakers in their own right, or as teams which embrace writers, directors and producers, alongside sales arms and local distribution operations or output deals. The trend has been that entrepreneurs have tended to focus on the international sales, distribution, fund-raising or the newly changing world of exhibition, rather than development and production.

Management of film businesses

The challenge of raising money, managing investors, and selling a business at the optimum time, while also carrying out the day-to-day job of managing a business, is demanding. Most truly talented entrepreneurs set up a business based on a potentially profitable business model, grow and develop it, and then attempt to sell it at a perceived maximum moment. Then they start again with a new concept and/or a new company, and not necessarily in the same sector.

Managing a film company, whatever specific sector in the business, demands the physical daily presence of that person where possible. This can create problems in some sectors – such as sales and distribution, where managers are part of the sales or buying process, and are forced to be absent from offices; or where producers have to be on set. Of course, strong delegation skills help a business run smoothly while an MD is away, but the day-to-day process can be interrupted if a manager is constantly away.

Other key roles of a manager include their ability to put the assumptions of a business plan into action, to hire and fire staff, and to report to a Board and/or owner. There is a tendency in the film business for managers who also own their business to fall into 'owner-drivers': part-entrepreneur, part-manager, and often compromised in their daily decision-making by also having to protect their shares and ownership.

Barriers and challenges to different types of film businesses

The production company

Barriers to entry are very low: a film producer does not have to pass any professional exams, or belong to a union in order to be in business. Indeed, they can print their name on a card and below it the words 'film producer' and set about their business. However, without underlying rights in potential projects, most producers need to raise seed money to get started. Why? Because a producer has to be in development, with scripts and packages, prior to being able to potentially create income via being in production.

It is interesting to look at the development/production business from an instinctive entrepreneur's point of view. The first point an entrepreneur might raise is: How long am I going to be in development before I start making money? Answer: almost certainly longer than any business plan projection might claim, as most newcomers are extremely optimistic. The next set of issues is the repayment of sunk costs (plus overheads) and the ability to reach the stage where a fee income is payable.

A producer is only rewarded via three main streams:

- repayment and possible premium of development money being repaid on first day of principal photography;
- a production fee (if not forced to defer or part-defer);
- net profits shared normally on a 50–50 basis with the financier(s), of which the producer has to take care of the talent (writer, director, cast), which normally amounts to 20 of the 50 points. Rarely does a producer negotiate box office kickers/bumps from excellent performance.

In light of the above streams, we should reconsider the risk attached to any initial seed money. Most entrants achieve a low level of development project conversions, and many are forced to part-defer or defer production fees. There is no collateral (e.g. library rights), no guarantee of product flow, and no guarantee of fee levels. The likelihood that a film achieves break-even now needs to be added into the mix. Cash break-even is the moment when the revenues of a film, following the deduction of fees and expenses incurred in distribution and the payment of gross participations to talent, equal the costs of production, including the overhead contributions and costs of finance. At that point, the film is able to repay its costs 100 per cent.

Following the break-even point being reached, all additional revenues, after the deduction of any additional cost of sales, contribute to profits. Until break-even, a film is a loss-making investment from the perspective of the producer/financier. As performance tails off, the film's generation of revenues will tend to lag behind the accumulating cost of the capital used to produce and distribute it.

The importance of the break-even point is that once it has occurred, given the marginal costs of distribution and exploitation being so low and the pricing of film at the consumer level being more or less fixed (e.g. volume can increase but prices do not drop), a film, once it has achieved break-even, will tend to generate increasing profits.

The sales company

Just as we examined the investment opportunities and issues in a production company, we now look at a sales company from a similar perspective. Unlike a producer/ production company, where the overhead can be kept tight and the costs rise and contract depending on the level of actual production activity (and associated fees and contracted staff via a production), a sales company has certain fixed overhead and operating costs that are more difficult to organize in a flexible manner.

The fact is that there is a significant level of outlay of cash made by a sales company prior to any fees/commissions from product sales. They include:

- overheads – which varies from boutique operations with around 4 staff, to major companies handling up to 30 films a year, with staff of 15 or more;
- materials, including poster, promotional material, trailer, etc.;
- attendance at major markets, including Cannes, the American Film Market, Berlin;
- attendance at launch festivals, and launch costs for each film;
- advances/minimum guarantees if the company is financed to enable it to put up investment in return for rights.

The standard level of 'sales and marketing' costs normally allowed by a producer/ financier has been around $150,000 over the past decade. However, with the erosion of the value of the dollar, most companies either budget in euros or insist on a sterling minimum of £100,000, or $200,000. This is outside the cost of the first festival launch, which in many cases can cost as much as the overall sales and marketing budget.

Hence, without a library of rights that can assist in annual turnover via television sales and reissue business, entry can be hard to justify given the 2–3 year turnaround prior to real income streams. The main issue is that although the sales company is higher up the revenue stream, it has considerable outlays prior to receiving repayment on its own sunk costs, let alone commission on final delivery of the film to distributors. And a smart entrepreneur will also raise the question of payment on delivery. Despite contract obligations, what forces a distributor to always accept delivery of a film? Cases have occurred when a distributor has decided that the final delivery of the film is not the screenplay on which they pre-bought the film. This tends to happen when the film itself is disappointing. What happens when the distributor goes out of business during the period between signature and delivery? The sales company has to find a new distributor and cancel the existing contract.

Making a business plan for a sales company is a more predictable exercise than for a production company. However, given the above variables and time-sensitivities, it still requires considerable collateral and underlying rights to help pin its business into a structure that ultimately becomes an attractive investment.

The distributor

Moving to the next level of the value chain, it is instructive to see the issue of risk, financial outlay and returns when examining an independent distributor's business plan. Despite being higher up the revenue chain, distribution is not a business for the strictly risk-adverse investor. To be in business, an independent distributor has to compete with peers and, in certain cases, mini-major and major distributors. A distributor needs to address the following issues:

- the need for a high level of outlay prior to income/fees from product;
- start-up costs (sunk);
- overhead;
- market and festival attendance;
- cost of advances/minimum guarantees;
- cost of prints and advertising (marketing material;
- booking of cinemas and collections.

The relationships that matter to the entrepreneur

The key relationships that the entrepreneur needs to develop and maintain include:

- Other like-minded, smart, rising talents with ideas. The best entrepreneurs take notice and include other talent rather than remain threatened and closeted. This way they build an idea, a team and/or a partnership.
- Advisors: strong entrepreneurs will seek out the best lawyers and accountants. They assume that business-minded lawyers and accountants are business savvy re-fund raising, and they need reputation and advice when putting together investment proposals.
- The great and good: investors like solid, experienced people on board. It is a price the entrepreneur pays for taking the investment.
- Bankers: most only join up once the money has been raised. A bank that is in from the start is a far better partner, even if they simply lend you a limited overdraft.
- Interesting and relevant managers will be crucial to the founding entrepreneur to bring on board.
- Sounding boards: people who have experience – in particular in the specific area you are targeting.
- The opportunity: what makes the proposition compelling has to be at the start, middle and end of the business plan that is being proposed.

The entrepreneur facing the investor (or manager)

What key questions is the entrepreneur being asked by an investor or potential manager? A manager is included in this assessment, as they too are often asked to make an investment in return for shares in an operation. Key issues that an investor will ask include:

- Why is the business opportunity compelling, and is it achievable with the resources being proposed – in particular the management?
- What is the rate of return? This is calculated as an IRR (internal rate of return on the investment per annum pre tax). If the IRR is too low (say below 15–20 per cent per annum depending on going interest rates), then most investors simply walk away from the business plan and do not take a meeting.
- What are the risk factors? Top entrepreneurs focus heavily on risk management in an effort to counteract risk factors that will inevitably be raised or assumed by any potential investor.
- What is the growth potential?
- What is the exit, and how realistic are the different opportunities?
- Are the assumptions made in terms of income, timing and profitability realistic? What happens when they are tested?
- What is the additional X-factor upside that could take the investment into super-profits? This is particularly important in film investments.

The entrepreneur and the management team

Any entrepreneur will have put a team together – consisting of:

a) a possible partner
b) investors
c) managers.

The senior managers and partner will be expected to put up what is called 'pain money' – for example, cash for shares (a share of the business ownership). Alternatively, managers will be given share options, at a price that should enable them to cash them up at a later date at a profit, but hence only at the point that the company has been successful. As the management does not pay upfront, it has less control over a manager leaving if the company has failed and the share prices are low. In the balance, the notion of manager/owners (rather than option holders) is more powerful in terms of key tests; including loyalty, tying management in, building success and being paid on a full exit.

The principle of 'pain money' is vital to the investor, and is seen as a commitment test. If managers are forced to come up with a token payment upfront, they will – theoretically – care more about the company and their decisions than if they just draw a salary with no initial investment. For entrepreneurs, it is obvious, and most do not expect to take any money out of the business until it has reached considerable success and profits. For managers, it sorts out the weak from the strongly committed.

The standard deal is around 20 per cent of the company, split out between a management team and the remaining 80 per cent held by investors if a start-up.

Sometimes an 'escalator' (which means that depending on the IRR, the management can earn back their shares and many more) can be applied to ultimately give the management a much bigger slice of the company. The ultimate new shareholding balance will depend on how well they perform.

Selling up and how to cope with failure

The exit is all important to an investor and to an entrepreneur. What are the typical options for film companies in the industry?

- A trade sale;
- private sale of shares to new investors (hard to find);
- going public (alternative investment market – most likely in the UK) – hard to achieve;
- a management buy-out.

What are the key issues from an entrepreneur's perspective?

- Write an action plan to keep a sale on track;
- choose top advisors;
- delegate to other managers while the sale is on;
- clean up the accounts and deal with any black holes/long-term debts;
- draw up a list of possible companies/investors;
- decide how involved you are going to be post the deal; this normally is a deal breaker, and will often require 'handcuffs' that force a manager/entrepreneur to still remain involved in some way;
- you only have one chance, so plan well ahead; never underestimate the time it will take to find the right buyer and the right price;
- always, in the film business, recognize that less of more may be better than remaining small: keep an open mind.

Issues around the notion and fact of failure

Never use the word failure with an entrepreneur. They do not get the concept. The fact that it is an integral part of business is not the point – it is just that entrepreneur's way of business life and psychology is to never give up and accept defeat.

How do entrepreneurs overcome a major problem, setback or closing down of a company?

- Acknowledge it fast;
- act on it fast;
- take insolvency advice early;
- look after staff on a close down/exit;
- move on fast but not so quickly as to repeat the mistakes;
- acknowledge what were mistakes, and be honest about which were yours, and which were beyond your control;
- remember it is only business.

Wisdom on how to proceed:

- Most deals go wrong at the start; a fact prevalent in the film business.
- Projections always override historical track record. Always put history first. Do not exaggerate. Or make promises you cannot keep.
- Try to put realistic milestones going forwards.
- Venture capitalists can be attracted to experienced Boards but actually back the wrong non-executive team for a film company.
- It is important to overcome reluctance to change management when a company needs to turn around or alter direction fast.
- Finance directors are most often replaced in the first year.
- CEOs are the next most replaced in the first year.
- Do not see the deal as an end point in itself: you are back at the starting line in nearly all respects.
- Spend time with investors pre the deal, get to know them.
- See the bigger picture and the market you are operating within as clearly as possible. This is very hard when you are struggling to close a deal to continue film business professionally.
- Relations with your investors are critical – if they understand the film business you are in less than 1 per cent of the entertainment investment market. They will understand setbacks and wider market problems and be more patient.

Case study interview: The Film Department's Mark Gill

The Film Department, an independent movie finance, production and international sales company – founded by former Warner Independent and Miramax Films president Mark Gill and former Miramax executive vice president and Yari Film Group COO Neil Sacker – raised $200m in June 2007. Mark Gill talked to the author about the challenge of raising private finance.[2]

The interview

Raising money for The Film Department was like doing a remedial MBA. We didn't know how much should be equity, how much debt, how much mezzanine, and what the pricing should look like. (In fact, we barely knew what mezzanine was!) The good news about having smart people in your life is that they will tell you. What they told us is that the bank debt is the easy part. Sure enough they were happy enough to line up and do that lending. The mezzanine is somewhat more difficult but manageable [financing that comes out after the bank, with higher pricing, and is out before the equity]. But when it came to equity we were told: 'Maybe we can help, but you are really on your own.' In our case it was an even split of $30m equity, $30m mezzanine, and then $140m of senior bank debt. What that means in practical terms is that for every movie we make, the cost is met by 15 per cent from equity, 15 per cent from mezzanine and 70 per cent from bank debt. The bank debt is covered in a combination of contracts that are to be discounted from foreign sales, with some gap against remaining rights. It's almost a single picture model, but the difference is that we already have our banking lined up, and they are anxious to put the money to work. From a film maker's point of view, you don't have to worry about any of that, which is the key problem with independent financing. There's always the worry that the money won't show up or that there are other pre-conditions at the last minute that make it impossible to close and start shooting. The money is our problem, not yours. We initially thought that we'd go out and find 4 x \$7.5m chunks and be done. Well, that was both naive and stupid. We did actually find two to each do that, but the rest of it was in chunks of \$5m, \$1m and the smallest were in chunks of \$250,000. It leaves you realizing that there's as much hand holding to find \$250k as there is as finding \$7.5m. We did some 580-odd meetings, to find 14 people. Almost everyone on Wall Street said, 'You Hollywood people, you're not really business people. How can we trust you? How do we know that anything you say is true? All you do is grab financiers by the ankles and turn them upside down and shake until all the money comes out of our pockets. Why would we ever do business with you?' And then most of them turned out to be far less reputable than even the most venal talent agent I've ever met. It's a truly gruesome process. Had anyone warned me prior to starting, I'd have never done it. The domino effect was very hard, as we had five key elements to hold together, and it fell over three times. On the fourth time we got lucky. But even on the day we were supposed to sign it nearly fell apart. I don't recommend it to anyone. What you tend to find is that people who invest want as much security as possible, which is a reasonable thought. Many said that they didn't want to invest with no distribution, but we finally found a few who did. Then, how do you figure out how the money can be spent, and what are the requirements, which is the key to it. You're going to be making one decision on a \$30–\$40m movie which is a big chunk of the money. Specifically, we have GE Capital, our underwriter, on the Board, along with three other investors, Neil and me. Of course the Board has controls. But when we get down to the green light word, what really matters is what we can do fast by ourselves. We agreed that five managers could green light a movie under certain conditions. There is a 6–7 page document on how to do that. If we over time fail in our numbers, then the Board can step in and have authority over that, but as long as we do what we said we were going to do, then we'll continue to have the authority to green light.

By the way, that approach was also considered a form of Marxism in Hollywood. It was truly terrifying to many investors, who said that we had to be kidding them. But the people who ultimately came in said: 'Okay, we're betting on you, so we should really bet on you rather than half bet on you and then cut you off at the knees.' What it means from a filmmaker's perspective and why we were finally able to sell it was we can move quickly. What the management wanted to achieve was the following:

• not to worry about going to a studio and getting that committee to approve something before we start;
• not to have to have made foreign sales and got contracts in, and notices of assignments signed, and the banks say fine and all the rest of it; and,
• not to have to explain where the other half of the money is.

The above reasons are mainly why two thirds of independent movies collapse. We explained the problem, and sold the ability to move and green light very quickly as a competitive advantage, and the investors saw that.

16 The challenge of creative management

> The view that good ideas are rarer and more valuable than good people is rooted in a misconception of creativity.
>
> (Ed Catmull, co-founder of Pixar and the president of Pixar and Disney Animation Studios)
>
> Historically we've been blinded by the genius of Shakespeare, but forget the fact that he was also a brilliant entrepreneur …
>
> (Marc Boothe, managing director, B3 Media)

Creative careers

Building a creative career in any artistic arena is a challenge; building a successful progression of work that grows to more than the sum of its parts in the film industry is tantamount to climbing Everest. You may think you are getting somewhere, and your goal appears closer, but all too quickly a setback pushes (and sometimes crashes) you back down again. Antagonizing peaks all too often lead to larger troughs, and many – understandably – fail to stick to the climb.

So how do creative, talented people stay the course? Retaining focus, confidence and a sense of direction all appear to be traits that are highly individual and idiosyncratic, but to enjoy the freedom to exercise talent requires dedicated and intuitive colleagues, dynamic teamwork and, essential to any filmmaker, strong creative management. These rules are not directed at directors only – for there is a multitude of creative talent that the industry itself all too often takes for granted and who rarely shine in the public limelight thanks to the hierarchical obsession with the cult of the 'director' in particular. Filmmaking is collaborative and requires reservoirs of creative talent to make ideas reach audiences in an effective manner.

There lies a potential contradiction in the notion of 'managing creativity',[1] but the meeting of business and art is what draws people to work and remain engaged in the movie business. This chapter looks at why creativity is absolutely central to film companies; from where generic sources of creativity emerge; ways that creativity is either obstructed or encouraged; and how the building of a creative environment, nearly always with the assistance of teams, can impact on how artists feel about their work and its associated value to both them and the wider world.

Without creativity – which in business frames of reference results in the creation of intellectual property rights – film companies and media business entities would have nothing with which to trade. Creativity is the axis around which all other filmmaking activity revolves. Far from being limited to ideas, creativity, to list just some of the most obvious areas of application, is required for writing, editing, pitching, producing, shooting, lighting, designing, editing, selling and marketing. Many creative talents are required on both a business-to-business basis (e.g. the positioning and selling of a film to a distributor/buyer) and for the task of designing a campaign to reach the end-user – the audience. This is how money is made, and how companies grow and thrive – through a churn of product, successful placement in the market and openness to reinvention. Without successfully harnessing creativity, companies and their managers have nowhere to go in the moving-picture industry.

Film organizations are heavily dependent on intellectual property to generate income. The key entrepreneurial equation is how to turn the creation of IPRs into value, which in turn demonstrates how interdependent the artist and the manager/ producer are when it comes to creating such a complex product as a movie. The variety and complexity of this 'business ecosystem'[2] starts not necessarily with the broad 'market' per se, with all its rivalry and competition, but within a tighter vortex that throws up subtle contradictions and insecurities. Companies are dependent on creative people – and the more talented they are, the easier it is for them to leave and take up work elsewhere. So from a manager's perspective, the aim is to work out how to find them, motivate them, get them working to the best of their ability and retain their loyalty so that they do not leave.

Sources of creativity

Sources of creativity in the film development process, listed in a simplified, utilitarian way, gradually brings us to the key umbrella that helps link intrinsic creativity with productivity: the team. However, different 'feeders' supply core initial starting points, hence the order suggested below:

1   the book/adapted to a screenplay
2   the original idea/treatment/screenplay
3   the writer
4   the writer/director
5   the producer
6   the director
7   third-party sources
8   the team.

Sources of inspiration imply ownership. But, given the inherent complexity of the film value chain, and the difficulties of moving ideas through development, into production, and to the market, creative talent that inspires ideas axiomatically finds itself in the hands of managers if they are to realize their ideas into reality. This leads creative filmmakers into a trap: 'Most clever people don't like to be led. This creates problems for leaders.' This statement, cited by Peter Bloore (a Senior Lecturer in Creativity at the University of East Anglia) in his lecture on Managing Creative People,[3] opens up the psychological issues at stake when management encounters creative people. Referencing Goffee and Jones's article 'Managing Clever/Creative

People – Herding Cats?' (2007), Bloore lists seven key factors that summarize clever/creative people's characteristics:

1   They know their worth and have tacit skills – knowledge that cannot be transferred independent of its holder – rather than skills that can be easily codified.
2   They are organizationally savvy and will seek the company context in which their interests are most generously funded.
3   They ignore corporate hierarchy. They care about intellectual status, not job titles, so you cannot lure them with promotions.
4   They expect instant access to top management and if they don't get it they may think that their work isn't being taken seriously.
5   They are well connected and are usually plugged into highly developed knowledge networks – who they know is often as important as what they know. This increases their value to the organization but also makes them more of a flight risk.
6   Creative people have a low boredom threshold and will leave if you don't inspire them with your organisation's purpose.
7   They won't thank you even when you lead them well. They don't like to feel that they are being led.[4]

Obstructing creativity

Encouraging the imagination is much harder than killing it. Typical ways to block or stifle creativity include:

1   Inability to listen and ignoring people's input. Managers who quickly override creative people actively disable them. Listening is a required skill if creatives are to flourish.
2   Alienating team members by allowing dominant, inexperienced (or unconnected) personalities to control the creative process.
3   The failure to provide accurate and timely information (especially when well-informed creative people have a habit of finding out). Sloppy work and late feedback kills confidence in creatives.
4   Not providing a forum for open debate and blue-sky thinking. Defensive, controlling behaviour does not inspire creatives.
5   Failing to read and consider the written work in full (e.g. producer or commissioning editor reading notes/coverage but not the screenplay). Inability to physically read is probably one of the biggest demotivators for a writer or writer/director.
6   A lack of discipline for agreeing, recording and acting on decisions. A critical path is quietly appreciated by creatives even if they verbally push against being actively controlled.
7   Instantly negative opening statements: 'We don't normally … it can't be done this way … '; 'That's not the way we work … '.
8   Setting up unrealistic timelines and deadlines that lead to unnecessary disappointment. There is enough rejection in the creative filmmaking mix without generating it unnecessarily.
9   Inefficiency over practical details: not covering/repaying expenses; paying late; general thoughtlessness for the person in question.
10 Stalling development and progress through lack of finance.

What attracts creative people?

Financial reward alone is not what drives creative people. Ownership, recognition, appreciation and responsibility tend to be more important and persuasive drivers than simply being paid large sums of money. 'They don't want to feel bought – they want to feel valued.'[5] That is not to suggest that financial reward is unimportant; but it tends not to be the primary motivating factor. There is an alignment of varying factors and influences that bear weight when motivating creative people. Attractants include: the people/peer group (e.g. a producer's track record); the challenge of the project/task; the chance and source of funding to see their ideas/vision realized; your vision; the external and internal environments; and the organizational culture.

Specifically, if management is to actively encourage creativity – especially in a team environment – it can choose to focus on the following actions: notice creativity; reward it (not necessarily in terms of money – it may be about working flexibility re hours, or shared ownership/credits, etc.); request it but do not demand it; delegate it; and build up both individual and team ownership. 'One of the key tasks of a leader is to understand the problem space and help people define it and then work within it to solve the problem', explains Stibbe.[6] Although directly referencing games rather than films, Stibbe also recommends managers to use the abstraction and objectivity of a 'partial outsider' to help put creative issues in context and help the team match the right solutions to the right problems and avoid false trails.

Putting mantras into successful action is the gold dust of managers.

> It's extremely difficult for an organization to analyze itself. It is uncomfortable and hard to be objective. Systematically fighting complacency and uncovering problems when your company is successful have got to be two of the toughest management challenges there are.

explains Ed Catmull about managing the animation production company Pixar.[7]

> Clear values, constant communication, routine post-mortems and the regular injection of outsiders who will challenge the status quo aren't enough. Strong leadership is also essential – to make sure that people don't pay lip service to the values, tune out the communications, game the processes, and automatically discount newcomer's observations and suggestions.

Intense post-mortems and welcoming 'fresh blood' are part of the Pixar's approach, but taking the organization back to its operating principles are where the real instruction lies. The three key Pixar principles are:

1   Everyone must have the freedom to communicate with anyone.
2   It must be safe for everyone to offer ideas.
3   We must stay close to innovations happening in the academic community.

The first two principles may be hard to put into real practice, but straightforward to comprehend as objectives. The third is more taxing for managers of film companies who tend to fire fight problems and challenges on a daily basis. Catmull explains that Pixar runs a collection of in-house courses which they call Pixar University:

It is responsible for training and cross-training people as they develop in their careers. But it also offers an array of optional classes – many of which I've taken – that give people from different disciplines the opportunity to mix and appreciate what everyone does.

And ultimately, by fusing technology with art, while enshrining the notion of learning at each stage, Pixar can attract the very best talent and keep it.[8]

There is a confidence and positivity to the Pixar model, but it is the management that took the lead and set (and has continued to re-set) the tone for the company. Most importantly, the Pixar creative environment enshrines a 'team democracy' approach. Attributes beyond the Pixar model for a creative environment might include:

- a building/office that encourages people to meet, exchange information, and share facilities;
- high standards that are commonly accepted;
- openness to new ideas, suggestions and outside commentary and analysis;
- ability to learn from mistakes – promoted by tolerance and positive introspection;
- allowing those more experienced to have a voice, while promoting mutual respect;
- considered and timely feedback;
- enjoyment and fun – which in turn promotes team-shared experience, communication, confidence, morale and a sense of living in the moment;
- the setting up of forums and communication rituals which are respected by all attendees.

Creative team management from a film producer's perspective

Conventional 'business teams' tend to have clear objectives, roles and positions of hierarchical power, which are established at the onset of a project. These roles and the overall format tend not to alter much during the lifecycle of the project. However, as Bloore points out, business team theory and creative team theory provide us with an interesting way of viewing the film development process. If we take it as given that a 'team' is whenever more than one person works together in a planned way towards a single purpose, that accurately describes what happens in film development. Whilst acknowledging that it is not fashionable to think of film development as a team activity, Bloore goes on to suggest that the film development process involves a creative team that grows and shrinks regularly: 'As it does so, the balance of power and control also shifts within the team. ... This is one of the many reasons why the film development process is more complex and potentially chaotic than "conventional" creative teams.'

So, from the producer's perspective, they normally maintain long-term relationships with more than one writer – certainly more than a director does. The producer also has to generate intellectual property – in this process created by the raw material of new screenplays or sources such as novels, plays, etc., to adapt. Directors, especially those established and successful, are often offered completed screenplays to work on.

The producer's task is to balance the writer and, initially, their relationship with the development team. However, the writer will want to have a primary, one-to-one relationship where available and possible with the producer. They will not want to take notes, feedback and direction from development staff on an ongoing basis. If the writer is not working already with a director (or is not a writer/director), the producer will have to be careful about the way the writer is introduced to the director. Directors select material but are also chosen due to commercial demands, most likely to do with the commercial imperative of financing a film on the back of an established and appropriate track record. The producer's director selection may not fit with the writer's view; an immediate point of creative conflict. Or the director may not be sympathetic and diplomatic about voicing creative input. And ultimately the director will be responsible for 'delivering' the film, not the writer, whose job has typically been phased out by the stage that the film is in front of the cameras. (Of course writers are often needed to re-write on set, and some directors are creatively open and inclusive in their treatment of writers rather than exclusive.)

The key to successful creative management of writers and directors is the ability to develop trust, and long-lasting bonds. In return, writers and directors are employed on a more regular and constructive basis, and slates of work emerge rather than ad hoc, one-off experiences. And when writer and director work in harness with a producer, as covered in Chapter 3, some fine results can emerge.[9]

Case study: Neil LaBute's *Vapor*

Taking an American piece of material and attached talent, and seeing what can occur when a European-based company commits to developing and financing that package, can illuminate the creative, cultural and financial hazards that are associated with ambitious cross-border investments in the film business. However, such ambitious projects that have high-value elements either attached or potentially likely to join such a project, often form part of the price of doing business in the higher end of the independent film business. Projects that can potentially drive a company's perception and reputation forwards are hard to come by, and entry comes at a premium. The following case study demonstrates many of the above issues.

The development package

Pretty Pictures, a Los Angeles-based production company run by producer Gail Mutrux (*Rain Man*, *Quiz Show*), approached Renaissance Films in 2001 to finance the development of a Neil LaBute project. The novella, written by a new writer, Amanda Fillapachi, is about a young wannabe actress in New York, who meets and falls for a strange scientist who ostensibly makes clouds for a living. They embark on a highly charged and challenged affair, while the story takes on fantasy-like Pygmalion aspects as the lead actress is re-shaped, literally, by her admiring scientist. In other words, *Vapor* is an off-beat, truly 'independent' project, not cut out for in-house Hollywood Studio development but potentially original enough to attract high-end talent given the status of the director and producer committed to developing the material.

The project came to light thanks to a vigilant acquisitions executive working at Renaissance during that time. Sarah Sulick had found out about the book and the attachments, and pitched it internally to Renaissance's co-managing directors, who were interested in pursuing the project.

After initial discussions, the agreement between Renaissance and Pretty Pictures stated that Neil LaBute (*In The Company of Men*, *Nurse Betty*), would adapt the novella, and direct the film. Pretty Pictures was to produce, and Renaissance was committed to financing, controlling world rights, and executive producing. The dates of writing commencement (two drafts and a polish) were initially left vague, as LaBute had some 'prior commitments', but Mutrux assured Renaissance that she would be able to get the writer/director to focus on the screenplay once his latest film, *Possession*, an A. S. Byatt adaptation, was completed.

During a meeting between Renaissance, Mutrux and LaBute, prior to signature of the three-way development deal, Renaissance stressed that some of the more extreme elements of the story needed to be handled carefully if the script was not to alienate both the potential cast and, ultimately, the project's intended audience. Renaissance internally debated whether it should consider including the right to appoint a third-party writer to the project as an insurance for timely delivery and a greater level of creative control – with LaBute writing a 'director's draft' rather than two full drafts and a polish, but nothing was decided upon. Renaissance decided, instead, to rely on a delivery date for the first draft (February 2002) in the long form development contract, which allowed LaBute more than six months from signature to deliver.

At this stage, a Los Angeles-based company, Catch 22, approached Renaissance about sharing the development costs 50–50, with a view to co-financing the project. Renaissance decided that this partnership would help offset the upfront risks of development, and a verbal agreement was established, but not papered (e.g. legally drawn up) in a timely manner. (Later, Catch 22 fell away as the company closed prior to any formal legal contract being in place, leaving Renaissance picking up the tab for the full development and pre-pre-production costs.)

Writing delays

The first draft of *Vapor* was delayed by 12 months (script delivery ended up being in February 2003) due to LaBute directing a new movie of one of his plays (*The Shape of Things*), a Working Title project that was not mentioned when the development deal was agreed. Although the first draft was potentially strong, it needed significant rewriting. Specifically, the writing in the more extreme and emotional scenes in the script required attention. Most problematic was that the first 40 pages read like a zestful and light romantic comedy; while the following 80 read like a noir psycho-thriller. To be specific, the male lead literally throws the female lead into a cage with a view to 'improving' and training her around p.48 of the screenplay, shortly followed by the character using an ice dart gun to control his muse: definitely edgy material.

Market pressure on the development process

After notes and a meeting with Renaissance, LaBute made some minor revisions. Renaissance, however, was under time pressure to package the film (i.e. attach key cast and agree a budget) prior to the imminent film market at Cannes. Why? Because that was where the film had its best chance to be financed, and because Renaissance was hoping that the project's launch into the marketplace would also lift the company's overall status and reputation with international distributors.

The one draft plus revisions version of *Vapor* was sent out by the Creative Artists Agency (CAA), acting on the behalf of Renaissance, to cast. After a 10-week period, Ralph Fiennes and Sandra Bullock committed to play the leads. The director assumed that now that key talent was attached, the script was in shape and required no major additional work.

Renaissance's sales team argued that the draft suffered from mixed-genre confusion, and was not yet in shape for key distributors to read. By this time sole managing director Finney pointed out that the script needed to be sent to North American and foreign distributors at least three weeks prior to the commencement of Cannes. Otherwise, the script would not be read, the project would not be considered and no crucial pre-sales and financing partners would be closed. In turn, the talent would move on to other projects.

What should Renaissance do?

1   Put project on hold, and request a new draft from LaBute as per his contract?
2   Put project on hold, and appoint a writer agreed by LaBute to make the changes in tone, etc., that Renaissance feels are crucial to the project working?
3   Request further work from LaBute on the screenplay right up to the eve of the market, and then deliver that draft to primed US and foreign distributors in the hope that they will read promptly given the attachments?
4   Allow the existing draft to go out three weeks prior to the market, and bring LaBute to Cannes to talk face-to-face with distributors about his vision for the film? Renaissance could then use a North American partner attracted to the project to bring pressure on the screenplay once they become partners.

What actually happened?

The script went out three weeks ahead of Cannes, and LaBute attended. However, whilst the project was taken very seriously, the script was not widely liked, mainly due to the mixed-genre problem.

What should have happened?

a)   Renaissance should have included and exercised the option to appoint a third-party writer in the original development contract. This might have avoided some of the delays and hence subsequent time pressures on Renaissance to finance the film so soon after first draft script delivery.
b)   Renaissance should have placed the project on hold rather than take a screenplay that was not ready to be read by distributors to the market.
c)   The writer and producer could then have had more time to work on a fully re-worked draft. If the script worked, new talent would have committed.

The packaging stage

After the previously mentioned false development starts, Renaissance decided that *Vapor* still held certain strong attractions re creative packaging. 'Creative packaging' refers to the writer, director and cast (potential or attached) that make up most of the key elements when planning a production. First, the writer was also the director. Second, the writer/director had a cast already in mind when the book was optioned and the screenplay commissioned.

The initial cast

The pitch from LaBute and Mutrux was that LaBute was intending to write the part for Rene Zellwegger, who had played the title lead in LaBute's *Nurse Betty*. Mutrux had a strong relationship with Ralph Fiennes (to whom she spoke on the phone regularly) thanks to their work on *Quiz Show*. Renaissance considered the cast combination commercially appealing – possibly to the tune of around $15–20m re a prospective budget. And Fiennes was extremely keen to work with Zellwegger.

Shortlisting

When the screenplay was deemed ready to go out to cast, CAA, who represented Zellwegger, (and Renaissance), gave the project to her agent and management on an exclusive basis. No time limit was set initially, as the director, producer, agent and Renaissance all expected Zellwegger to read promptly. She was aware of the project, and LaBute had spoken to her on the phone about the role and the concept. Zellwegger had the script the first week of March 2003. Concurrently, she had been nominated for a Best Actress Oscar for her role in *Chicago*. Despite repeated calls from Mutrux, LaBute and Renaissance, CAA and Zellwegger's management continued to ask for 'more time'. What became clear was that Zellwegger was not going to make a decision about her next role until she knew if she had won the Oscar. CAA rang the producer six weeks after the initial submission, and told Mutrux that Zellwegger 'was passing'.

Renaissance had just four weeks prior to the Cannes market to package *Vapor* to a level that would attract pre-sales and an American financing partner. A shortlist was drawn up, that included Cameron Diaz at the top. It became clear quickly that Diaz was not available. ICM's CEO Jeff Berg rang Renaissance suggesting Julia Roberts, but by that stage (three weeks prior to Cannes), CAA had got LaBute to focus on Sandra Bullock, also a CAA client. Bullock read the script within four days. Bullock has a very close relationship with Warners, including a production company with her sister that operated on the studio lot. Bullock was scheduled to play the lead in *Miss Congeniality 2* for Warners, but the shoot was not starting until January 2004 – leaving a gap that autumn for the actress to do *Vapor*.

Suitability

LaBute met Bullock, who liked the screenplay and her character very much. She spoke to Fiennes about their prospective partnership, and that seemed to go well. Renaissance had little time to consider whether Bullock was the right commercial fit for the project – as the creative elements (writer/director, producer, existing cast), appeared convinced. So too was CAA, as the agency was mindful of the timing issues re getting the project out to distributors prior to the Cannes market.

Cannes

A letter from CAA with the draft and cast attachments confirmed, was sent out ten days prior to the Cannes market. John Ptak, the lead agent representing the project, put a budget price of $25m on the film in his letter. (This number was an issue for Renaissance's sales head, as she was concerned that it was placing the project at a higher level than the material could justify, despite the cast attachments.) Renaissance managed to get an announcement about *Vapor*, with Bullock and Fiennes attached, onto the front page of *Screen International*'s first daily magazine of the market. Everything seemed on be on track.

The distributors' reaction

Vapor is a particularly demanding screenplay. Most key territory buyers did read the screenplay prior to attending Cannes. But many were confused, as they understood Bullock's casting up to p.48 of the script, but at the point that Fiennes' character 'forces her into a cage', many became confused about genre and casting suitability. With the exception of two key distributors, Renaissance failed to make any pre-sales at Cannes.

Post-Cannes, what should Renaissance do?

1   Re-cast Bullock, and relaunch the film later that year at MIFED?
2   Stick with the casting, and try to close a Warners' North American deal and a deal with Icon (an international distributor that operated in the United Kingdom and Australasia) for the United Kingdom/Australia/New Zealand with existing cast?
3   Go back to Zellwegger, when she did not win the Best Actress Oscar?

What actually happened?

Renaissance tried to close Warners and Icon, and also tried to pre-sell during the summer of 2003 by visiting distributors in Spain, Germany and France face-to-face, but to no avail.

What should have happened?

Renaissance should have kept control over the project much more tightly at the point that Zellwegger 'passed'. Instead of being rushed into a creative decision chosen by the creatives, the financier should have been cautious and patient. As an international sales company, it should have been aware of the dangerous juxtaposition that Bullock's casting represented: 'Light, comedic actress in dangerous, indie movie from auteur ... .' It should have said no to Bullock prior to her coming on board.

The financing stage

It is relevant now we come to examine the budget issues and finance that had to be raised, to recall that Mutrux and LaBute had worked previously on *Nurse Betty* ($32m) and *Possession* ($30m). These budget levels provided the executive producer with an indication of the director's potential 'value' in the independent marketplace.

Cast

The two leads by May 2003 attached to *Vapor* were Sandra Bullock and Ralph Fiennes. However, despite the high level of casting for an independent film, Renaissance had indicated to Mutrux that no more than $20–22m was likely to be available to *Vapor* from the marketplace due to the challenging material and LaBute's recent track record.

The budget

Renaissance asked Pretty Pictures to deliver a production budget on the draft that distributors read at Cannes 2003. The first production budget submitted totalled $33m without financing costs. In Renaissance's opinion, this budget was at least $10m too high. Renaissance decided to fix on what they thought was a realistic figure for distributors and financiers, and re-work the script, schedule and budget while the financing was being raised. A figure of $25m was arrived at, including financing costs (e.g. cost of banking gap, loans, interest, and financing fees, etc.).

Finance plan(s)

Renaissance had two potential plans for raising the finance for *Vapor*, based on the need to raise $25m. Both first required a North American deal, that could be announced and promote the film to the attention of key foreign buyers. These financial components would, potentially, be the cornerstone financing of the film:

1   North American deal (plus Australasia and South Africa) with Paramount Pictures (33.3 per cent of budget), German tax fund (20 per cent), further foreign pre-sales (30 per cent) and bank 'gap' against remaining sales estimates (17–22 per cent), requiring 200 per cent coverage.
2   North American deal at $5m (20 per cent), further foreign pre-sales at 40 per cent (including the United Kingdom/Australasia; Germany; France and Italy); German 'super' tax fund (30 per cent), and bank gap against remaining sales estimates (10 per cent), requiring 200 per cent coverage.

Finance plan 1 – Paramount

This plan stemmed from a first look deal Renaissance had secured with Paramount Pictures in 2001. The agreement was to cover projects owned and submitted by Renaissance, whereby on presentation of script, director, budget and two lead actors, Paramount would have the option to co-finance 33.3 per cent of the film's budget. The Studio would take North America, Australasia and South Africa (the territory). Paramount considered *Vapor* carefully, and their head of business affairs, Bill Bernstein, co-ordinated the financial assessment. However, despite the numbers looking promising, the Studio did not feel that Neil LaBute was a director they wanted to work with given his art house and literary credentials. The Studio passed two days prior to the start of the Cannes market.

Finance plan 2 – Warners

Sandra Bullock had a production company on the Warners' lot, and the actress was signed up to do *Miss Congeniality 2* for the studio starting winter 2003. When it became clear to Renaissance that all other Studios and US independent buyers were passing on *Vapor* during the market, Renaissance asked the producer to call Warners' CEO Alan Horn's office and request their support. Horn responded with an offer of $5m (later upped to $5.5m), but the deal was not agreed until the second to last day of Cannes. All major foreign distributors had left the market by then. The Warners' deal was also not agreed in any detail, limiting its use as an announcement.

Renaissance set about trying to close the Warners' deal in May/June, and visited in person key distributors that summer in German, Italy, France, Spain and Japan. Nearly all distributors slowly passed, based on a) script, b) director, c) Bullock's casting. Any still keen were later put off when the project was moved from Warners to WIP (Warners Independent Pictures, the newly created specialist distribution platform), with its vastly reduced theatrical opening. WIP's head Mark Gill was not keen to inherit the project. He called Icon, who were keen to pre-buy United Kingdom and Australasia, and explained that WIP was not going to do the movie. Finance plan 2 was dead.

Finance plan 3 – equity

When it became clear that no North American deal was going to work, Renaissance then tried to find equity for the film, and to bring the budget down. The producer and director worked hard to bring the film down to $21m, and relocated the film to Toronto to cut New York City shoot costs, and pick up Canadian benefits. However, as the budget dropped, so too did the percentage commitments of some of the cornerstone financing, including the German 'super tax' plan. The plan looked as follows:

Budget:	$22.5m including financing
German tax:	$6.75m (30 per cent)
Canadian benefits:	$2.25m (10 per cent)
Pre-sales:	$3.4m (mainly medium and minor territories, including the Benelux countries, Eastern Europe/CIS, Middle East, Israel, etc.) (15 per cent approx)
Bank gap:	$3.4m (15 per cent) – in first position re recoupment
Equity required:	$6.75m

Renaissance attended Toronto in September 2003 with a view to trying to close the above financial package. It was under pressure to get the production into principal photography, and was starting to spend money on pre-production to keep the cast.

What happened next?

1   More than six potential equity partners requested in-depth meetings. Most focused on the strength of the cast, and why the project had not managed to close significant pre-sale territories.

2   All equity players focused on the bank gap being repaid prior to their equity being recouped.

3   No equity players decided to come into the project.

4   The German 'super' tax fund dropped its offer from 30 per cent to 20 per cent.

What should have happened?

1   Renaissance should have never spent monies beyond development and certain pre-production items such as the budget and location work.

2   Renaissance should have been much more concerned about the mismatch of Sandra Bullock in a project that was mixed genre – and far from a standard romantic comedy. This is in no way a criticism of the actress, but a realization post-distributor testing.

3   Once there was no North American distributor for the film, *Vapor* should have been closed down. Equity partners were unlikely to come to the table by that stage.

4   When the first budget at $33m was submitted, Renaissance should have confronted both the producer and writer/director much more specifically about the financing challenge and the need for a) script work and b) a reduced budget that correlated to the complexity of the material.

17 Project management

In Italy for thirty years under the Borgias they had warfare, terror, murder, bloodshed. They produced Michaelangelo, Leonardo de Vinci and the Renaissance. In Switzerland they had brotherly love, 500 years of democracy and peace, and what did they produce? The cuckoo clock … .

(Orson Welles in *The Third Man*)

Introduction to project management

'Nobody knows anything', wrote William Goldman, in his infamous book *Adventures in the Screen Trade*[1] some 25 years ago. Written with his tongue partly in his cheek, Goldman's dictum has been thrown up as a blanket by 'the business' to help obscure how much film professionals really *do* know about developing and managing projects from a concept, to the written page, on to film and all the way to the box office and beyond. The key role that projects play as a focal point for knowledge creation and integration in many industries is vital and relatively transparent. By stark contrast, due to the fragmented, dislocated structure of the independent film business, efforts to create a sustainable advantage through the collective experience of project management are almost non-existent. Gathering and sharing experience is anathema to many film practitioners; while the complex demands facing film producers in a highly disintegrated business tends to work against neat, concrete rules and models for success. Instead, obscurity and dictums such as Goldman's famous phrase tend to rule the day. The purpose of this chapter is to explore what light 'project management' can shed on a highly demanding and systemically fragmented and dysfunctional industry. It then leads to an in-depth case study involving well known and, in cases, highly successful filmmakers, and their collective failure to bring a major project to the screen.

Project management is a central pillar within the film business. The distinctive challenge of managing through projects in the film sector benefits from a simple starting point: each film is a 'project' in itself. Professionals even refer to films as 'projects' per se on a daily basis. The key project manager, from start to completion, is the film producer.

So notwithstanding Goldman's comment (which is really driving at how little Hollywood Studios know about a film's potential performance prior to its release), what do we know about how to manage projects in the film industry? First, in principle, managing the film project should start and end with the film producer. Every decision the producer makes (or avoids) will impact on the way each level of a project advances. Managing the creative development process – meaning concept, story and screenplay – effectively begins early. This critical stage of the management process can be compared to the design and laying of a foundation for a tall building. If it is slightly out at the start, the rest will collapse later.

The ambitious producer is also a deal-maker, and there is considerable need for entrepreneurial skills in the film business as we saw in Chapter 15. An experienced producer understands the overall business plan: they know the number of projects he or she is able to successfully manage. From the perspective of a hands-on film producer (who is dedicated to the making of films rather than acting in a more removed, finance-focused 'executive producer' capacity), he or she will only be able to make one feature film a year, and at a stretch, two, though they are unlikely not to spill over the 12 months. More might indeed impact on the effectiveness of their 'project management'. By contrast, a top Hollywood producer making blockbusters – meaning films of budgets north of $50m, but now normally more than $120m, excluding prints and advertising release costs – can normally manage one film every two years or so due to the sheer scale and demands of each project. If they achieve more, they probably fall into the Hollywood 'A list' category.

A producer is by definition in the business of multi-tasking; but their focus is in three key areas when managing a film project. Those areas are development, production and distribution. At the development stage, an established producer would be reading (and where appropriate optioning) a range of books for adaptation, considering film treatment outlines, commissioning scripts, reading original screenplays, and packaging more advanced films. These activities form the R&D element of their business. So while overseeing the physical production process on any given film project, a producer should be concurrently developing a slate of projects at varying stages of advancement.

As films come closer to achieving financing and entering the preparation-for-production stage, the producer needs to identify and attach value to the project. For example, by attaching 'elements' such as a director, cast, etc., financiers and distributors are able to assess the project's market potential. That same producer is also responsible for securing distribution for his/her film – a challenge that they should be considering from the early stage of a project's conception. Alongside the distribution stage is the marketing and commercial exploitation of each completed film through a series of windows, albeit that the detailed management is delegated to third-party distributors around the world.

So far, I have examined the project management process from the perspective of the producer. However, part of the central management role of a producer is to co-ordinate and organize a range of other players, also carrying out key roles on a film project. For example, the perspective of an 'executive producer' will be seen as the person responsible for raising part or all of the finances for the film. He or she will be expected to be attached to a project from a financing, strategic and exploitation perspective (the latter meaning how to maximize revenues from all formats and windows), and to complement and assist each respective producer's day-to-day management of the project.

An international or local distributor – either responsible for selling films to each territory around the world, or for releasing films in a specific territory – sees the product at a later stage and from a different perspective to the producer. Their over-riding challenge is to manage both specific film projects and their overall slate, with a market, an audience and their own company's business development in mind. Often an international distributor also plays the role of an executive producer, bringing finance from individual distributors to the film's finance plan.

Within each film project's cycle, a range of additional practitioners play a role. They divide into four key sectors: a) creative, including writers, directors and actors; b) the physical crew who make the film; c) third-party financiers, including banks, investors, broadcasters, etc., and d) 'services', including lawyers, accountants and agents.

The producer, to summarize,[2] is managing the following key areas when running with a project:

1   the production company's entire slate of projects;
2   the project's inception and research and development;
3   creative development and attachments (to achieve a 'package');
4   financing/investor parties and execution of contracts;
5   additional executives (executive producers, etc.);
6   lawyers, agents, accountants (services);
7   budget, locations, schedule, etc.;
8   physical production crew;
9   the distribution and marketing plan;
10 launch of the film to the market followed by long tail monitoring.

No producer is expected to be a leading expert in the above headline areas (and I have simplified the key areas for the purposes of comprehension). But their respective project management skills will dictate which they control and lead directly; and which they delegate, including what appropriate teams and levels of responsibility are given down the line.

Each area is extremely demanding. A producer who is inexperienced in certain areas will fail if they do not delegate effectively; a producer who cannot co-ordinate executives and representatives and drive timelines will be unable to achieve financing. A producer who can complete the package and finance for a film but has not consid-ered the market for distribution and exploitation will almost inevitably fail to recoup. In summary, the producer needs to know a huge amount about a) themselves, and b) effective, specialized project management, if they are to succeed. We have moved a long way from Goldman's assertion that nobody knows anything.

Project management is often personified by the producer's struggle for control over the filmmaking process. The overriding challenge of managing each and all of these three stages – development, production and distribution – requires a strong producer who can see both the 'bigger picture' and the demands of the specific film in question. He or she also needs to be making the project with a market and business objective in mind, beyond just pocketing the production fee. Given the fragmented nature of the management, financing and talent structure in the independent film industry, coherence and consolidation are difficult to find. As one works up the value chain, however, and start to reach integrated companies that control the three main areas of development, production and distribution, the structural gaps start to be covered, and the risk lowered to some extent.

While it is often said that 'the buck stops with the producer', the truth is that unless that same producer is an A-list, heavyweight power-broker, or backed by a heavyweight entity in the form of a Studio or major independent, he or she will find it harder to manage and control the range of tasks and differing third parties to achieve a successful outcome. That is what Bill Mechanic meant when he explained that all 'Independent Producers' are really 'dependent'.[3] While there are important lessons to be learnt for analysis of project management within the independent film industry, mistakes and problems can only shed light up to a limited glass ceiling. The producer's experience and personality has much sway over the process. Each film project has a huge number of individual variables and each 'sub-manager' along the film cycle often has conflicting interests.

There is also an inherent paradox that lies at the centre of the film business – as management has to contend with both 'creative' and 'commercial' imperatives. Managing the creative process and 'talent', while at the same time trying to control large sums of money and ensure returns on investment, makes for a highly challenging environment.

Case study: Terry Gilliam's *Good Omens*

The purpose of this case study is to analyse a range of issues that arise from an in-depth examination of a larger scale, European-based movie project through development and a significant period of packaging and financing. The case study involves analysis of: a) project management; b) talent management; c) development challenges when managing films aimed at the independent big-budget market; d) the financing strategy for larger independent films; and e) the problem of 'closing' a complex film – with numerous elements – that have to reach a 'nexus' for the project to go into production.

The pitching stage

It was a typical producer–financier lunch meeting in Milan in early November 1999, at a traditional Italian eating-house just outside the grey gates of the MIFED film market, that the first pitch to Renaissance for *Good Omens* took place. Marc and Peter Samuelson, the experienced English-born producers who traversed the Atlantic, with Peter based in Los Angeles and Marc operating out of London, left their most ambitious project until last on their development slate hit list. Finney, co-managing director of Renaissance Films with Stephen Evans, who together had raised some $40m earlier that year from a single source of capital, Hermes Pension Fund Management, was immediately interested. Investing equity in larger budget films was not part of their business plan. Developing potentially commercial projects and then financing them from third parties, and putting those projects through Renaissance's international sales operation, however, was a strategy that appeared worthy of exploring.

Co-written by Terry Pratchett and Neil Gaiman, *Good Omens* is a sprawling, multi-character novel woven around a 'reconstructed' Apocalypse. The book's central characters, Crowley – a slick, cunning earth devil – and Aziraphale – a confused and bookish angel – represent good and evil. Except that they have been drinking friends for more than 400 years, and have jointly decided that the world is far too good a place to abolish and that the Apocalypse needs aborting. That means they have to find the Antichrist – in the form of a 'normal' 11-year-old boy called Adam living in a quintessential English village – very quickly if the Four Horsemen of the Apocalypse and the final reckoning are to be stopped. The story is distinctive, original, and thrives off heady elements of anarchy and morality in equal doses.

The Samuelson brothers had optioned the lengthy book some years previously, but had found it hard to tap the right director. Despite Warner Brothers controlling the project for a period, no script had been commissioned. Warners had made it clear that the material would need to be set in North America rather than the United Kingdom if they were to even consider financing the project.

What made the Samuelsons' pitch ride above the typical market hawking was the scale of ambition and, in particular, the director they had potentially secured. Terry Gilliam had expressed a genuine interest in co-writing and directing *Good Omens*, but only if the film was to be developed, financed and predominantly shot in Europe. His writing partner, Tony Grisoni (co-writer with Gilliam of *Fear and Loathing in Las Vegas*), was also keen to have a go at jointly adapting the novel. Marc explained to Finney:

> What Terry wants is to make this film in England. He's not interested in setting the story in America and having a studio controlling everything. He's been through all that before. This time he wants to finish each day and go to bed in his home in North London.

The Samuelson brothers estimated that the film would cost around about $25m to produce, a number that seemed low in terms of the ambition of the project but also low enough to convince Finney's partner Evans when it came to considering a pitch to set *Good Omens* up at Renaissance. At the end of the Milan lunch, it was agreed that the Samuelsons would set up a meeting for Renaissance with Gilliam, Grisoni, and Marc. When Finney got back to London, he ran Evans through the pitch, and the partners agreed that hearing Gilliam's take on a Pratchett novel was an experience not to be missed. Sure enough, in late November, Gilliam performed an imaginative, energetic and high octane pitch – supported by a more cautious Grisoni, who patiently explained that the book was going to be difficult to shape into a workable screenplay and might take some time to conquer. The discussion skipped quickly over what sections and elements of the book would need to be pruned or cut; instead it was lifted by Gilliam's infectious humour derived from the material and his own peculiar vision.

By now, privately, the Samuelsons had indicated to Renaissance that the budget was more likely to be around $40m, nearly double the initial $25m mentioned in the original discussion in Milan. Work on the screenplay was not going to start for some while, as Gilliam was busy setting up his 'passion' project, *Don Quixote*, with a view to shooting the film in Spain the following year. But Evans and Finney were not put off, especially after being seduced by Gilliam's luminous performance. It was decided that Sophie Janson, the deputy development executive at Renaissance, should be the 'point person' on the project. She was to strike up a strong relationship with Grisoni, which was to prove important during the coming months. Finney and Evans were to be attached as Executive Producers, in light of their financial commitment, ownership of the forthcoming script, and intention to work with the Samuelsons to package and finance the project.

The development deal

Developing *Good Omens* was not to come cheap. A stepped development deal was agreed in principal; with Gilliam and Grisoni being guaranteed a total of £360,000 to deliver two drafts and a polish. The initial payment was £30,000 to each writer on commencement of the first draft; £60,000 each on delivery of the first draft; £60,000 on delivery of the second draft, and £30,000 each for the polish. Once that polish was completed, each further polish was to cost an additional £40,000.
   The book option deal was as follows:

- 1st 18 months (14 November 1997–15 May 1999): $25,000 on account of purchase price (at this point the book was optioned by the Samuelsons)
- 2nd 18 months (16 May 1999–15 November 2000): $25,000 (50 per cent) on account (and here Renaissance took over)
- 3rd 18 months (16 November 2000–15 May 2002): $25,000 not on account (Renaissance paid)
- 4th 12 months (16 May 2002–15 May 2003): $50,000 not on account
- The purchase price (that is to be paid on first day of principal photography – and effectively 'exercises' the option): 2.5 per cent of budget, floor of $250,000, and a ceiling of $400,000 and 5 per cent of 100 per cent of net profits.

Jenne Casarotto, an experienced London-based talent agent, who had handled Gilliam for some years (among other clients, including Stephen Frears, Neil Jordan, Nick Hornby, etc.), had stressed to Finney that the overall commitment, whilst 'appreciated' from a UK company, was 'far less than a Hollywood Studio would have been prepared to pay to develop the project'. The implication was that Renaissance was 'getting it cheap', and that she would have been asking for more than $1m in writing fees (around £700,000 in 1999) if a Studio was paying. The one exception to the supposed 'cut price' was the costly further polish fees. She stated that it was an attempt to stop her client (and later Grisoni was added to her client list) being stuck in 'perpetual development hell' and to force the producers to focus on getting the film into production. Ironically, writing work did not start on *Good Omens* for nearly one year after the agreement was completed, thanks to Gilliam's unfortunate experience on *Don Quixote* (recorded in heartbreaking detail in the documentary *Lost In La Mancha*).
   In addition to the cost of commissioning the screenplay, Renaissance picked up the Samuelson's historical costs, totalling around £110,000; and agreed to fund the book options (see above). The overall commitment from the UK company was more than £500,000 by the time all the contracts had been tied up. What was not included or set out in the development negotiations was the implicit understanding that Renaissance was to be 'on the hook' for all further development and pre-production costs right up to first day of principal photography. In other words, Renaissance had effectively become the 'studio' for setting up *Good Omens*, with associated cost and control implications that had not been considered in full by Finney.

The producer mix

Within a matter of days, a new element was added to the producer mix, although one that had been very clearly planned by the Gilliam camp. Jenne Casarotto told

Evans that Gilliam was concerned about the Samuelson brothers producing the film as lone lead producers. Gilliam's *Twelve Monkeys*, which had starred Bruce Willis, Brad Pitt and Madelaine Stowe, had been produced by an A-list Hollywood Studio producer, Charles Roven (later to go on to produce *Scooby Doo* and the later *Batman* franchise among other blockbusters). Gilliam was insisting that Roven was to be brought into the film as a lead producer, according to Casarotto. She also stressed that all parties would need Roven's script skills if the project was to be developed successfully to the point of raising the picture's budget.

A meeting was finally held at the Samuelsons' lawyers, Olswang, in early 2000. The intention was to map out how the project in principal would be financed; how much each parties' fees would be per their respective work and financing, and how Roven would work with the Samuelsons and Renaissance. An in-depth three-way agreement between the parties was going to need to be drawn up. (In addition, a separate producer deal between Roven and the Samuelson brothers was also going to have to be documented – something that took a lengthy amount of time and caused considerable divisions between the two producing parties.)

Before the meeting had really started, Roven asked bluntly whom Renaissance's distribution partners were in order to guarantee at least 40 per cent of the production's finance. The question exposed the fledgling sales operation that Renaissance had added to its development and production interests when closing its deal with Hermes. The sales arm had no experience of pre-selling a film at a $40m budget level. Roven, in turn, explained how he had financed the $29m *Twelve Monkeys* (to be ultimately delivered at around $32m) through four key distribution partners, which included UGC PH (France), Toho Towa (Japan), Concorde (Germany) and Lauren (Spain). The deal was split 25 per cent four ways, and had effectively left North America 'open' for a sale at a later point. As a result, in part, to the budget being controlled when compared to the challenging material – and fronted by A list stars – *Twelve Monkeys* had made considerable profits for the investor-distributors and producers. 'Angus, here's the thing. I receive a seven figure cheque every year thanks to the financial structure of that film', Roven explained later. *Twelve Monkeys* had gone on to take more than $160m worldwide during its theatrical release and far more from video and DVD revenue streams.

Whilst some of Roven's *Twelve Monkeys*' partners had either moved on or been changed (with Helkon replacing Concorde, and UGC PH looking unlikely to be involved in a larger budgeted Gilliam film), his experience and relationships far outweighed Renaissance's. Roven stated that he could bring Germany and Japan to the *Good Omens* table. Renaissance had nothing to match this. With the exception of an output deal with Entertainment Film Distributors, where no advance was paid in return for a modest 25 per cent distribution fee and a strong share of the ancillary income, Renaissance had no long-standing foreign distributor relationships. On the other hand, given that Renaissance was stumping up the entire development and pre-production risk, the company's managers felt that they should have a fair shot at trying to pre-sell and sell-and-service the majority of the sales on the film and be paid commission accordingly. A deal was later agreed that gave Roven/Samuelson a 5 per cent commission on key foreign territories (defined as France, Germany, Spain, Italy, Australasia and Japan) if they made the deal; and 5 per cent to Renaissance if in turn they closed the territory. It was agreed that Renaissance would handle the remaining Rest of the World for a 10 per cent commission.

No commission was due to be paid until the negative cost of the film had been met, so in practice all commissions were to be deferred and would only be paid out if: a) sales and finance came to more than the negative cost prior on first day of principal photography; or b) were placed in a recoupment agreement once the financing had been raised. The deal also allowed Roven's company the opportunity to control and exploit music-publishing rights in return for a share of royalties. That left North America to be dealt with.

'Controlling' North America

Roven, as was to be expected, had a 'deal' with a major Studio. He had recently moved away from Warners, and had set up a deal at MGM. The terms of the financing and distribution terms with MGM were undisclosed, and were vaguely understood by Renaissance to be negotiated on a film-by-film basis. The 'deal', in standard Hollywood practice, did however outline Roven's producing fees and profit position. Roven, rather than insisting that MGM had an automatic first look at *Good Omens*, openly acknowledged that he did not own the project. Therefore it was agreed that whichever party brought a North American deal to the table was to be entitled to a further 5 per cent fee post the full negative cost of the film being raised.

Thanks to Evans' relationship with Ruth Vitale, then president of Paramount Classics, Renaissance had been approached by Paramount Studios to work more closely on its slate financing. Finney and Evans were invited to a meeting with Paramount president Sherry Lansing and production chief John Goldwyn during the summer of 2000. Following the 'get-to-know-you' meeting, Finney and his director of finance picked up the baton, and started to close a first look deal with Paramount Studios through Bill Bernstein's Business Affairs office. (The deal was not to cover any submissions to Paramount Classics, the specialist arm of the studio.) The agreement was to cover projects owned and submitted by Renaissance, whereby on presentation of script, director, budget and two lead actors, Paramount would have the option to co-finance a third of the film's budget. The Studio would take North America, Australasia and South Africa (the territory), and charge a 25 per cent distribution fee across all income streams (e.g. theatrical, video, ancillaries and television). The deal's structure was particularly attractive in terms of potential video and DVD income from Renaissance's perspective. The Studio would fund the P&A, to be determined on a film-by-film basis, which was to be recouped off the top. Post full recoupment from the Territory, Paramount was to take a 2/3–1/3 split from overages; and keep the Territory in perpetuity. Three rejections in a row by Paramount would lead to the deal being cancelled at Renaissance's election.

Paramount's original intention had been to have an option over English-speaking territories, but Renaissance had successfully kept the United Kingdom out of the deal, hence protecting its output deal with Entertainment Film Distributors in the United Kingdom. On paper, the deal looked fair. In reality, what it represented was 'an agreement to agree' rather than any significant commitment from Paramount towards co-financing Renaissance's larger, more commercial projects. And Renaissance was at risk for all development, overhead and pre-production costs.

Roven was gracious about the Paramount deal, and was pleased that *Good Omens* was to have two potential North American backers, rather than just MGM. However, before any realistic approach could be made to any Studios, financiers and international distributors, the screenplay, budget, locations and star attachments needed to be in place. A 'package' needed to be constructed, which was to require considerable project management, time and money over the coming months.

Screenplay development

The first draft of *Good Omens* came in at more than 170 pages long. It also was delivered in the late autumn of 2000, many months later than anticipated thanks to Gilliam's commitment to *Don Quixote* and subsequent (and understandable) depression following that film's collapse. Delivery would have been even later had it not been for Grisoni's working methods and dedication to the project. The writer had devised a workable structure with Gilliam, and was able to get a number of pages down, send them to Gilliam, get his notes and comments, rewrite, and then move on to the next section. Once a draft was in place, both of them then reviewed, discussed and refined the screenplay. 'Let me be clear. Terry doesn't actually write anything, but he's right there all the way through the process', explained Grisoni.

In addition to the length, each page was extremely dense, packed with action, images and detailed effects and touches. (Months later, a senior Fox executive explained to Finney that whilst he 'loved the script, every page read like it was costing a million dollars'.) While the story's structure was starting to take shape, the multiple characters and density made the read slow and confusing. And whenever the devil and angel were not in the action, the story tended to drag. As Janson pointed out in her notes on the draft, 'we miss Crowley and Aziraphale when they aren't on the page, as they are the heart and action of the story'.

A development meeting was held, where Renaissance made it clear that the script needed to come down to no more than 120 pages. In Gilliam's directors' contract, it was stated that the film would be no longer than 120 minutes; and that financiers/producers would have final cut. (The standard industry estimate is that a script page matches around one minute of completed film.) Gilliam paid scant lip service to the length, and was already arguing about favourite scenes and characters that he did not want to lose in the new draft. Grisoni tried to reason with the director during that meeting, recognizing that the project was fenced in by practical realities. Extensive notes from Janson were passed on to the writers, suggesting specific cuts and character removals and reductions, many of which Grisoni appreciated. A new draft was embarked upon.

Early concept marketing

When the first draft of *Good Omens* arrived at Renaissance, it was read by the sales and marketing team. Despite the screenplay's length, the company's executives could all see the rich commercial potential. It was agreed with the producers that Renaissance could design a 'concept poster', which would include the name of the project, director, writers and producers. A concept poster makes distributors aware of a project's existence, and acquisition executives start to 'track' its progress and note the imminent arrival of a screenplay to read and provide 'coverage' for their senior management. In the case of *Good Omens*, the book's jacket cover was adapted and a large fiery red poster was designed with gothic black lettering. It was placed within the Renaissance offices at the American Film Market in February 2001 as a way of introducing the project to the market. It was also agreed between the parties that the first draft, under no circumstances, should be circulated to even selected buyers at this stage. Renaissance and the producers were aware of the damage often done in the marketplace when early screenplay drafts, which require considerably more work, are released and read before they are ready. And re-reading screenplays is an unpopular task within the film-buying community.

Between the American Film Market and Cannes 2001, Renaissance made some significant changes in staffing. Finney took over the international sales team. The shift in senior management made the producers understandably wary of whether Renaissance had the experience and clout to raise significant foreign pre-sales on the film.

Drafts and casting

The second draft materialized some five months after the arrival of the first. More than 30 pages had been cut, with the length now at 137 pages. Whilst decisions had been made about certain scenes to omit, the screenplay was still packed with a wide range of characters, and still 'challenging' to read through without having to go back and check on names and places, etc. Roven, however, felt that it had improved considerably, and began to work more closely on the script. He also appreciated Janson's notes, many of which he agreed with. Crowley (the devil), and Aziraphale (the angel), were now much more central and present within the structure. But Renaissance and the producers all agreed that one of the characters (Shadwell, a witch finder) needed to either be cut completely or edited back, as he cluttered the third act; while the role of witch (Anathema Device) needed clarifying and more characterization. A polish was embarked upon, with the intention that the script would be considerably reduced. A draft needed to be ready for casting and distributor-financiers if the project was not to lose momentum. However, what occurred was a 'dance' of a few pages coming out, and certain scenes that Gilliam was keen on, going back in. 'What the experience made me realize was how important it is, when script editing, to make your points really clearly about cuts right from the start', explained Janson later. 'I should have been stronger.' In fairness, Finney and Evans should have been more verbal and aggressive if this situation was to have been resolved.

Gilliam's casting

Gilliam had always been clear that he wanted Johnny Depp to play Crowley. He had become close to the actor during their work on *Fear and Loathing in Las Vegas*, and Depp had been a lead character in *Don Quixote*. He had subsequently witnessed the film's collapse at first hand. Unfortunately, the producers and Renaissance were mindful that in 2001, Depp was unable to 'open' a movie. His credits over the previous three years ranged between lower budget independent films to large-budget-but-mediocre results. The producers drew up alternative lists, that included: George Clooney (who read, and liked the script but was too busy to commit); Brad Pitt (with whom Gilliam had fallen out with following a quote in a book following *Twelve Monkeys*); Mel Gibson (who was more focused on his own directing career, with *The Passion of the Christ* on the horizon); and Eddie Murphy. Will Smith was added to Murphy's name on the list, and a debate between the North American and the UK partners about whether it was politically offensive to cast a black person as a devil ensued. The Americans were against; the Europeans did not see the problem. Neither black star took up the role anyway. *Good*

Omens' Crowley role kept coming back to Depp, in part because Gilliam had not personally pushed the script with any other of the above A-list stars.

Aziraphale, the angel role, was more straightforward, at least to start with. Robin Williams, who had worked with Gilliam on *The Fisher King*, had been pencilled in by the director from day one. Unfortunately, Williams was also going through a difficult period re his relationship to box office performance. Renaissance had hoped that an A-list Crowley would solve the problem, but that was not forthcoming. The third key role was Anathema, the witch. While Renaissance and the producers felt the role might be able to attract a star such as Cameron Diaz, Gilliam was keen on Kirsten Dunst, who showed great potential to become an A-list star, but had not reached her *Superman* status back in 2001. He met with the actress in Los Angeles, and she was keen to be attached.

A fluctuating budget and rising costs

By now, Renaissance had commissioned a budget. A schedule – essential for any realistic budget to be compiled – was drawn up by the experienced line producer David Brown, and after a number of meetings with Gilliam, Brown produced the first full budget for *Good Omens*. It came in at $93m: $10m was reserved for the two lead roles, at $5m each (fee levels that were nominal rather than established with the actors' agents as agreed); $15m was earmarked for computer-generated imagery (CGI) and special effects; and the overall shoot period was to last 18 weeks. The physical and technical demands of the complex and lengthy screenplay were the most important factors re the new 'blockbuster' budget. Evans and Finney were extremely worried at the level of this budget, and the schedule informing it was on a script that had not been nailed down, making it an unreliable number.

In reaction, Renaissance and the producers focused once again on the screenplay. The new polish brought the screenplay down by a further six pages. Every cut, however, was becoming a personal fight with Gilliam – even when Roven stepped in to take up the cause. Ultimately, the polish removed Shadwell, the witch finder, from the third act. The screenplay was sent out to a shortlist of buyers, including MGM and Paramount. However, rather than commission a new schedule and budget, the producers and Renaissance told Gilliam that they could raise a maximum of $60m for this film, and that he would have to work within that parameter. Whilst the budget, through considerable skill on the part of Brown, was reduced downwards, at no point was a full, completed schedule and budget completed to fit the nominal $60m cap.

Part of the problem facing the project was that different elements required for a film of this size were not coming together at the same time. The script was still not at 120 pages; the cast was unofficially attached to the project rather than formally signed up; and despite different budgets being compiled around a) a UK shoot, b) a UK and Isle of Man shoot, c) an Australian shoot, d) a German shoot, and e) an Eastern European shoot, Gilliam was clear that he wanted the United Kingdom only. This was communicated only after a trip to Studio Babelsberg in Berlin, and after Marc Samuelson and David Brown did a research trip to the Isle of Man. The Isle of Man was very clearly not to the directors' satisfaction. Considerable sums of money were now being spent in addition to Renaissance's development costs. For example, all Roven's travel costs, phone bills, trips to London, etc., were being charged back to Renaissance. (Finney even had an invoice for $25 from Roven's office many months later when meeting the producer in Los Angeles, which he offered to clear in cash. Roven said to forget it, 'but I'm really glad my guys are right on the case'.) Heads of departments and a casting director were being approached and attached. Gilliam and Brown were working out of Radical Media's Soho offices – given gratis thanks to Gilliam and the director's work with the company. But the offices and momentum gave the producers and director the feeling that the film was about to happen.

Certain heads were not working out. Production designer Assheton Gorton, for example, could never 'get' the Apocalypse as a concept let alone design it, and was working in a very out-moded way though nobody would really come out and say so. Overall, from one executive assistant's perspective, all the people who were brought in at this unofficial prep stage were half-hearted about it because the film was not cast or financed and they therefore did not throw themselves into it.

Pre-selling Good Omens

Despite interest in the project from major foreign distributors, it became clear to Finney from his experience at Cannes 2001 that for a project of this size, foreign distributors would only believe that it was financed and worth stepping up for once a North American Studio was attached. Roven agreed with him that a North American deal was essential if the film was to proceed. He too was mindful of his ability to bring his foreign partners to the table without the USA secured. The finance plan for *Good Omens* was still vague at this point. The general strategy was as follows: If 25–33 per cent of the finance could be raised from North America, it was presumed that five major foreign territories could be pre-sold. Say, France, Italy, Germany, Japan and Australasia – bringing in by Finney's estimate around 40 per cent of the budget (or $24.5m, see Table 17.1). In addition, if the film was to shoot in the United Kingdom a tax deal would be done, bringing in a further 8 per cent approximately. On the back of this level of pre-sales, a bank gap would be made to work if there was enough value in the remaining territories to provide 200 per cent coverage on the gap loan. So the plan looked in theory as shown in Table 17.1.

Finney and Roven went out to Paramount and MGM, respectively, at the same time. Finney had developed a relationship with a senior Paramount production executive, who in turn pressured the vastly experienced Rob Friedman, executive vice president of Marketing and Distribution, to consider the project under the terms of the Renaissance–Paramount deal. Friedman did not like the script. In particular, he did not like the ending, which he found offensive (Adam's young friends are killed in a variety of gory ways when the Four Horsemen of the Apocalypse arrive on earth). 'You can't do that to children on a big screen', explained Friedman to Finney. 'Definitely not on a project costing this much.' 'Would you meet Terry and tell him that?' asked Finney. 'Yes, but only on the grounds that Paramount is not making this movie at this point. I don't want a misunderstanding where we fall out with Terry', said Friedman.

Over at MGM, Roven engaged the Studio's head of production in the project. A new budget was requested that bore a resemblance to the $60m pitch, but before that was drawn up, MGM's president Alex Yemidjiian took a view on the project. 'Unfortunately, it's just not his kind of thing. He doesn't get it', explained Roven. 'They're passing.'

Table 17.1 *Good Omens* finance plan

Budget: $60m	
Paramount (or another):	$20m
Pre-sales:	
France	$5m
Germany	$6m
Italy	$4.5m
Japan	$6m
Australasia	$3m
Subtotal	($24.5m)
	$44.5m
UK tax deal (8%):	$4.8m[a]
Total funds raised:	$49.3m
Bank gap:	$10.7m (with a need for more than $22m in remaining sales estimates from Rest of World)[b]
Total:	$60m

a There was some debate over the amount possible to raise in the United Kingdom through tax deals. This figure was reached on the conservative assumption of any break allowable to a film of more than £15m. A more aggressive deal may have been possible, but for the purposes of the finance plan, this was the figure assumed.

b Territories left included: Spain, Scandinavia, Russia/Eastern Europe, Latin America, South Korea, South East Asia.

Most other Studios had politely passed – always with the proviso that they would 'love to see the film when completed' – but Evans had a strong relationship with Fox chief Tom Rothman. The two had become friends while Rothman was head of production at Samuel Goldwyn, and *Much Ado about Nothing* was one of the successful fruits of their work together. Evans managed to get Rothman and his partner, Jim Gianapolous, to read the screenplay and take a meeting with Gilliam, Roven, Evans and Finney. The meeting took place a few weeks after 9/11 – an event that Roven viewed as a world political watershed. 'The world will never be the same again', Roven stated darkly. The Europeans working on *Good Omens* took a much more relaxed view. Surely there could not be a connection between the World Trade Centre bombings and *Good Omens*, they thought.

The pitch seemed to be going well in Rothman's airy office on the Fox lot. Forty minutes into the meeting, Gilliam took out a large artists' pad. As he flipped each page, Rothman and Gianapolous took an increasing interest in the wild and scary images, beautifully drawn by Gilliam's hand. Then the page turned again: an image that none of the producers had seen loomed off the page. Two huge towers, close to each other, with angels flying from one, while devils and evil beings scampered around the other, filled the room. Rothman suppressed a gasp, and appeared to pale as he sank back in his chair. Fox were going to pass. No North American deal was available to *Good Omens* in the autumn of 2001.

Shortly after the Fox meeting, Finney and Evans met with Roven at his offices on Sunset Boulevard. Roven was unequivocal: 'Guys, we're finished. My advice is that you absolutely have to close this film down. We're dead.'

18 Business models 2.0

> Whether you are a writer, agent, producer, broadcaster or distributor you will
> need to re-evaluate your business model to adapt to the changing landscape.
> You need to do something about it now. The pace of change is accelerating, as
> is the economic impact on your business.
>
> (Patrick McKenna, CEO, Ingenious Media[1])
>
> The trick is not to look for new landscapes, but to look with new eyes … .
>
> (Marcel Proust)

New media business models

Business models are one of the Internet's most discussed and debated elements. The
new environment they operate in, however, leaves them often as one of the least
understood aspects of the Web. Traditional 'old-style' entertainment business models
are being forced to change or die, and yet, in the words of Professor Michael Rappa,
there is very little clear-cut evidence of what this means precisely in the current 'tran-
sitional' stage.[2]

Before examining the implications arising from the shift from 'old' to 'new' media,
it is key to set out: a) how the overall media environment has been changing; and b)
given the changing universe, what a 'business model' actually means. Of course, in its
simplest form, it means a way of doing business that throws off cash. The associated
model should demonstrate how those revenues are generated by marking where that
business is positioned in the value chain. But as we will see later, the value chain itself
is being significantly restructured through the radical nature of the Internet and associated change.

This chapter examines both the changing media environment and the challenge of
new business models. It looks at which sectors are most likely to succeed in adapting,
but most importantly, views the entire new landscape with fresh eyes that throw up
a myriad of opportunities. A conceptual starting point, thanks to the new geography
of the Internet, is to move away from the notion of 'consumers' and usher in the term
'users'. (Consumer assumes a direct commodity transaction, while the Internet is
governed by a wider predominantly 'free' space.)

Methods of investment are also being forced to change due in part to the changing
dynamics of the changing economy. It is this author's view that old-style 'invest and

exit' strategies over set periods of time are coming unhinged. On the one hand, sources of seed and growth capital have been drying up; on the other hand, new entrepreneurs have been quick to use the Internet to create new models from a 'bottom-up', garage-business starting point. The old 'five years and out' exit model has been recently criticized by Warren Buffett and others.[3] The argument goes that venture capitalists are overly attracted to 'concepts' and assume an 80–90 per cent failure rate on all start-ups. The venture capitalist is seen as a commodity rather than a partner.

One answer to the breakdown is that emerging entrepreneurs are honing their skills at embracing new net models, while keeping their overheads as low as possible. Once sales and hence cash flows are up, profit starts to look realistic rather than towards the back-end of a five-year plan. Through new and adapted business modelling, combined with efforts to solve the tension between commodities and gifts in the digitally networked environment,[4] film and other media industries are starting to navigate a socially and commercially profitable nexus.

The changing scene

The overall media environment, which includes film, television, music, games and user-generated content, is under considerable and increasing pressure with many competitors for people's time, attention, money and loyalty. The production and distribution of audiovisual content in particular has been affected in the past decade by:

- technological change, including a considerable increase in bandwidth specifically within Western Europe and North America, but also many first and second world regions across the globe;
- audience fragmentation and migration;
- an increase in multi-tasking skills and multi-absorption of varying media simultaneously;
- a rise in social networking and associated user-generated content and collaboration;
- a rise in multi-channel, interactive broadcasting;
- an increase in populist, interactive programming involving the public as lead players and contestants;
- a change in payment/billing mechanisms;
- a rise in the public's ability to produce and distribute (often cost-free) their own creative endeavours, including music, words, photographs and video;
- an increase in file sharing and an associated increase in piracy;
- inter-changeability between mediums, with decreasing and less clear boundaries between online networks, short films, recorded music, photos, etc.

In a highly focused and incumbent-critical report by the British Screen Advisory Council's (BSAC) Blue Skies Group, the effect of the above changes has not in large been driven by 'old style broadcasters and filmmakers but by a range of new companies meeting consumer demands in ways the old systems did not'.[5] The supply-led to demand-led business trend is changing the exclusivity of existing suppliers and gatekeepers. And while broadcasters and filmmakers have habitually referred to 'choice', what they usually mean is a choice of content. Films and programmes tend to be prototypical – one-offs that demonstrate little indication of future success. Hence the entertainment industries have downplayed retail management and failed to deliver customer service to a level that competitive high-street brands have aimed to perfect. Control over distribution is now being forced to give way to retail branding and servicing power. BSAC's Blue Skies Group goes further, arguing that 'share of mind' is the concept that captures the reality of the new market ... replacing the conventional concepts of share of time and share of voice. 'Owners of mind have the power to decide what, when and how to pay attention to what is on offer. Producers and distributors have to maximize their share of mind, and monetise it.' In conclusion (and I refer to the ensuing debate later in this chapter), the BSAC group suggested two key trends to note and benchmark:

> *A New Ecology*: The new ecology consists of TV, film and video, the music industry, Internet Service Providers (ISPs like Orange, BT and Virgin), investors, computers, games and other sectors in puzzling and often volatile relationships. The new ecology is systemic in that it is not possible to isolate one niche from another. In order to make sense of what is happening, industry and regulators have to understand the new relationships, both of content and cash, between producers, distributors, users and re-users, as we have tried to do. There is a real danger that by focussing on preservation, it will be impossible to relish the new. Attack is often the best form of defence and always better than accepting failure.

> *Winners and Losers*: All organisations have to work out how to establish a foothold in the new landscape. Revenues will be cannibalised as traditional business revenues begin to fail. We believe organisations that have a secure revenue base (e.g. the BBC) and newcomers that have no revenue base to cannibalise (e.g. Google) are the best placed.

Developing business models

Given the scale of challenge, it is important to note that despite the impact of the Internet, to date the successful monetization of new models has not emerged quickly. Part of the problem may lie in over-simplistic (and optimistic) business modelling or models that are built on the wrong set of assumptions and goals. Many entrepreneurs start the wrong way round. A useful, in-depth definition was posted in an essay in the *Harvard Business Review* in December 2008.[6] The authors recommend that one should start by developing a strong 'customer value proposition (CVP)'. Many companies begin with a product idea and a business model, and then go in search of a market. Success, according to the authors, comes from figuring out how to satisfy a real customer who needs to get a real job done – and not just what and how much is sold but more precisely 'how' it is sold. The next step is to construct a profit formula that allows you to deliver value to your company. You need to decide what resources and processes you will need. A CVP without a profit formula is useless, 'as many dotcom start up found out'. The authors' advice is to start with a goal for total profits and work back from there. If you are an incumbent, then the last step is to compare the new model to the current one you are employing. This will determine whether it can be implemented with the existing organization or needs to be set up as a new separate unit.

By placing the customer first, and the profit formula, resources and processes behind him/her, the authors stressed that market knowledge and product expertise still gives incumbents insight and competitive advantages when trying to go 'new'. The challenge, however, is how to 'tap into expertise without importing the old-rules mind set'.

Today's media incumbents are having considerable difficulty changing their own predispositions, assumptions and entrenched mindsets. Media companies creating, licensing and distributing IPRs have tended to rely on relatively complex business models, traditionally based on a mixture of advertising, subscription, licence fee (e.g. free-TV), pay-per-view, sponsorship and sub-licensing, etc. None of these models necessarily placed the CVP in poll position. And now the 'traditional' models are starting to either struggle or go bankrupt. In the United Kingdom alone, witness the BBC fighting to retain the licence fee; while ITV's advertising-dependent business model is collapsing and Channel 4 fights for its right to survive.

The Internet itself, and associated business models, is not immune to the challenge of monetization. *The Economist* summed up the business model challenge facing the World Wide Web itself, stating in an article titled 'The end of the free lunch – again,'[7] that

> Internet companies are again laying off following the last bubble of 2001, scaling back, shutting down or trying to sell themselves to deep-pocketed industry giants or talking of charging for their content or services. [MySpace and YouTube managed to sell to News Corp and Google before the cooling of the market.] The idea that you can give things away online, and hope that advertising revenue will somehow materialise later on, undoubtedly appeals to users, who enjoy free services as a result. But there is no business logic to it, too. The nature of the Internet means that the barrier to entry for new companies is very low – indeed, thanks to technological improvements, it is even lower in the Web 2.0 era than it was in the dotcom era. The Internet also allows companies to exploit network effects to attract and retain users very quickly and cheaply. So it is not surprising that rival search engines, social networks or video-sharing sites give their services away in order to attract users, and put the difficult question of how to make money to one side. If you worry too much about a revenue model early on, you risk being left behind. Ultimately, though, every business needs revenues – and advertising, it transpires, is not going to provide enough.

So if it is not 'advertising', the multi-billion dollar question is what is it, and how is it to be achieved? A central element to the challenge is that the fundamental shift is in 'user' behaviour, brought about by 'socializing' technology and deregulation, not the mechanics of the digital technology itself. The only clear winner to emerge from the digital age so far is indeed the 'user': he/she has an ever expanding choice of what is now available anytime and anywhere, and at an even lower cost – including a plethora of 'free' if you include pirated and user-generated content, etc. Consumers are diverse and have as wide a set of behaviours, tastes and attitudes as those of producers or business-to-business buyers. Traditional models have chased the Pareto 20:80 principle – the larger the audience, the more justification for higher ad rates or retaining licence fees, etc. And gatekeepers controlled distribution and had the consumer in a stranglehold. But today and tomorrow the Internet allows people to operate either by themselves or in smaller groups, or in focused fan-based flocks, rather than gravitating axiomatically to mass audience levels.

In the BSAC seminar on 'Future Trends: Life and Death Post 2012', the Blue Skies Working Group pointed to the four Basic Demands (as do a host of academics and commentators): Everybody wants to choose what they want to watch, when they want it, how they want to watch it and how they want to pay for it:

> That might be a one-off cash payment, a subscription payment, a payment to rent, view or keep, or it might be free. It might be paid for by advertising if the consumer is happy to have advertising around content. We're talking about consumers who want to buy and use a film or television programme in pretty much the same way as they can go onto Amazon, click and have books delivered within 24 hours. It's really as simple as that. And as we all know *the industry is so set up that that is a long way from being provided.* ... Broadcasters, filmmakers and entertainment companies often talk about choice but they usually mean a choice of content. Consumers are more ambitious and want choice in each of the Basic Demands.[8]

What is impressive about BSAC's Blue Skies fearless analysis is that as a practitioner group, it leaves most trade and industry bodies way behind in critical thinking. Ironically, it has been academic and journalistic work, research and non-film practitioners who have offered fresh thinking and added to the critical debate about the Internet and new business models.

The Long Tail model and debate

There are new suggested guidelines that govern present and future business in this new multi-window of commercial opportunity. One of the more extrapolated theories on how to exploit rights was coined by journalist Chris Anderson, editor of *Wired*, when his initial article (2004) and subsequent book (2006)[9] drew on research and analysis of several companies in the entertainment sector. The argument put forward went as follows: commercialization on the Internet is not a marginal market; instead, it is an emerging market with ongoing built-in increasing value. The commercial argument is rooted in three main observations: 1) the Internet draws together a fragmented and dispersed audience which, when consolidated as a whole, makes up a very significant market; 2) the costs and limitations of physical distribution are eliminated and product consumption becomes more personalized and in tune with the demands of the net-generation; and 3) the 80:20 Pareto principle (20 per cent of products account for 80 per cent of sales) no longer dominates. Popularity is no longer the main or only driver of market value; relatively unknown or minority interest products can be found and bought with ease. Their availability and acquisition by fragmented users form a key part of the new virtual economy.

Anderson went on to outline three rules that oversee his new business model concept, all focused on the user's leading role and individuality: 1) 'make everything available' – meaning the availability of a wide range of titles; 2) 'cut price in half, now lower it' – which enshrines competitive pricing in contrast to other distribution channels; and 3) 'help me find it ... ' – which relates to branding, retail action and personalized consumption. 'The companies that will prosper', Anderson declared, 'are those that switch out of the lowest-common-denominator mode and figure out how to address niches.'

This statement and his accompanying work were directly attacked by Anita Elberse, an associate professor of business administration at Harvard Business School.[10] Her own conducted research indicated the opposite to Anderson's conclusions. While acknowledging that the Internet allowed for

> more obscure products being made available for purchase everyday, the tail is likely to be extremely flat and populated by titles that are mostly a diversion for consumers whose appetite for true blockbusters continues to grow. It is therefore highly disputable that much money can be made in the tail. In sales of both videos and recorded music – in many ways the perfect products to test the long-tail theory – we see that hits are and probably will remain dominant. That is the reality that should inform retailers as they struggle to offer their customers a satisfying assortment cost-efficiently. And it's the unavoidable challenge to producers. The companies that will prosper are the ones most capable of capitalizing on individual best sellers.

Anderson patiently batted back Elberse's curve ball in an ensuing blogging exchange, but the key point was that Elberse was taking the side of the 80:20 rule and supporting the notion that powerful incumbents have most to gain ultimately from the new global dissemination game the Internet throws up.

Factors impacting films' transition from old to new media – The independent incumbent's perspective: Stewart Till

Some players are not convinced that the advent of digital signifies a revolution or instant change. In a Cass Business School address,[11] Icon CEO Stewart Till set out the key issues facing the changing film landscape from his perspective:

> Film understands multi-window distribution, and controls all forms of exploitation. The production and distribution of film involves millions of dollars, and is not easily accessible to the guerrilla creator. Even once the product exists, film still incurs a significant cash outlay to bring to the market. Convergence will significantly accelerate in-home, easy film renting through downloading and streaming, but piracy (theft) needs to be combated. Most of the old rules will still prevail. For example, simply creating something does not mean that it will be watched. The consumer looks to film to get something that is not available in their everyday life or from other forms of entertainment.

The Studios will continue to prevail as their size and muscle is still valuable, but there will still be room for independents. While business will improve thanks to easier, more accessible distribution (both through digital screens and Internet home delivery), Till argues that it is crucial from a distribution standpoint to always look to a multi-territory strategy. He also makes the point that while there is no perfect correlation between the production budget and size of audience, there is still a relationship.

While the new digital world is of course going to change the film landscape and offer more choice to the user, it's important to remain clear about the product: Film will always be 'a film', not a short or a video installation or a television drama.

In terms of fresh opportunities, Till sees digital production and post-production as endless in terms of possibilities, but there will be even more importance on the marketing of product, with shorter windows and simultaneous worldwide release dates to contend with. The migration from television to the Internet will give rise to a 'fantastic' VOD offering and an encouraging Long Tail.

So will it change the film industry as we know it? Not really, according to Till: 'Film will always be about effective distribution of great storytelling. The arrival of digital is a transition not a revolution or panacea, and the change in the media world is going to happen much more slowly than the industry and business schools predict.'

The 360-degree approach and integrated opportunities

While there are key inherent dangers lurking in the bipolar positioning discussed in this chapter (where both sides may be well off the future mark), there are also positive areas of potential advancement. Specifically, barriers to entry for smaller and independent companies are lowering; and opportunities for creative talent to develop with less sunk-cost risks associated with physical production are promising. The arrival of a new, increasingly efficient market that is responding to the needs of new users provides for new commercial opportunities; which in turn also offer potential cross-media synergies for the entertainment industry; and lastly, but not least, the scope for interaction with other markets linked to core product, and able to be exploited and disseminated simultaneously across new platforms and accessed (and even paid for) by a myriad of user-friendly systems.

Ultimately, the adoption of a more holistic approach towards exploitation and multi-platform promotion will be essential if the cost of new content is to be successfully amortized. Hardly new (the Studios have been operating it for decades), is the much discussed '360-degree' model. In the 'future is now' multi-channel world, where the user has infinite choice, creative businesses need to compete not just against rival product and other entertainment providers, but with other non-media businesses competing for the user's 'share of mind'. This requires early consideration and assessment of all potential forms of exploitation, adaption and promotion of film in particular, if the changing value chain is to be conquered.

Vertically integrated and multi-channel exploitation remains vital to commercial development. New product and projects have the potential to be positioned and accessed through a multiplicity of revenue channels. This strategy does of course require a certain level of knowledge of the market for each opportunity, but it is also possible to acquire this through a series of partnerships or joint ventures. The integrated approach adopted in such examples can create a virtuous circle as each strand of exploitation promotes and reinforces each other.[12]

The new way forward

'No matter how grand our request to become global entertainment giants or pioneers of revolutionary technologies, we cannot forget that it is the story that lies at the root of every successful form of entertainment.' When Peter Guber, film producer, chairman of Mandalay and former chair of Sony Pictures Entertainment, pronounced those words some 15 years ago,[13] this author had no real notion of the enormity of user changes that were to be brought about through the Internet. Nevertheless, content for the film business specifically remains 'king', while scale and 'reach' remains 'queen', to use the words of Terry Ilott. The creation of compelling, distinctive, emotionally alluring and moving content carries a premium that transcends all existing and future delivery systems. The informational networking ecology of the Internet serves to promote and expand outstanding content, not bury it.

Leading creative organizations lead because they produce outstanding content. The challenge producers and creative organizations now face is how best to deliver that around the 360-degree clock, across as many different channels, outlets and platforms as possible, and how best to find that blend between commoditizing and gifting. But without strands of significant monetizing, the creative economy will dry up.

Case study interview: Pierre-Ange Le Pogam, co-founder of EuropaCorp[14]

> Critics often have trouble accepting that you can like Jean-Luc Godard and Walt Disney. Normal people like both.
>
> (Luc Besson, filmmaker and co-founder, EuropaCorp)

Luc Besson and Pierre-Ange Le Pogam were natural business and creative partners from the start. 'I know what Luc likes, and he knows what I like,' explains Le Pogam. 'We're not fully satisfied by French culture and cinema. We both share the aim of reaching an international audience for our films.' Following a significant falling out between Besson and then Gaumont distribution chief Le Pogam, on the one side, and on the other their producer/distributor partner Gaumont, which had passed on *Taxi 2* (and blocked the two working as producers and distributors on the successful original version), the director/producer/distributor duo decided to go it alone. They turned entrepreneurs and set up EuropaCorp in September 2000. The company was designed to be an independent, vertically integrated studio from its inception, and to offer an alternative way of producing and exploiting films from a French hub.

A discipline was enshrined: avoid owning and operating cinemas or being involved in broadcasting and staggering under the weight of a huge corporation. Instead, the key model was to concentrate on making around ten feature films a year, with average budgets of around €12m, and to control distribution and associated publishing links generated by all creative production.

'The plan was to capture the margins from the distribution business. There also comes a point when you match artistic ambition with financing, and you come to a final number, say 10. We will always try to make that an 8 without cutting anything from the artistic merit or input of the project.'

The vertically integrated business model was central to Besson and Le Pogam's concept. 'We operate like an American studio,' Besson has explained. 'The entire process of making our films, from pre-financing to video release, by way of screenwriting, poster design and export, is vertically integrated and grouped together in the same place. We are the only ones in France working like that.' However, Le Pogam stresses that after his many years with the heavy management system at Gaumont, the microstructure model adopted by EuropaCorp not only needed flexibility and speed of decision-making, but was essential if the company was to achieve a new vision and creative ecology. Commentators have suggested that the system is more akin to the old Hollywood of the 1920s and 1930s, where Mayer, Warner, Zanuck, Thallberg and the leading independent producer of that generation, Goldwyn, ran autocracies rather than the executive decision-making committees found inside the Studios of today.

Underpinning the structure was the need to reach users across all spectrums of exploitation. Le Pogam took his extensive experience of marketing and distribution and his obsession with reaching wider audiences at Gaumont – exemplified by *The Fifth Element*'s global impact – to both a national, and international level with EuropaCorp. More than 40 per cent of EuropaCorp's turnover is from outside France, while French box office receipts make up between 5 per cent and 10 per cent of the annual turnover – underlining the strategy of a wide 360° wheel incorporating horizontal and vertical receipts and a range of revenue streams.

The EuropaCorp studio employs approximately 120 full-time people. The overall model's key areas can be broken down as follows:

- Development – rights acquisitions of material and creative development.
- Production and finance – ten films a year, significant pre-sales within and outside France. Tight above the line and below the line management systems to control costs. Slate mix (genre films, auteur films, super productions at €20–60m).
- Sales/distribution and marketing-in-house sales operation. Strong distribution operation, video through GIE FPE (Fox/Pathe/EC).
- 360° exploitation of licences and rights – books (Intervista), music, and licences and merchandising.
- Commercials – development of new talent and techniques through publicity films.
- Video-on-demand – MovieSystem, a partnership between Canal Plus and Orange [sold to CP with EC minority interest (25 per cent – participation sold)].
- A multiplex cinema and Saint-Denis Studios – future projects.

Many areas within the above structure are kept tight, often through strategic links to third parties and joint ventures. And the avoidance of profligacy shapes the production planning stages of all EuropaCorp films. The company has around four producers in-house capable of fully developing, planning and delivering a project. Although it tracks third-party independent producers carefully, it avoids first look and in-house producer deals – in stark contrast to the on-the-lot production labels paid for by the Hollywood Studios.

'Give a producer too much food and they get fat,' explains Le Pogam.

We don't believe the company is the star, the movies are the star. To stay in business, we need to have the best people with us to be able to guess what the right price is, meaning the money you need to have to be able to make that movie happen at the best artistic potential. And then you need to have the best people to make sure that movie becomes the best vehicle to create revenues. So we've created an industrial system around the movies – with everyone working under this system and each movie proving again and again that we have the capacity to be taking care of all aspects of that product.

EuropaCorp generates a large amount of original ideas, and material often emerges from writer and director meetings. It approaches the development stage through a fusion of writer/director and producer. Le Pogam is adamant that it is preferable to have the director involved in the writing of the screenplay at the earliest possible stage. In addition to in-house material, the company receives around 900 projects a year. These are analysed and reported on by a group of around 20 readers from various backgrounds and interests, with each covering around 3–5 projects a month. Ultimately, material that moves forwards to a packaging and pre-production stage has to be signed off by Besson and Le Pogam.

Above the line costs are controlled by lower advance salaries to top talent in exchange for meaningful profit participations. Le Pogam cites the example of Chinese star Jet Li, who commands a Hollywood price of around $8m a film (as compared with $200,000 per EuropaCorp film and a percentage of future receipts). Below the line costs are rigorously controlled, with each scene broken down, and all production costs analysed and scaled back to a level that still maintains the creative vision but no fat. 'If you go over budget by $5m, you've got to find another $70m of revenues to restore $5m in profit. You need a miracle, and we're not in the miracle business.' He explains the risk profile opportunity by reference to Hollywood:

> The Hollywood Studio may go for a movie with a $50m budget. By contrast, we are able to provide the same movie for $35m, so some of our movies find an easy home in the United States and across their worldwide distribution operations, because they need to feed these networks. When they distribute our films, they limit their risk exposure. And for the major independents or the good independents, it's more and more difficult for them to have access to the films of the Hollywood Studios, so they need to find the level of product to compete, and hence they come to us.

That situation has grown even more acute with the closure of New Line, Picture House, Warners Independent Pictures, Paramount Classics and the scaling back of Paramount Vantage since 2006/2007.

A good example of the risk-management role of the in-house sales operation is in Besson's *The Extraordinary Adventures of Adele Blanc-Sec*. The $33m film was pre-sold at Cannes 2009 on director, script, pitch and concept – and of course the track record of the company delivering the film, covering 80 per cent of available territories outside France, the United Kingdom and North America. Green lighting films beyond a $15m budget will normally require a North American pre-sale, or Besson and Le Pogam will put the film on hold. This strategy has worked especially well when harnessed with Fox: *Taken*, an action picture directed by Pierre Morel, cost $37m and grossed $140m in the North American market and a further $90m from 'foreign'.

The importance of 360° exploitation is central to EuropaCorp's business plan. The release in 2009 of original movie soundtracks, the publishing of film-related books, and the production of commercials made up more than 10 per cent of total sales activities for the group. Rather than these activities being viewed as diversification, as mistakenly viewed by French academic commentators, the strategy mirrors the Studio exploitation model. EuropaCorp Diffusion develops DVD publishing product, and handles DVD distribution; Intervista publishes screenplays and books of the films; Ydeo manages all advertising campaigns, and EuropaCorp Music Publishing handles original soundtracks. Besson's *Arthur and the Invisibles*, which was sold to 71 countries, in 37 languages, and grossed more than $100m internationally, was also subject to 60 licensing agreements, requiring 20 different international agents under the supervision of a former Disney executive. Mobisodes, combining short edited scenes from *Arthur*, were played on Orange cell phones for €0.50 per episode, and more than 100,000 videos were viewed through streamed media. Orange subscribers were offered exclusive interviews with the film crew; and an agreement with BNP Paribas allowed the bank to use the characters from the film through to the end of 2007.

In May 2007 Besson and Le Pogam took EuropaCorp public by listing it on the Paris Stock Exchange. By mid-2007 the share price had hit $21 then sank back to around $7, but the $100m line of credit was seen as critical to the partners if the company was to be able to consolidate.

At that time Luc and I were the two major owners. Firstly, as entrepreneurs, how could we be sure that one day we would see a personal upside from our project? Number two, we know a lot of people in Hollywood, but still we know the limit, we are French, we are not American. We needed a kind of recognition beyond the good reputation of Luc Besson and Pierre-Ange Le Pogam that was to give the market proof that we are real, we exist: that we are concrete. Plus, in French business culture, a public company provides a system that you can trust because who is going to cheat with the results and with the allocation of receipts in such company if we are public? It was a chance to create cash and provide respect in the French economy because suddenly everybody knew about the value of the company.

Le Pogam concedes that neither Besson nor himself were aware of the 'crazy' roller-coaster ride going public was going to instigate.

We didn't know how difficult it was going to be, but we needed to do something for our reputation. That reputation could come from two places: one was going public; the second was welcoming onboard some beautiful institutional partners. But if we are public we remain the bosses of the company, if we welcome other partners who knows if five, ten years from now if we are still making the decisions? If our only goal was personal money, then we could have attracted a couple of American investors for around 25 per cent, and then after achieving the best possible value everybody sells everything after say ten years. But the goal was to establish a studio. So we guessed that that was going to be a more painful way, but we accepted [going public] as a necessary evil.

Management has been shared out, in particular with regards to the day-to-day running of the company and the finances.

We learn every day. And as you know that we need to identify the people capable to run the company with us and after us, and we have the taste of sharing with some people. I don't want to lie: it's hard because this is still a company inside of which for many decisions you need Luc or myself. We are learning how to live with that and we are making progress maybe not every day but every month. The beautiful system doesn't exist in any company. A company always has many defaults in terms of management, whatever that company is.

EuropaCorp: key figures

Year	Apr. 1 2007– Mar. 31 2008 €,000	Apr. 1 2006– Mar. 31 2007 €,000	Apr. 1 2005– Mar. 31 2006 €,000
Revenue	128,546	147,100	158,661
Operating profit	7,441	10,607	11,517
Net profit	9,361	6,945	8,218
Shareholder's equity	145,390	136,503	62,890
Total assets	469,761	388,828	226,966
Accounting standards	IFRS	IFRS	IFRS

Source: COFISEM – 20/06/09 and EuropaCorp

Note: Net profit explanation – the net (after tax) profit for the entire group as a whole. Includes group's share of the net profit, as well as the net profit for the minority interests.

Shareholders	Percentage
Front line	61.98
Other shareholders	22.82
Pierre-Ange Le Pogam	8.05
CNCEP	4.2
Achille Delahaye	2.8
Company-owned shares	0.12
Luc Besson	0.02

Source: COFISEM – 20/06/09 and EuropaCorp

19 Case study: interview with Simon Franks, Redbus Group

> In business, many people can have a great idea, do something well and make money once. Sometimes you just have the right idea at the right time. But good business people have something innate and that allows them to make money again and again. Curiosity is what allows you to be a serial entrepreneur, and your understanding of cycles means you know there's always a time to be a seller and always a time to be a buyer.
>
> (Simon Franks, founder and chairman of Redbus Group)

Simon Franks sold his first business at the tender age of 11. During chilly winter lunch-breaks at his North London school children were forced to play outside. Franks set up a business selling chicken soup , aided by a teacher who would bring him boiling water and he would fill cuppa soups and sell them at a hefty margin. A busy trade ensued, to the point of such success that a group of other kids bought the 'business' from him. Some 20 years later, Franks sold 51 per cent of Redbus Distribution first to Helkon for $23m, and then the same company again four years later to Lionsgate for $35m in cash plus $7m of stock. This case study, from an interview with the author, examines Franks' entrepreneurial ride with Redbus Film Distribution.

Simon Franks has a thing about playing games. He likes the self-discipline because he knows deep down he is not really a very disciplined human being. Left to his own devices or nature for that matter, and he will fail to do the things he needs to do on time and on schedule. Wasting time in his book is a negative: life is short, and why feel the guilt that goes with laziness?

One of the first things you find out about setting up business is that no one calls you back because you're not relevant yet to their livelihood. I understand that. They don't need you. They don't see how you can help them along their journey, so your phone doesn't ring. When you call people they often don't take your call and you get into this funk: get out of bed, get showered, get changed, walk into my office (i.e. the spare bedroom), remove the laundry that my girlfriend has dumped there the night before, and go right through the list of things to do. I'd do all those things and it'd be ten past ten and I'm finished. You have to be very careful what you do next, between ten past ten and six o'clock, whenever it is you finish, as it's critical to the success of your business. I had a time between 2.30 and 4.30 which was sacrosanct. It was the time when I played soccer on my Playstation. By doing this I didn't feel I was wasting time but instead enjoying a scheduled break.

Many of my friends would laugh and say 'he doesn't have a job, he just sits at home playing Playstation', and to an extent they were right, but there was a method to that madness. And I remember thinking that I would know when the business was getting off the ground because I would have to make appointments in my Playstation time. And that was a very significant moment, some six-to-nine months in. I actually realized that there was no purpose anymore to that game time.

Franks had always told himself that he would go to work in the City purely to make money. He came from 'quite a modest background', and he was committed to starting up his own business once he had made some seed money. He worked in the City on a five-year plan, after which he had paid off his mortgage and had around £200,000 spare to invest.

It's a lot of money for a 26 year old but it's not millions. And with that I looked around and I thought 'What business should I turn my attentions to? What are the parameters for me?' One was: it has to be something interesting. And secondly, it had to be a serious challenge. The odds needed to be stacked against me. For in those situations the risk reward equation is often positive and you are most able to leverage your efforts and skill. I like those kinds of situations. ...

Switching from a production fund to a distribution plan

One of the first people Simon Franks met in the film business was a UK producer, Richard Holmes, who had just completed a film called *Shooting Fish*. 'The project seems to be going great and yet I'm not making any money', Holmes complained to Franks. 'The distributors are making all the money.' Franks listened carefully, and given how smart he thought the producer was, decided to ditch his plans to raise a production fund, convincing himself that 'distribution is the business I'm interested in'.

Shifting focus from a production fund to distribution allowed Franks to get higher up the film business revenue stream. But he was still perplexed by the specific vagaries of the film business.

Even in distribution it can be very scary – besides the cost of acquiring the rights to films, you have to cover a large overhead. In the essence the overhead represents the cost of the group of resources – people ready to take finished product A and put it into the shops, effectively. In other consumer focused businesses you see your design, you see your prototype, you push a button and in two months time you're selling it. You know what you're going to be getting, you know when you're going to be getting it and you know what your marketplace is. But you don't know those things when you acquire the rights to a new film. Often you're going to have a terrible film come through which means, not only have you lost money in what you've bought, but your resource is waiting around because they have nothing to do. Why? Because the product's not good enough and you're not going to release it. Though sometimes you have to accept that it's bad and then flog the dead horse anyway.

So what I said when I entered the business was two things: One, the kind of people who in the past had been running film businesses in the UK were people who wanted to be in the creative part of the industry. Now, although film is my passion – I see many films every week and have thousands of DVDs, a cinema in my home, etc. – this had nothing to do with me being in the film business. What we looked for, firstly, was to avoid the wrong people in the wrong place who couldn't be unemotional and have perspective. The second thing was that people thought film was utterly random, and so serious UK business people shunned it. No one had really sat down and said, okay, can you model films? Can you build a process in a risk-adjusted way as you can do in other businesses? And so I built a very complicated spreadsheet which tried to model returns. We used to model things by budget sizes, by very developed strictly defined genres and certain actors that had certain values that were revenue drivers. Very often the revenue drivers were not what would make a film a theatrical success. Some films are more likely to do well theatrically but they don't do so well on DVD and they don't do well on TV and hence, through that matrix, you come through to a few types of films that are lower risk. That's what we focused on. Our model showed the best risk reward situations to be in horror and then teen comedy. The third was British indie films, but I'm talking for the general international markets, and that's where we focused. Because if you work on the presumption that most films that we were going to acquire were going to be poor, then I'd rather have a poor horror film than a poor drama, because you'll make zero from a poor drama. TV and DVD sales for poor dramas are so low that they are meaningless financially.

For Franks, it was the buoyant video market that attracted him as a revenue stream that threw off enough cash to potentially 'manage' some of the inherent risks.

The only people I could see making money were doing so thanks to the video market. And I started to think, there's a lot of money in this business if you do it right. In the City I was an arbitrager, doing debt restructuring and working out the relative values between X and Y. So when I started to look at film rights I wondered why no one valued them like music rights? So the first thing I did was to go to all these independent producers and buy their rights. But as it turned out, instead of going to say, ten producers and having ten films each, each UK producer's got one film and they can't sell you that because they've given away all the rights in making the film, so I'm thinking: 'Hell, this is going to take me years to get ten films together just buying rights.'

Distribution's business model attracted Franks. The portfolio approach – allowing for around 12–15 films a year to be exploited – in contrast to one or two a year via production, was much more attractive.

Not because I thought distribution was necessarily better than production but I do prefer to have a portfolio approach. If you're good at organizational administration – which I think is what I excel at – you can have a disciplined business, keep costs low compared to competitors and be very tight. That way, even in an average year, you can make money.

The early acquisition strategy

According to Franks, picking up product was a lot easier in the early to mid-1990s than it is today.

> In my day there were no big alliances but now many of the big product sellers are aligned and not selling their products to third parties. Lionsgate's product is gone, they were one of the biggest providers, Summits product has gone, they were another of the biggest providers, the Miramax product has gone, the New Line Deal has gone ... There's almost no product around, so when something does come around the price rate is astronomical, because everyone needs it. Unless you're one of the distributors aligned with one of those product providers, you are in trouble.

The first Redbus UK acquisition was *The Tichbourne Claimant*. A large screening was held with many distributors attending, and the UK asking price was a multiple of millions at the start of the process. Franks worked the producer over, bringing the numbers down but it remained seven figures. Then his partner, Zygi Kamasa, got involved in the process.

> I remember Zygi going to see him, when we were first talking about starting up and the producer said: 'Look, I'll be honest with you, I've had some knocks, obviously, I'll do the UK, on its own, for one and a half million.' Zygi's response was a simple: 'How can we afford that, it's so much for this kind of film?' A year went by, and the company was established by this stage. A call came in from the producer, explaining that he's 'desperate to do a deal for half a million'. Zygi, who was a brilliant negotiator, probably the best I've ever met, and I went to see him. He just sat there very quietly and I was shocked when Zygi got it down to single digits. Zygi was looking at me, and I was trying not to giggle, as I get very embarrassed in these situations. He bought our first film for seven grand ... .

The first thing the producer asked was whether Redbus was going to release the film theatrically? 'Absolutely', said Franks, who explained that 'Martin Sorrell unknowingly had ("sort of") financed Redbus because WPP had provided them with a large credit line for advertising spend.' Franks had £100,000–£200,000 in the bank.

> If any of those early films had failed we'd have been out of business pretty quickly and wouldn't have been able to pay them back I guess. But it didn't and you know what, they must have made a good profit out of us over the years. Last year we spent over twelve million pounds with them. Fortunately their faith in us has been repaid, thank god. The producer didn't really ask detailed questions, so we guaranteed a theatrically release, but of course we could do that on one screen. In the end we did it on just under 20 screens.

Redbus released *The Tichbourne Claimant*, and it grossed a very modest £150,000 at the UK box office. Redbus, on the back of a very strong period story and decent cast – perfect for TV – cut an impressive trailer. So when the BBC offered around £70,000 for it, they said 'great, we'll come back to you'. Then a call came in from the office of the chief executive of Channel 4 asking if the film was still available, and that a buyer at Channel 4 will be in touch. 'So this is great fun, an introduction to someone we didn't even know, saying that they had to have the film!' Franks explained that they had a deal with the BBC.

> 'Is it signed?' No, but 'we're a young company, so it's not our place to be pissing people off'. 'Well let me tell you the situation: the chief executive of Channel 4 was out last night and he and his wife went to see your film, which they've fallen in love with and he has to have it. He's promised his wife.'

Channel 4 offered £120,000 for the film.

So what could Redbus do? Bid the two channels up? Go with the BBC who had been decent in the first place? Take the higher offer? Franks and Kamasa went back to the BBC, and told them exactly what had happened. The BBC took some time to think about it, then came back and said: 'If you promise to sign here, then we'll match what Channel 4 has offered.' Franks is sure that Channel 4 would have paid more if given the chance, but

> now that we were in profit on our first film ... we dealt with Channel 4, and sat down with them, and explained exactly why we couldn't sell to them. We wish we could but it would be wrong. And you know what? The head of film said 'I want you to know that, a) I didn't really want the film anyway, and b) I really respect you for coming to see us and being honest about it'.

As a result of Redbus' experience on *The Tichbourne Claimant*, the executives got to know all the TV buyers and they got on well. Franks even took to making it his policy to sit next to the BBC's chief film buyer, Steve Jenkins.

> He's got an encyclopedic knowledge of film. And whether I enjoy the film or don't enjoy the film he's the biggest buyer of films in the country; all the other distributors were chatting to each other but instead Zygi and I were gauging his view and reaction to the film we had just seen.

Aggression also played its role in Redbus' rise. *Cabin Fever* was being repped by William Morris agent Cassian Elwes in 2001 at the Toronto Film Festival. Kamasa caught an early flight home, but Franks decided to stay on, intrigued following Redbus' hit film *Jeepers Creepers*.

> I moved my flight to the last one possible, but I could still only see 15 minutes. He caught Cassian on his way out: 'You know what? It's not bad ... it's not bad ... what do you want for it?' And he said 'Well, to be honest I was looking for x, y, z'. I knew it was made for next to nothing, around $400,000 dollars. I paid $100,000 dollars for UK rights, which was more like a typical straight to video fee. So we signed a deal on the back of a napkin, there and then. Subsequently, the producers tried to get out of the deal (not Elwes). ... We've still got the napkin in the safe, with the *Cabin Fever* deal on it. Thank god. It was a huge hit, and we made millions from it. From that point onwards, if I stayed in a film screening, people thought I must hate the movie!

Redbus focused on going to festivals and picking completed films. 'Because we didn't have money to lose many times over, and I found it much scarier to pick scripts – finished films was a good way to go at the beginning', explained Franks. 'Eventually, as we became bigger, that became impossible. All the really good projects have gone at script stage. And many of the films we did subsequently were acquired at script stage.'

The challenge of cash flow

Cash flow management is critical in any business and is a nightmare if you are not on top of it. Especially in the film business. Even the most exceptionally bright people don't seem to be able to understand cash: it's the lifeblood of any business. A good starting point is to take your existing assumptions on cash flow and push all income back by six months and bring up all the bills three months earlier. And then you still should probably halve what you've got. For example, it was a shock to me when the BBC told me 'by the way', on *The Tichborne Claimant*, 'here's your deal for £120k', and I'm like 'in the money', ... then they explained: 'We're paying you in three and a half year's time.' I'm like 'What are you talking about three and a half year's time, pay the money now. You can't pay in three and a half year's time!' Answer: 'We pay when we play.'

No one told me that. I went into distribution knowing nothing about the business. Obviously I tried to bluff it but it caught me out massively. Within a year and a half of us trading, by late 2000, we were technically trading 'off the top'. Now, we did nothing wrong by that because as long as you can explain that you had good reason to believe you'd be fine then that is acceptable. But drawing the line can be complex. There were times when we sat down and discussed whether we could make it. The fact was that we would have gone bust, profitable, which is just crazy. We were owed a fortune yet no one would lend to us. We had proper money by year two, you know, £300k to £400k owed to us by broadcasters, blue chip solid guarantees and Barclays offered us a total facility of £200k and no overdraft on top of that. Then overnight they took the overdraft away around the time of the dotcom bubble.

Franks went to three friends and borrowed £50,000 from each to remain in business. It did not take him long to find Coutts,

not because I was posh, but because their media division is incredibly supportive if they believe in the management of a company. We went from having a £200 grand facility to zero, and then thanks to Coutts to having a £3 million overdraft. And that was the difference between survival and failure.

Franks explained that drawing down on a facility can be a very demanding process. Coutts would use projected estimate on video revenues; so while that would create a positive for the drawdown level, the overall level would be reduced by any committed expenditure for acquisitions.

It was a tricky thing, especially if the seller was looking for letters of credit, which is what almost everyone uses in the business. LCs are basically cash, I mean, you can convince yourself that they are not, but they effectively block up your credit lines. Finance is the heart of any business, and I spent a huge amount of my time managing our cash flow and focusing on planning on when we could do things and we couldn't do things … and sometimes a film's release would have to be moved.

However, Redbus struck gold not just once, but three times over two key years in 2001 and 2002.

> We were very lucky. Over these two incredible years our total investment in terms of advances was around $2.3m in three hit films, and those films probably did $100m in total revenues: *Bend It Like Beckham*, *Jeepers Creepers* and *The Gift*.

It was the video business, which was huge for all three, which created serious cash inside Redbus. 'And that's when everything changes.'

Marketing and handling the United Kingdom's exhibition circuit

Dealing with the exhibitors in the United Kingdom as an independent is extremely challenging. As Franks sees it,

> cinemas favour Hollywood Studios in their terms of trade and that's just a fact. These very low, basic rentals (Redbus received around 26–28 per cent of each box office ticket) and then very high hit targets, basically means that the good deals go to all the big Studios that have all the huge hit potential. I think only once in our history in 12 years we made money at the theatrical stage of a film's life. Independents don't have special terms because we don't have films that excite in advance as much as big budget Studio fare.

In terms of expanding the Redbus brand and clout in the market, Franks was given a golden opportunity when PolyGram Filmed Entertainment's UK distribution operation was effectively closed down in 2000 when Universal acquired the company. With the necessary financing, and its first success in the bag, Franks went after Chris Bailey and Carla Smith and their 14-strong distribution and marketing team. It took nine months for Bailey to join up, and the condition was that Redbus had to hire every single person in PolyGram's UK distribution outfit other than the top executives who were moving on. Franks recalls that it was

> like, uh, okay, a) I'm still working out of my apartment at the moment, b) I have £200 grand in the bank and your combined wage bill is definitely more than that, so how am I going to finance this? This is what I was thinking in my head, but I told Chris: 'done', and I told myself, they are the best marketing team out there, always have been the best, and this is a chance in a lifetime, so go for it. And I did.

The promise of hiring such a large team without knowing necessarily he could afford their contracted periods did worry Franks.

At our company we have a paid ethical advisor, who is someone, who is a lay person, who specializes in religion, ethics and all this stuff and it's to him we said 'in this situation can we hire these people? Do I have to declare our financial situation?' If I did declare I didn't have the money they wouldn't have come, and he said that if any of them were in a situation whereby they were turning something else down by coming to us they should be allowed to go, but if they weren't (none of them had anything lined up), then it was okay. And so we said to Chris: 'You need to tell everybody that we only want people that have no other current job offers.'

Firstly, marketing is about the right people. Secondly, if you are going to be an independent distributor, spend less money buying films and more money marketing them, which is what we did. At the time that was quite novel, although everyone thinks that way now. And with what I believed to be the best marketers in the business we were now ready to take on the market.

The German deal that closed and then opened again

Rebus was finding business extremely tough during its first two years. 'We were suffering real cash flow trouble. Not that we weren't profitable, but cash flow-wise we were basically on the edge', recalled Franks.

> I bumped into this guy called Werner Koenig who immediately I loved, and who ran a company called Helkon Media. The German distribution company was basically the same type as my business, except he'd floated it, somehow, and it was suddenly worth $500 million, you know? $500 million on the Neue Market bubble! Helkon only had double our revenues. It was pathetic ... but those were the times.

Koenig told Franks: 'I've always wanted to have a UK distributor, so why don't I buy your company.' To which an astonished Franks replied: 'But I've just met you! I'm not selling you my fucking company ... .' Franks and Koenig went out a few times and they hit it off.

> I really liked him; he was a great character, like a film star in many ways: he was full of charisma and dynamism. He was one of very few people I'd be happily subservient to: Werner was the real deal. Anyone who didn't get him, I didn't get either.

A year later, Franks was at nearing 'death's door' with the business, unable to pay his bills despite strong performances. Franks called Koenig, and said: 'You know what, maybe I will sell you the business.'

The two met at the Four Seasons in Berlin and instead of getting on with a deal, Koenig insisted that they had a two-hour massage. Then they sat down.

> Although I owned the majority of the shares, Zygi and I had talked everything through. We'd agreed that if we could get $3 or $4 million we'd take it, as it would have got us out whole and made a profit for those who had supported us in the beginning. (We also wanted a big earn out over time going forwards, as we felt that we were on the verge of an exponential growth in profitability if not cash generation.)

'Look, you know what? I really like you Simon. I want to be in business with you. I'll make you an offer, I won't negotiate, you take it, or you leave it. If you don't take it I'm walking out.' And I start thinking between three or four, please be four, be five even, go on. ... He went: 'Sixteen million dollars.'

Our balance sheet was less than two. And we were 2 years old. Inside I'm dancing with the angels, but externally I went very quiet. Then I said: 'No. You know what? Your business is at best double the size of mine and you are worth according to the stock market $500 million dollars and yet you think we're only worth sixteen? That's an insult. Don't treat me that way.' I got up to leave. And he grabbed my arm, and said 'Alright, how much?' I said '23 – but only for half.' 'Done.' And that was it, 51 per cent was now owned by Helkon.

A year later Werner Koenig died in a skiing accident before the last tranche of the deal was paid. By then $16m had been paid, but Helkon was unraveling.

> They were in a hell of a mess. Unfortunately there was a couple of Germans who were Werner's partners who had been with him since the beginning. They basically didn't trust any of us and wouldn't let us do what we wanted to do to try and save the thing.

Although by then Helkon's financial problems were north of $250 million. Redbus was never paid the last seven million dollars.

In this interim year, Franks became very disillusioned with the film business. His company had become owned by a foreign company now bankrupt, and the key person who had done the deal was now dead. And whilst $16 million dollars received seemed a lot, the reality was that the majority was used to pay off debt and guarantees and to buy out other shareholders, and once Helkon was in administration, the entire freedom of Redbus to operate became almost completely frozen. 'I need to do something else', thought Franks, so he started buying other companies – mostly distressed media businesses that needed restructuring but had potential cash flows and ultimately value. Most of the money from Helkon was reinvested rather than spent. Franks still drove the same car; lived in the same apartment, and although wealthy by now, he reinvested considerable sums rather than go 'crazy'.

Two years later Redbus got the UK distributor back thanks to a small, hidden-away clause in the original contract enabling Redbus to wrest control in the event of a Helkon liquidation. Under these circumstances, Redbus could be bought back at a substantial discount to the acquisition price. During the protracted and frustrating process, in particular dealing with administrators, and insolvency practitioners, and all the banks that deal with loans that are in distress or in default, Franks learnt a great deal about the process. Instead of obsessing about the distribution company, he took the opportunity to set up the Redbus Group as a business, specializing in picking up distressed companies, which remains its main activity today.

What was learned from the Helkon deal?

> I would say to any owner do not sell 51 one per cent of your business to anybody. Unless the quoted price is crazy, in which case take it but know that 51 per cent is a bad number to sell because you got a lot to lose still but you don't have any control. The interim period was very horrible because I was dealing with this

German accountancy in Hamburg, and they didn't get me, they didn't get the business, it was very difficult.

Having repurchased the company, Franks – who owned 80 per cent of the company – and his minority partner Kamasa decided to sell to Lionsgate in October 2005. The deal was reported by Lionsgate at $35m plus debt, but according to Franks the debt was quite substantial – 'many millions which was owed to us plus cash drain, and we were a cash positive company so in total it was a lot of money. And we'd only bought it back at single digit millions from Helkon'.

The deal came at the right time, explained Franks. The video market was flattening, the risk re P&A was higher than ever, and Redbus was witnessing a consolidation in the UK distribution market. Bigger players, larger pockets, and higher barriers to entry all played their part in the decision to sell. And if Redbus had turned the offer down, Lionsgate may have bought a rival, making life more uncomfortable and leaving no option but to go back and reconsider the offer.

In summary, Franks did two very personal things on closing the Lionsgate deal. He established a charity foundation, the Franks Family Foundation. And he put aside more than $1m to be shared out between some 20 staff even though there was no contractual need to make any bonus payments.

> I expect paid staff to work their bollocks off and treat my money, the company's money, like their own money. We don't like wasting things. When we went through a downturn, we didn't make any people redundant. Thank god, but almost everyone else did. And you know why we didn't have to? Because we keep things tight so that we can afford to keep people, but they don't see that in the good times, they think you are being tight with them. When we sold the company, I paid a special non-contractual bonus, which was in total over a million. Remember they didn't even work for me now. They worked for Lionsgate by this point, so it wasn't even as a motivational thing. But it was the right thing to do and I'm proud that we did it. The Redbus Film Distribution team was always a pleasure to work with. To be honest the thing I miss most about the business is spending time with them. Without the like of Carla Smith, Chris Bailey or Guy Avshalom, Redbus would not have been the successful company it was. I consider the time I had working with them and their teams a pleasure and a privilege for me.

Redbus distribution titles (all media unless stated)

Like Minds (2006) – distributor (2005) (UK) (theatrical)
The Best Man (2006) – distributor (2005) (UK)
The Contract (2006) – distributor (2006) (USA) (theatrical)
An American Haunting (2005) – distributor (2006) (UK)
Diameter of the Bomb (2005) – distributor (2005) (UK) (theatrical)
Revolver (2005) – distributor (2005) (UK)
Good Night, and Good Luck (2005) – distributor (2006) (UK) (theatrical)
Mortuary (2005) – distributor (2005) (UK) (theatrical)
Edison (2005) – distributor (2005) (UK)

Gypo (2005) – distributor (2005) (UK)
The All Together (2005) – distributor (2006) (UK)
Enron: The Smartest Guys in the Room (2005) – distributor (2005) (UK)
Hard Candy (2005) – distributor (2006) (UK)
Rize (2005) – distributor (2005) (UK)
Taking 5 (2005) – distributor (2006) (UK) (theatrical)
Zemanovaload (2005) – distributor (2005) (UK) (DVD)
Man About Dog (2004) – distributor (2004) (UK) (theatrical)
It's All Gone Pete Tong (2004) – distributor (2005) (UK) (theatrical)
Oyster Farmer (2004) – distributor (2006) (UK) (theatrical)
Madhouse (2004) – distributor (2004) (UK)
Ushpizin, Ha- (2004) – distributor (2005) (UK)
School for Seduction (2004) – distributor (2004) (UK)
Tooth (2004) – distributor (UK)
Walk on Water (2004) – distributor (2005) (UK)
We Don't Live Here Anymore (2004) – distributor (2004) (UK)
Touch of Pink (2004) – distributor (2004) (UK)
Grand Theft Parsons (2003) – distributor (UK)
Open Water (2003) – distributor (UK)
The Republic of Love (2003) – distributor (2003-) (UK)
Emile (2003) – distributor (2003-) (UK)
11:14 (2003) – distributor (2005) (UK)
The Hunted (2003) – distributor (2003-) (UK)
Live Forever (2003) – distributor (UK)
House of the Dead (2003) – distributor (2004) (UK)
Monsieur N. (2003) – distributor (UK)
Levity (2003) – distributor (2004) (UK)
Asonot Shel Nina, Ha- (2003) – distributor (2005) (UK)
Bollywood Queen (2002) – distributor (UK)
Cabin Fever (2002) – distributor (UK)
White Oleander (2002) – distributor (2003-) (UK)
Welcome to Collinwood (2002) – distributor (UK)
Stark Raving Mad (2002) – distributor (2003) (UK)
Spider (2002) – distributor (UK)
Ash Wednesday (2002) – distributor (UK)
Riders (2002) – distributor (2003-) (UK)
Bend It Like Beckham (2002) – distributor (2003-) (UK)
The Mothman Prophecies (2002) – distributor (2003-) (UK)
A Walk to Remember (2002) – distributor (2003-) (UK)
Repli-Kate (2002) – distributor (2004) (UK)
Jeepers Creepers (2001) – distributor (UK)
Chica de Río (2001) – distributor (UK)
Sidewalks of New York (2001) – distributor (UK)
The Gift (2000) – distributor (2001) (UK) (theatrical)
Dead Babies (2000) – distributor (UK)
Nasty Neighbours (2000) – distributor (UK)
State and Main (2000) – distributor (2001) (UK) (theatrical)
Maybe Baby (2000) – distributor (UK)

Under Suspicion (2000) – distributor (UK)
Being Considered (2000) – distributor (UK)
Gun Shy (2000) – distributor (UK)
What's Cooking? (2000) – distributor (UK)
Play It to the Bone (1999) – distributor (UK)
One Day in September (1999) – distributor (2000) (UK)
Strange Planet (1999) – distributor (UK)
The Big Kahuna (1999) – distributor (UK)
The Rage: Carrie 2 (1999) – distributor
The Tichborne Claimant (1998) – distributor (UK)
Abre los ojos (1997) – distributor (UK)

20 Conclusion: the new looking glass – a changing wonderland

> The error of those who rely on practice without knowledge. Those who are enamoured of practice without knowledge are like pilots who embark without a helm or compass, and never know for certain where they are going.
>
> (Leonardo da Vinci, *Prophecies*)[1]

The weakest links

Before re-examining the film value chain, the recurring focus of this book, it is instructive to reflect on some of the challenges facing the independent film business beyond Hollywood. In the opening sections of this book (Chapters 1 and 2), we analysed a connecting theme: that the independent film sector suffers from a range of strategic and economic shortcomings that fail to complete the vertical and horizontal challenges required to build a sustainable model. The film value chain is vertically 'disintegrated', taking its form in a protracted series of fragmented links – all carried out a considerable distance from the final market destination: the user. Some argue that dependency on public subsidy, fiscal bail-outs, quotas and broadcaster support, as opposed to an active, vertically integrated range of companies and strategic investment sources, has dissipated in particular the European approach to filmmaking and industrial exploitation. Others point to heavily supported models, such as that in France, as the way to go. As respected film veteran Jakes Eberts argues, 'The French system, for all its warts, provides France with an industry. I think Europe should dupe the French system: it would create lots of jobs, enthusiasm and business.'

The 'auteur' model – one driven by the artist (often in the form of the writer/director/producer) – rather than the market-driven producer has led to a gap between film product and audiences. Specifically, in my book *Developing Feature Films in Europe*,[2] the argument is made that Europe has undervalued the development process both financially and strategically. Around 7 per cent of the US's total audiovisual revenue, and up to 10 per cent of each film's budget, is invested in development. In contrast, Europe tends to spend a much lower percentage, estimated at 1–2 per cent. Two decades ago (*c.*1985), the development process within Europe's film industry was a poorly defined, secondary element to the notion of entering film production. Most practitioners would have assumed that development had something to do with scripts and left it at that. Script editing, producer involvement, adding elements such as the director, talent, etc., to form a package that has financial value are all undervalued and often poorly executed. Part of Europe's problem stems from a very strongly developed 'auteur' culture, where film directors have enjoyed the majority of the power in the filmmaking process. Private sources have remained hard to attract. The risks involved in feature film development are extremely high, hence private investors expect to take stakes that are rewarded both from production budgets and any eventual net profits, if available.

Research and qualitative analysis pointed to the weaknesses in key parts of the early value chain. Writers in particular have tended to be isolated, and cut off from the main arteries of the production/finance value chain. Specifically, not enough time is being given to the development and preparation of films in Europe. The fact that producers only get their production fee on the first day of principal photography, along with repayment of sunk costs in development, has tended to push films into production before fully developed and effectively packaged.

Specifically, independent film production companies operate an inherently weak business model. The independent industry's modus operandi requires them to invest in the development of film projects and pay their associated overhead costs at their own risk. The business plan will normally follow a route whereby they assume that if they can develop a sufficient level of projects that can be placed into production, they can both recoup their development costs, and create sufficient production fees to cover both the work in producing and delivering the film, along with the sunk costs in overheads to date. This is an inherently unstable model and despite considerable public intervention through state aid, the vast majority of the industry is unsustainable on a commercial basis. In addition, the scale and level of scattered, small production entities leaves no leverage for the spreading of risk through portfolio management (e.g. slates of films rather than one-off productions).

In addition, as we have witnessed in detail in this text, the extended film value chain leaves the producer far away from the consumer, and often uninformed about the market demands. Worse than that, emerging producers from around the world are all too often resentful of the roles of sales companies, distributors and their marketing executives – wasting time ignoring or second guessing them rather than understanding the need to work with each link to reach the end-user.

Just as I have addressed issues in the production sector, I have also examined the strategic weaknesses in the sales and distribution sectors, as part of my recurring interest in the different parts of the film value chain. Sunk costs require considerable outlays prior to a sales or distribution operation receiving repayment on its outlays. The producer/sales distributor relationship is inherently unstable; while the distribution sector – albeit a gatekeeper link between product and the audience – is highly competitive and lives under the dominant shadow of the Hollywood global oligopoly. The correlation between the unstable value chain and the difficulties faced by investors in understanding and interfacing strategically with the film business are inextricably linked.

Last, a note about the considerable divide that exists between academic research and formal teaching methods, and the practitioner's role and experience across the film market. Frankly, much of what is published in the academic spectrum is poorly informed, relies heavily on quantitative research rather than qualitative work, and is designed in such a way that bears little to no relevance to the industry and its very pressing strategic challenges. In addition, academic practices appear to insist that research papers and texts are written in a language and syntax that few mortals can join up. I struggle to comprehend much of what has been written to date (with notable exceptions), so those of you out there are not alone. More effort is required to build a new architecture that links academia's insights and the practitioner's world of experience, much in the way that Pixar, the animation studio, for example, fuses the two sides into one productive whole.

Restructuring the value chain

The global film industry is currently experiencing a total restructuring of its value chain. This 'user' and digitally driven restructuring provides a dynamic framework for business strategy analysis, with lessons and future indicators that have wider implications for global industrial strategy. Practitioners are painfully aware of the changing status quo, but all too often, the silo-mentality of the different sections of the industry (the fragmented value chain) means that people see change from only their specific viewpoint, rather than from an informed overview. In addition, practitioners face their own marginal utility challenge – running production, finance, sales or distribution operations, etc., does not allow much time for 'wonderland' research, let alone implementing restructuring programmes to take account of changing demands.

The independent film industry needs relevant research on the restructuring value chain, expedited in a rigorous manner if it is to have real impact. This book's focus and scope was designed to be the forerunner to such a project. The first part of such a project should ideally explore previous and current academic research on value chains, and specifically focus on 'value chain restructuring'. This section will reference and analyse value chain restructuring within significant global industries outside film, while looking at potential similarities with the film industry sector. Recent research and analyses of the software industry all indicate the importance of changing technologies of globalization and its relationship to value chain restructuring. How to analyse the way managers and organizations cope with major change points in their specific sector value chains – notably those restructured as a result of changing technology and consumer demand trends – will form a key element of subsequent methodology to the case study element of this project.

This section will utilize the Learning School's approach to strategy, management and organizing around significant moments of change.[3] It will also draw on tools of study and enquiry emerging from the Cognitive School, notably re management behaviour in response to the pressure of a changing market over a period of time. At a secondary level, it will draw on Henry Mintzberg's Entrepreneurial School – in particular examining entrepreneurial actions re subject matter in terms of 'strategic thinking as seeing' in this changing value chain environment.

Studying the value chain as if its sequences are governed by one entity or organization does not reflect the reality of many industries. Many products are not created and delivered to the end-user by a single company. To accommodate this, Michael Porter (1985)[4] created the concept of the 'value system', which includes the individual value chains of all the separate companies or players who are co-operating within an industry to deliver a final product. Perhaps reflecting that integration, writers and academics in the media sector have gradually dispensed with the distinction between the value chain and the value system, and refer to them both as the value chain, encompassing all the separate stages of value addition, whether within one company or several. As a result, this chapter will follow current usage, and will use the value chain concept to apply to all the various stages of product creation, distribution and exploitation across the global film business footprint. Methodological approaches to the study of multi-territory and global value chains will also inform the subsequent research design.

The research site: the case of the global film industry

The global film industry is potentially able to provide a rich and fruitful research basket for those wishing in particular to straddle industrial practice with academic study. The entertainment business as a whole has a high economic and strategic importance, along with high media visibility. Specifically, the film business offers up rich data that traverse both an entire product's lifecycle and a range of connected products (prequels, sequels, spin-offs, merchandising, etc.), and because it has a global reach that offers the potential to throw light on emerging questions that remain unanswered.

Value chain models cited by previous and current academics have been predominantly concerned with major Studio films and Hollywood Studios, as opposed to 'independent' films (which are more widespread in European production in particular). Academic research has arguably had negligible impact on practice despite considerable interest and focus over the past two decades. It is my view that the changing film value chain will have a significant impact on future windows, revenue streams and film business strategies far into the twenty-first century – both in the Hollywood studio sector and in the independent film business. The impact of these shifts and what the industry (and its key sectors) is both currently doing and strategically planning have interest far beyond the film sector alone.

Historically, film distribution has been the main risk-taker in the film value chain. It has acted as a 'gatekeeper', essentially selecting and determining which films get made, marketed and distributed. The distributor – whether a Hollywood Studio or a powerful integrated independent company – has invested (often co-invested rather than putting up 100 per cent of a budget) in production costs, and has borne the majority of the prints and advertising costs (e.g. marketing costs). In turn, the distributor has been the principal beneficiary of success in the marketplace. Distributors enter into sliding-scale deals in exhibition, royalty deals in the home entertainment and performance-related deals in pay-TV, etc. A studio recovers its marketing costs in first position and takes significant distribution fees before passing any revenues back to the producer or his/her sales agent.

This pivotal role has arisen because of the specific economic characteristics of the film industry. Huge rising costs on production and marketing (keeping a film's recoupment far away from cash break-even), the high failure rate and, until recently, the capacity constraints in exhibition, have all enabled the distributor to remain the key lynchpin that dictates the majority of what gets made, and who gets what.

The above model and its associated value chain are under increasing pressure to change. The arrival of direct links between the producer and the consumer, in particular via the Internet, is now fundamentally changing the economic characteristics, but also its architecture. Production and publishing roles, as per the music and book publishing models, are becoming increasingly important at the cost of distribution's previously dominant position. Just as television broadcasters are being forced to adapt to a consumer who wants a programme instantly, rather than follow a forced schedule (or anachronistically copy a show for later viewing), so too is the distributor finding pressure on what the film consumer demands within their own pressurized leisure time zones, rather than what suits the distributor's time scale of delivery.

The compression of the film value chain, whereby the producer is brought much closer to the consumer is of significant interest. Niche audiences, once able to be tapped and marketed directly, have significant value if able to be reached less expensively. Communities offer major core audiences.

The 'opening' of the market, with the distributor's role being taken over either side – both by the producer and the exhibitor – changes strategic approaches and thinking on a significant scale. Internet marketing and its growth in sophistication and specific demographic reach, will encourage end-users such as cinema owners and chains, pay-TV operators and even video game operators to enter the production market themselves. A world where these players commission development and feature film production, which in turn help drive their respective platforms, would appear to cut out third-party distribution completely. The cost of marketing will be borne by the production financier or the exhibitor rather than the distributor.

The new film value chain is likely to become considerably truncated. Theatrical release of feature film product will continue to play a dominant role. However, the complex system of connected windows for exploitation is going to look considerably flatter, as we witnessed in Chapter 2:

New film exploitation value chain

1 Theatrical release
2 Video-on-demand via the Internet
    (All previous rights and windows, including DVD, home video, pay-TV, free-TV, etc., are likely to be submerged into one set of exploitation rights – VOD through the Internet, which in turn will be downloadable within a household and onto a television screen, etc.)

The arrival of such a new 'flattening' landscape is both intriguing and perplexing. Such radical upheaval directly challenges the entire economic and strategic preconceptions upon which the film industry has been built. The general challenge has been to overcome the pyrotechnical drag; hence the profit has always been derived from re-selling the same product again and again, through a range of different windows. But Internet distribution directly challenges that model. From a distributor's perspective, they will demand a larger price from 'second media' because they know that less than 5 per cent of films break-even at the box office stage of exploitation.

'You're facing a situation where you make a film', explains Redbus's chairman Simon Franks.

> Let's say it does £5m at the UK box office, which is always the hurdle to profitability in most films, and there is still a prints and advertising loss at that level.

But now you need to make all your P&A back and pay for the film and the profit just from one source, which is the second and now only window. I think that is probably going to be Apple, but we don't know yet. I don't like the idea of that. I don't like the idea of having to rely on just one window and one entity in order to become profitable.

The upheaval of the film value chain, and the shrinking of the exploitation windows are changing the film industry beyond recognition. As technological tipping points arrive – such as the speed and ease of downloading and moving images across a range of household screens – old industry structures will need to be challenged and re-drawn. And with the changes in recoupment and exploitation structures will come significant changes in the way financing structures fund films outside the Hollywood Studio system. And so the independent film industry is going have to be smart, reinvent itself, and do some real fusing between research and practice if it is to curb 'watching the old win'.

Further reading

Books

Acland, Charles, *Screen Traffic: Movies, Multiplexes, and Global Culture*, Duke University Press, 2003.
Adler, Tim, *The Producers*, Methuen Drama, 2004.
Bilton, Chris, *Management and Creativity: From Creative Industries to Creative Management*, Wiley-Blackwell, 2006.
Burke, Rory and Barron, Steve, *Project Management Leadership: Building Creative Teams*, Burke Publishing, 2007.
Epstein, J. Edward, *The Big Picture: The New Logic of Money and Power in Hollywood*, Random House, 2005.
Goffee, Rob and Jones, Gareth, *Harvard Business Review on Managing People*, Harvard Business School Press, 1999.
Gomery, Douglas, *Shared Pleasures: A History of Movie Presentation in the United States*, University of Wisconsin Press, 1992.
Hanson, Stuart, *From Silent Screen to Multi-Screen: A History of Cinema Exhibition in Britain since 1896*, Manchester University Press, 2007.
Hark, Ina Rae, *Exhibition, the Film Reader*, 1st edn, Routledge, 2001.
Henry, Jane, *Creative Management*, Sage Publications, 2001.
Ilott, Terry and Puttnam, David, *Budgets and Markets: Study of the Budgeting of European Films*, Routledge, 1996.
Jancovich, Mark, *The Place of the Audience: Cultural Geographies of Film Consumption*, British Film Institute, January 2008.
Kent, Nicolas, *Naked Hollywood: Money and Power in the Movies Today*, St Martin's Press, 1991.
Kula, Sam, *Appraising Moving Images: Assessing the Archival and Monetary Value of Film and Video Records*, Scarecrow Press, 2002.
Mintzberg, H., Ahlstrand, B. and Lampel, J., *Strategy Safari*, 2nd edn, 2009.
Silber, Lee, *Career Management for the Creative Person*, Three Rivers Press, 1999.
Squire, J. E., *The Movie Business Book*, 2nd edn, Open University Press, 1992.
Tolkin, Michael, *The Player*, Avalon Publishing, 1988.
Torr, Gordon, *Managing Creative People: Lessons in Leadership for the Ideas Economy*, Wiley, 2008.

Vogel, Harold, *Entertainment Industry Economics: A Guide for Financial Analysis*, Cambridge University Press, 2007.

Waller, A. Gregory, *Movie Going in America: A Sourcebook in the History of Film Exhibition*, Wiley-Blackwell, 2001.

Wasko, Janet and McDonald, Paul, *Movies and Money: Financing the American Film Industry*, Sage Publications, 1982.

Wasko, Janet and McDonald, Paul, *The Contemporary Hollywood Film Industry*, Blackwell Publishing, 2008.

Academic articles

Bakhshi, Hasan, 'The Plateau in Cinema Attendances and Drop in Video Sales in the UK: The Role of Digital Leisure Substitutes', October 2006, UKFC.

Bloore, Peter, 'Re-defining the Independent Film Value Chain', February 2009, UKFC.

Catmull, Ed, 'How Pixar Fosters Collective Creativity', *Harvard Business Review*, September 2008.

Chapman, Eli, 'Models for Sustainable Cinema', 2005, www. Chapmanlogic.com

Elberse, Anita and Eliashberg, Jehoshua, 'Demand and Supply Dynamics for Sequentially Released Products in International Markets: The Case of Motion Pictures', *Marketing Science*, 22(3), 2003, pp.329–354.

Eliashberg, Jehoshua and Sawhney, Mohanbir S., 'Modeling Goes to Hollywood: Predicting Individual Differences in Movie Enjoyment', *Management Science*, 40(9), 1994, pp.1151–1173.

Eliashberg, Jehoshua and Shugan, Steven M., 'Film critics: Influencers or predictors?', *Journal of Marketing*, 61(April), 1997, pp.68–78.

Eliashberg, Jehoshua, Elberse, Anita and Leenders, Mark, 'The Motion Picture Industry: Critical Issues in Practice, Current Research & New Research Directions', Erasmus Research Institute of Management, Harvard Business School, 2005.

Hennig-Thurau, Thorsten, Henning, Victor, Sattler, Henrik, Eggers, Felix and Houston, Mark B., 'Optimizing the Sequential Distribution Model for Motion Pictures', American Marketing Association, Summer 2006.

Hutton, Will and Schneider, Phillipe, 'The Failure of Market Failure', NESTA, November 2008.

Introna, Lucas D., Moore, Hope and Cushman, Mike, 'The Virtual Organisation – Technical or Social Innovation? Lessons from the Industry', London School of Economics, 1999.

Knapp, S. and Sherman, B. L., 'Motion Picture Attendance: A Market Segmentation Approach', in B. A. Austin (Ed.), *Current Research in Film: Audiences, Economics, and Law* (vol. 2), Ablex, 1986, pp.35–46.

Lampel, J. and Shamsie, J., 'Critical Push: Strategies for Creating Momentum in the Motion Picture Industry', *Journal of Management*, 26(2), 2000, pp.233–257.

Miller, D., 'Strategic Responses to the Three Kinds of Uncertainty: Product Line Simplicity at the Hollywood Film Studios', *Journal of Management*, 25(1), 1999, p.97.

Miller, D. and Shamsie, J., 'Learning Across the Life Cycle: Experimentation and Performance Among the Hollywood Studio Heads', *Strategic Management Journal*, 22, 2001, pp.725–745.

Pautz, Michelle, 'The Decline in Average Weekly Cinema Attendance: 1930–2000', *Issues in Political Economy*, vol. 11, 2002.

'Screen Digest Report on the Implications of Digital Technology for the Film Industry', United Kingdom Department for Culture, Media and Sport, Creative Industries Division, September 2002.

Zufryden, F. S., 'Linking Advertising to Box Office Performance of New Film Releases: A Marketing Planning Model', *Journal of Advertising Research*, July–August, 1996.

Other – newspaper articles, DVD, etc.

Amdur, Meredith, 'Is H'wood's biz model outdated?', *Variety*, December 2002.

Barnes, Brooks, 'Pixar's Art has Profit Watchers Edgy', *The New York Times*, 5 April 2009.

Fritz, Ben, 'Net Heads Finally Get Some Respect', *Variety*, April 2004.

Guider, Elizabeth, 'The Incredible Shrinking Aud', *Variety*, January 2004.

Iwerks, Leslie, 'The Pixar Story', Buena Vista International, DVD Release November 2008.

Glossary

Above-the-line Usually refers to the key cast, director, writer and producer of a project. These are considered above-the-line costs in a film's budget.

Adjusted gross receipts formula The same deal as in the gross receipts formula, but with costs taken off the top. Normally used to refer to gross receipts less all distribution costs through the exploitation chain.

Admissions Term detailing the audience numbers of a film through its theatrical release in cinemas.

Ancillary markets Generally meant to describe any markets outside of the film industry's original one of theatrical exploitation in cinemas. This is usually home video or television, but includes airlines and shipping, etc.

Angel investors Individuals who invest in projects on a one-off basis rather than as part of an overall strategy, and have low overheads and tend to trust their own judgement and instincts on an investment.

Assumptions A key component of a business plan, particularly as it is one of the most contentious. Assumptions are dependent on the managers'/entrepreneurs' commercial estimates (at their simplest) of costs versus income, next to timelines. Assumptions are the strategic a priori positions the business managers take on the different variables necessary for the running of the business, such as budgets, numbers, level of commissions, projected fees, P&A budgets, etc.

Avids Denotes a type of audience member that is a regular filmgoer compared to the rest of the population.

Back-end The profits generated by a film after all costs have been repaid and said film reaches the cash break-even point. However back-end is sometimes also defined more broadly as a participation in the revenues generated by the distribution of a film, and in the case of certain talent this may come before the film itself reaches break-even.

Balance sheet A financial statement that lists the assets, liabilities and ownership equity of a business. It is meant to provide a snapshot of a business at a specific point in time, usually the end of the year.

Below-the-line Usually refers to the direct costs of a production, and cast and crew hired once the pre-production stage is underway.

Block booking The practice, now illegal, of selling a group of films to an exhibitor as a 'block' or single unit. It was prevalent among studios until outlawed by the *United States v Paramount Pictures* Supreme Court decision of 1948.

Board A team including executive directors and non-executive directors, plus company secretary that oversee a company's operation. Executive directors run the company on a day-to-day basis. Non-executive directors attend board meetings and advise on the overall strategy of the company.

Break-even point   The point at which a production has paid back all its costs and is entering the net profits stage of exploitation.

Business model   The strategic framework that outlines how an idea/company/partnership can generate money. A business will use such a model to potentially create value in the marketplace.

Business plan   A plan of the cash flow, returns, costs and sources of revenue for a business, often expanded to cover a projected five years of lifetime for the business. Will include an executive summary, business opportunity and model, exit strategy for investors, market analysis, management team, organizational structure, assumptions and financials, etc.

Buzz   A marketing measure designed to represent the amount of discussion and public interest an upcoming film is generating, mainly by tracking Internet outlets such as blogs.

Cash flow   A term used to refer to the movement of cash within a business. It is a particularly useful concept in determining the liquidity of a business and whether it can meet overheads and debtors.

Cash-flow statement   A financial statement meant to show how the company will manage incoming revenues into the business as related to its outgoing costs. This is often done on a year-by-year basis or weekly in more detailed cash-flow plans. The cash-flow statement should reveal the point at which the company will be most in the red throughout the operation of its business, a key component in deciding the amount of capital the business will need to operate.

Catchment area   The radius around a cinema from which an exhibitor can expect to draw an audience, taking into account drive times, competitors and location.

Chain of title   The documentation that establishes the producer's ownership of the rights in the script, and which entitles the producer to make and market the film. This set of documents usually includes the scriptwriters' agreements, development agreements with funding agencies and options or rights assignments. In some cases the set comprises many documents, especially where a project has been in development over a long period of time, or where the script has been adapted from other sources, or where a number of writers have contributed to the script. In others, the set may simply be one document.

Classification   The practice of assigning different age ratings to movies in order to denote the intended audience for a given film and keep younger audiences from watching mature content. In the United States, this is governed by the MPA and was originally a pre-emptive measure to avoid censorship from government.

CNC   Centre National de la Cinematographie, the main government body administering France's film industry regulations and practices, as well as funds intended to support said industry.

Completion guarantee   Also known as a completion bond, this is a legal undertaking by a guarantor that a film production, based on preapproved specifications, will be completed and delivered by a certain date in the financiers' contract with the producer. The guarantee is not an insurance bond, but the guarantor commits to finding the best way for a project to reach completion and effective delivery or for the film's financial partners to an agreed price committed and advanced up to that point.

Concept poster   A poster meant for business-to-business marketing conveying the idea and 'feel' of a project in order to raise funds, before it goes into production.

Concession sales   Sales at cinemas that do not come directly from selling film tickets, such as drinks, sweets and popcorn.

Co-production   A film that involves more than one party in the production process, through co-operation as a joint venture or partnership, or as part of an officially sanctioned co-production treaty.

Counter-programming   The practice of releasing a film with a target audience different from that of another major release that weekend, usually during a spot in the calendar that is in high demand.

Coverage   A document that analyses a screenplay on behalf of a production company and recommends 'passing' on the property or considering it for investment or at least further development. Some coverage documents have detailed script notes sometimes used by producers in the development process.

Cross-collateralization   A method by which companies that have bought rights licences can 'cross' these separate rights in their accounting so that the gains in one offset the losses in another. For example, a distributor that has the rights to a film in both France and Italy, and makes money in one territory and losses in another, can use the gains in one to offset the losses in another before handing overages to a producer or sales agent.

Day and date release   Describes the simultaneous theatrical release of a film across a range of territories. Also used to describe a release strategy for a film in which a title is released simultaneously in its theatrical and home entertainment formats, with no 'windows' system.

Deliverables   The contractually agreed items that a producer needs to deliver to distributors for them to accede full delivery and successfully place and market a film. Will include items such as chain of title, all key contracts, stills photography, concept art, transcript of all dialogue in the film, technical materials, copies, etc.

Delivery   The contractually agreed point at which a distributor acknowledges full technical receipt of a film (creative, legal and technical) and begins its task of releasing and marketing the film.

Development   The stage of filmmaking where a script is put together or written, underlying rights are acquired, a treatment is created, key cast and crew are decided on, a preliminary budget and schedule crafted, and the overall package of what the film will be is put together. Some parts of marketing may begin during this stage.

Digital inter-positive   A digital copy of a film before a 35mm film print is struck for theatrical exhibition. It is considered more flexible to edit than the old film interpositives.

Digital rights management (DRM)   An umbrella term that refers to any technology intended to protect digital content from piracy or unlawful access.

Distributor   A distributor of a film is any company that buys the licence of exploitation of a film in order to be able to exploit the title in the theatrical and/or subsidiary markets. Distributors are therefore the final intermediary between a production and the exhibitor that will show the film on its screens.

Domestic   A key geographical sector of the film market that usually refers to the United States and also commonly Canada. Its economic power and large audiences makes it a key territory in film contracts, although a hard one to break into outside the Hollywood majors. Confusion arises when other territories are referred to as domestic, so that UK producers and distributors would consider that to be their 'domestic market'.

DVD   Or 'digital versatile disc', is a format for storing images and sound that uses an optical disc to store larger amounts of data than the similar CD-ROM.

Electronic press kit   The digital/video tape version of all marketing materials, often included in a CD-ROM or DVD. Will include interviews with director, stars, etc., and key sound bites cut for out-takes on TV, etc.

Elements   The key components of a film's package: director, producer, stars, script, budget, etc. Also used to describe key elements of a marketing campaign, usually referring to stars, notable crew, genre or other outstanding features.

When describing key talent, they are sometimes referred to contractually as 'essential elements' which has considerable impact on contracts, insurance and the bond.

Entrepreneur   An individual who is initiator, owner and leader of a business venture and therefore often has a large stake in seeing it succeed. Normally they step to one side and appoint day-to-day managers once a new venture is launched. Also refers to an angel investor whose primary source of wealth was through leading businesses in this manner.

Equity   Film investment that owns a portion of the film property, and therefore its profits or back-end.

Eurimages   The pan-European fund for multilateral co-productions. To qualify projects have to be signatory members of Eurimages, the only major European territory not currently a signatory being the United Kingdom. Founded by the Council of Europe, it is based in Strasbourg. Eurimages also provides distribution support in addition to production funding.

Exhibition   The stage of the film value chain where films are exhibited at cinemas, often referred to as 'theatrical'. Exhibition is generally considered a retail business, different in terms of commercial forces from the rest of the film value chain.

Exit   For an investment, the point at which an investor's capital invested is returned and he exits the business. Often described as five years in most business plans but some investors look for much faster exits (Hedge funds typically). A subject of much strategic debate post the financial crisis.

Facility deal   A deal where an investor provides facilities in exchange (or part) for copyright ownerships in a film, usually referring to post-production houses lending a production their services for free or a cut rate in exchange for an equity position.

Film copyright   The copyright created by the making of a filmed production. Copyrighted elements included in the film may comprise the soundtrack, costumes or characters. These rights are exploited by their licensing to third parties.

Film franchise   A term relating to the intellectual property involving the characters, settings and trademarks of an original film. This is built by creating a series of films and promoting its characters, settings and trademarks through advertising and merchandising. Film franchises thus often cross over to other forms of media and different types of products.

Film licensing agreement   Term referring to the standard agreement between a distributor and exhibitor, detailing the film rental fee, the split of gross box office takings that the exhibitor will pass on to the distributor, after taxes.

Film value chain   This term applies to the chain of processes including the key creative and financial steps that are undertaken through conception to completion of a film product. Ultimately, each step theoretically adds 'value' to a film product, enabling completion and ultimately its delivery to an end-user.

Finance   Film finance is loans towards a production or slate of productions provided against as high a position of security as possible. Film finance has no position in the underlying rights of a film once its loan and cost of the deal has been repaid.

Floor   The maximum share of the gross box office paid by the exhibitor to the distributor, after taxes.

Foreign, or international   Considered to be defining any territories outside North America. An 'international' sales agent, then, is a company whose business model is predicated on handling rights outside North America.

Four wall deal   A deal made with an exhibitor in which a screen is completely rented out by the distributor, so that all receipts go straight to that party. The exhibitor only charges a small administration cost. Rare, unless a distributor is trying to show the film in a minimum number of screens to qualify it as a theatrical picture.

Free-TV   A television business model that is 'free', as the main source of revenue is from advertising or arguably public licence fee, rather than directly from viewers paying commercial subscriptions or pay-per-view fees.

GATT   The General Agreement on Trade and Tariffs signed in 1993, which left out film and television audiovisual productions due to the inability of the USA and Europe to come to a satisfying agreement on whether film should be treated as a cultural or commercial product.

Genre   The 'type' of narrative followed by a motion picture, e.g. horror, thriller, romantic comedy. Often a key component in a film's marketing strategy.

Green light   The point at which a film or movie is given the go ahead by its financiers to begin drawing cash flow from the production account and start the production process.

Gross box office The amount of takings (usually expressed in dollars) a film makes during its theatrical run, before taxes. This is also before cinemas have taken their share, and costs.

Gross receipts formula   An arrangement between distributor and exhibitor where the distributor receives a specific percentage of box office receipts for a film, with the percentage dropping over time as the exhibitor keeps holding on to the movie.

Hedge fund   A fund specialized in generating outsized returns through the practice of leveraging after having raised large sums thanks to cheap debt (when available).

Hollywood   Once a specific geographic location where all of California's studios are based, the term now loosely refers to the Los Angeles-based film community and the studio system.

Home video   A film or other media that is rented or bought in order to be used privately at home. The term 'video' was originally meant to describe the mode of delivery, the VHS or Betamax tape, but now most commonly refers to DVD. The term has been uncomfortably adapted to include 'video-on-demand', which applies to the availability of films via the Internet.

Horizontal An approach of looking at the exploitation of film rights across independent territories where those rights may be exploited separately from other geographically defined territories or apply to entire footprints, such as Universe, World, etc.

House nut Also called the 'house allowance', the basic costs of running screenings for a film, which the exhibitor takes out of the gross box office take for that film.

In kind Payment to a production that is based on goods and services provided, rather than cash which the producer can draw from an account.

Intellectual property (IP) Legal property rights over creations of the mind, both artistic and commercial, and the corresponding fields of law.

Internal rate of return Most commonly referred to as IRR, the annualized effective compounded rate of an investment, the return that an investment returns to its investor each year from said investment, as described by a percentage of the original.

Investment Film investment is money invested in a film with a view to being recouped behind finance in the recoupment order but taking a share in the backend of the film's profits in perpetuity.

IPR Intellectual Property Rights is a legal definition of property rights over the creations of the mind. The creative industries primarily revolve around the exploitation of intellectual property rights.

Library of rights A collection of rights to productions that have gone through their first cycle of exploitation (meaning all first run windows, from cinema to free-TV), owned by a company in the film business in order to cash flow future productions or leverage to raise money and expand on further investments.

Loan capital Money raised for a business through the acquisition of a loan, to be repaid at a later date together with interest accrued.

Logline The description of a project in either one or a few short lines, often as an introduction to a treatment or script when presented to financiers or distributors.

Manager An executive director, appointed by a Board to run a company on a day-to-day basis. Many have a stake in the company either through shares or share options.

Market screenings Screenings are often set up by sales agents at a market in order to show a film, portions of a film, rushes or promos to distributors and thus secure a deal. Screenings can be restricted to distributors of certain territories or specific distributors within a territory. Most market screenings still take place at the Cannes, Berlin and the American Film Market.

MEDIA MEDIA is the programme established by the European Commission to support the audiovisual industries in Europe. It covers training, development, promotion, distribution and the support of film festivals, etc.

Minimum guarantee Also termed an 'Advance', this is an advance payment to the producers of a film by rights-based financiers in exchange for the rights to a territory or territories. Minimum guarantees are usually based on expected receipts from the exploitation of rights in those territories.

MPAA (or MPA) The Motion Picture Association of America, the body founded in 1922 to represent the business interests of the six major studios.

Multiplex A complex of multiple screens, generally ten or more. The multiplex concept began in the United States in the 1970s and 1980s with the development of larger malls and big box stores like Walmart. Some multiplexes, such as the Kinepolis in Brussels, have as many as twenty screens.

Net profits Returns after taxes, exhibitor's cut, distributor's expenses and fee, collection agents' fees and royalty, sales agents' expenses and royalties, and the production budget and costs of financing have been taken off. Given all these parties to be paid beforehand, reaching break-even point and profitability is a challenging task in the film business.

New media A catch-all term now outdated given that much of this media has existed for a number of years. It is meant to define new forms of delivery of media, such as video-on-demand, Internet Protocol television (IPTV), mobile/cell phone film downloads or digital projection.

Off-balance sheet financing A form of funding that avoids placing an owner's equity, liabilities or assets on the company's balance sheet. Generally this is achieved by placing these items in some other company's balance sheet.

On-the-lot deal A deal where a production company has offices on the lot of a Studio and usually has its development costs and annual overheads paid by said Studio.

Opening weekend The first weekend of release in theatrical exhibition of a film production, usually in its domestic market. Thought to be the most important determinant of a film's eventual success at the box office, although this tends to apply to Studio and larger budget pictures rather than specialized product.

Overhead The direct cost of running a business, be it office space rental, office materials, travels, etc. For example, for a sales agent these would be the main office, costs of paying staff, travelling to festivals and markets, and creating initial promotional materials. Some of that overhead is offset by sales and marketing budgets, which allow the sales company to effectively reclaim marketing costs to an agreed level, and apportion main market overheads against its slate of films.

P&A budget The budget a distributor will use to release a film at theatres, referring to 'prints and advertising', i.e. the cost of new prints and the advertising needed to support the release of those prints. The 'prints' part of the formula might become outdated with the introduction of digital distribution.

Package A collection of the essential elements of a film, usually including the screenplay or treatment, cast, director and budget.

Pari passu A Latin phrase meaning 'in equal step', referring to a recoupment order where investors recoup equal to all other investors.

Pay-TV A television business model that is based on a subscription service and/or pay-per-view. Usually offered by cable and satellite channels.

Peer to peer (P2P) A system of networking computers so that the resources of the whole network can be pooled together, usually for the purpose of file sharing. Unlike client–server networks, a central server or host is not needed.

Pitch The strategy and presentation used to sell a project or idea to financiers, sales companies and distributors. Actually, each part of the player value chain finds itself pitching to each other (e.g. distributor to exhibitor, sales to distributor, sales to financier, producer to sales, etc.).

Platform A segment of the audience to which the film will initially be targeted and from which it can ideally be launched to pick up wider audiences. Ultimately the aim is to widen to become a 'cross-over' hit.

Playability   A film marketing term meant to determine how much a movie will satisfy its core audience, and the chance of repeat viewings from that audience.

Points   A term used when referring to the percentages of net profits allotted to each investor. Points can also be awarded for services rendered, as is often done with above-the-line talent.

Pre-production   The stage of filmmaking where preparation for the shooting period begins, generally meant to be funded by cash flow from the production account but often drawdown comes very late in independent film productions. During this period, a full team is put together, and salaries are paid to the production staff to begin prepping their work.

Pre-sales   Sales made to distributors internationally prior to the film beginning production, therefore contributing to the budget of said film.

Print   A copy of a filmed production meant for theatrical exhibition developed from the dupe negative, developed from the inter-positive print, itself developed from the original film negative.

Private equity   Refers to institutional investors who take an equity position on a film, providing production finance in exchange for a portion of that film's copyright.

Producer   A film producer is the manager of the process of creating a film. He or she is usually the first person involved in a project and the last person to follow it through to completion. The producer initiates, co-ordinates, supervises and controls matters such as fund-raising, hiring key personnel and arranging for distributors. The producer is involved throughout all phases of the filmmaking process from development to completion of a project.

Production   Film production is the stage of filmmaking when the film begins to be shot and for which most of the elements of the film have been budgeted for. It is sometimes used as a synonym for 'film' or 'movie'. Not to be confused with the wider-ranging role of the producer, which involves many other stages of filmmaking.

Production screening   A preview screening of a film that is not near completion and will probably be missing visual effects, soundtrack or an editing polish. These screenings attempt to gauge an audience's reactions to specific aspects of a film that could be improved before the film's edit is locked.

Profit and loss account   A financial statement that describes how the company will transform revenue into net income, by showing the sources of revenue and the costs that will have to be taken out for the business to be operational.

Pro-rata   Money recouped in proportion to money invested in a film project, i.e. if an investor has put up half the budget of a film, the pro rata share would be 50 per cent.

Quota protection   Protecting a local market by imposing quotas that limit the number of films foreign to that market that are allowed to be screened in it.

R&D   Research and development, an upfront initial investment normally described as sunk costs in order to research possible innovations and practices necessary for the success of the business.

Recoupment position   The placement of each party's repayment, whether finance or investment. For example, the recoupment order at which an investor in a film begins to see a return for their investment, as relative to the other partners in the film.

Release pattern   Denotes the number of screens or prints, the date, seasonal period and cities chosen for the release of a film. Screenings at a large number of cities across the country are described as 'wide releases' while targeting specific screens and cities for a larger expansions are 'platform releases'.

Rental   Industry slang for film rental fee, the distributor's share of the gross box office, after taxes and the exhibitor takes its own share and house nut. This number is quite wide, and can range from low 20s to a 50–50 share.

Right of authorship   A feature of European continental law that considers the author of a work to be its first owner. This is in contrast to Anglo-Saxon law, where the producer holds this position.

Rights-based financiers   Financiers that exist within the film value chain and whose business model is essentially based on the acquisition of these rights. Examples would be distributors and broadcasters.

Run   A film's run is the amount of weeks said film keeps showing at the theatres.

Sale and leaseback   A now obsolete tax arrangement under sections 42 and 48 of UK law in which the producer sold the film to an investor with taxable profits sufficient to utilize the tax relief – typically a film partnership of individuals with higher rate tax liability – and leased the film back over 15 years. Most of the sale price is placed on deposit to secure the repayment instalments, with the remainder the producer's net benefit. Copyright and exploitation rights then returned to the producer.

Sales agent   A sales agent is appointed to represent a producer/financier to sell/license a film to distributors internationally. If the company buys rights rather than just represents it is technically an 'international distributor'. Sales agents are often credited in the independent market as executive producers, as they are key to financing films even if not putting up an advance for rights.

Sales estimates   A document detailing what the sales agent expects to receive from distributors in each territory for a given title. These are often broken down into two columns, the 'Ask', what the sales agent hopes to get, and the 'Take', the least the sales agent is ready to accept for a given title.

Screen average   The average earned by a film at each screen during a run at the cinemas. This is an important indicator of a film's success beyond its gross numbers, and highly relevant to specialized pictures' benchmarking of success.

Script editor   As with many publishing editors, a role meant for an experienced script reader, which encompasses pointing out structural and stylistic problems within a screenplay.

Scriptment   Popularized by James Cameron, a longer version of a treatment, of about 20 to 40 pages, including dialogue and more detailed descriptions of each scene.

Sensitivity testing   The process of testing the assumptions contained within a business plan given research into its specific market, or variation of the timings, hits and failures projected.

Share capital   Money raised through selling a stake in a business, done by the selling of shares that represent a stake that an investor holds.

Slate deal   A deal with investors, usually by a producer or sales agent, to deliver a certain number of films over a specified time period, committing to more than the usual one single project.

Slate/portfolio management   In film, a strategy used to spread the risk of a singular investment by spreading that investment across many projects. Studios commit to this strategy by releasing around 25–40 films a year, not being overly exposed to failure by any single one.

Spec script　A script written not for a fee but with the hope of it being sold to a studio or production company.

Special purpose vehicle (SPV)　Also known as a 'special purpose entity', it is a legal entity created for a temporary, circumstantial purpose. In film, this is often a limited partnership set up to handle all the accounts and place rights for one specific project.

Split rights　The practice of companies coming together to acquire a totality of rights, which are then split among the different parties. For example, two studios could fund the totality of a film's budget, then split the revenues these rights create horizontally, having one handle domestic distribution and the other international (aka foreign). Rights can also be split vertically, having for example one company handle theatrical distribution and the other home entertainment rights. Studio rights are normally completely cross-collateralized.

Still photography　Photographs taken throughout a production in order to give an idea of concept and atmosphere and to be used as key marketing tools. A key component of a film's marketing campaign, and one often neglected by independent producers.

Studio　One of the major six distribution companies, based in California, that currently dominate the film market. These include Disney, Sony, 20th Century Fox, Universal, Paramount and Warner Brothers. Once part of this club, Metro Goldwyn Mayer was acquired by Sony in 2005, leaving United Artists behind as an independent entity. These Studios are defined by their ability to distribute films worldwide and therefore being able to fund the entirety of the budget of a film and control the creation of all rights from development onwards. They have large libraries that allow them to take higher risks and operate 360 degree business models that are considerably wider than just feature film exploitation.

Studios are considered primarily distribution entities.

Sunk costs　Costs committed to a project (or company) that are non-recoverable and are therefore 'sunk' into the production (or company).

Tagline　A slogan, often placed prominently in the poster for a film and related marketing materials, meant to encapsulate the films' 'feel' or 'hook' to an audience quickly and directly.

Tax fund investors　Investors who leverage tax regulation in order to see returns.

Tax funding　Film financing agencies based around government tax credits for film projects.

Teaser trailer　A trailer considerably less long that a usual trailer (a trailer is normally around 90–120 seconds, and a teaser maybe 15–30 seconds) and made up of a series of images from the film with no narrative line, teasing the elements of the full-length trailer.

Tent pole films　Films of a large budget (generally US$100m and up, but rising each year) that are traditionally released in the summer and meant to play with a wide range of audience demographics and both domestically and internationally.

Territory　A contractually defined geographical area where a set of film rights may be individually exploited. Note that territories as contractually defined usually but not always relate to how they are defined politically. For example, the United

Kingdom and Ireland, Australia and New Zealand, are often considered one territory in contracts even if they are separate political entities. The French Territory often includes its overseas colonies, as do a number of larger territories.

Theatrical   Usually the first stage of exploitation of a film, that of a theatrical showing in cinemas. Also known as the 'exhibition' window.

Track record   The financial performance of the films released by a company or with the talent and critical review in question. Awards play a key role in track record in addition to performance.

Tracking   The practice of weekly surveys of potential film audiences, conducted mainly by Studios, meant to gauge what upcoming releases are in the public consciousness.

Trade press   Magazines and dailies that purely focus on covering the film and entertainment industry, and do so usually with a business-to-business perspective. Significant titles include *Variety*, *The Hollywood Reporter* and *Screen International*.

Trailer   Initially placed at the end of another film's showing (hence 'trailer') but now of course shown before the main presentation, these short advertisements for a film seek to convey to an audience in a few minutes (no more than 2 normally) the plot and essential elements, and highlights stars/performances if in the film.

Treatment   A long-form summary of the intended screenplay's plot. This rarely ever includes dialogue and set pieces, which are normally written in the full work later.

Underlying rights   The bundle of rights in the copyright of the script acquired by the producer through the chain of title and which includes all or some of the right to make and license film rights based on the script, the ancillary rights and the right to sequels, spin-off or remakes.

Venture capital   A type of private equity provided to early-stage companies with a high potential for growth, with a view to earn back the investment through an Initial Public Offering, a trade sale and sometimes a management buyout.

Vertical   An approach of looking at the exploitation of film rights up and down the different stages of such exploitation, starting with theatrical, then home video rental and sales, television, etc.

Vertical integration   The strategy is for a company to hold as much of the processes of the film value chain under one roof in order to minimize overhead costs and maximize profits. Studios are vertically integrated companies that control everything from development to distribution.

Video-on-demand   A system using video compression to allow television programmes and films to be delivered to an audience on demand, rather than at a set schedule. The term is now used widely for all film downloads on the Internet.

Waterfall   A term that is used to describe a range of re-payment and profit sharing orders in which different creditors/investors receive interest and principal payments at different stages of recoupment and in some cases lower-tiered creditors may receive only interest payments, etc.

Windows   The different chronological stages at which a film is exploited, starting with theatrical, then home video, pay-TV and free-TV, etc.

World   Or more precisely 'world rights', when all countries are bundled into one territory. Licensing world rights essentially means giving a licence to exploit a film in all known territories across the world.

Notes

1 Global film: a changing world

1 Flat Earth Mission Statement: http://www.alaska.net/~clund/e_djublonskopf/FlatMisStat.htm
2 Thomas L. Friedman, *The World is Flat: The Globalized World in the Twenty-First Century*, London: Penguin, 2007.
3 A. Scott Berg, *Goldwyn*, London: Hamish Hamilton, 1989.
4 Including Paramount, Fox, Sony/Columbia, Universal, Warner Brothers and Disney. Historically also MGM, though not currently counted as a studio.
5 T. Ilott, 'Film Industry Economics', lecture given at the Film Business Academy, Cass Business School, The City University, January 2009.
6 P. Bart's 'First Look' column, *Variety*, 2–8 November 2009, p.4.
7 A. Finney, *A New Dose of Reality – The State Of European Cinema*, London: Cassel, 1996.
8 B. Mechanic, Keynote Address, IFTA, September 2009.
9 Ilott, op.cit.

2 The film value chain

1 P. Bloore, 'Re-defining the Independent Film Value Chain', London: UK Film Council, February 2009. http://www.ukfilmcouncil.org/12384 [accessed on 5 June 2009].
2 T. Ilott, 'Understanding the Film Business', Film Business Academy lecture, Cass Business School, The City University, January 2009.
3 T. Ilott, 'Film Industry Economics', lecture given at the Film Business Academy, Cass Business School, The City University, January 2009.

3 Film development

1 A. Macdonald, MSc class, Film Business Academy, Cass Business School, The City University, April 2008.
2 A. Finney, *A New Dose of Reality: The State of European Cinema*, London: Cassel, 1996, p.18.
3 A. Finney, *Developing Feature Films in Europe: A Practical Guide*, London/Madrid: Routledge/Media Business School, 1996, p.7.
4 G. Pisano and A. Berkley Wagonfeld, 'Pacific Coast Studios', *Harvard Business Review*, 10 January 2006, pp.7–8.
5 S. Ferarrai, G. Cattani and C. Baden-Fuller, 'Building Projects through Collaborative Networks: A Study on the Determinants of Project-entrepreneurs' Performance', working draft, 2008, p.13.

6   Federation of Screenwriters Europe, policy paper, 2008, p.4.
7   A. Harries, in interview with A. Finney, Circle Conference, Abu Dhabi, 9 October 2009.
8   A. Finney, *A Bag Full of Tricks*, Berlin: European Film Academy, 1994, p.14.

4 Green lighting films

1   A. Finney, *The Egos Have Landed: The Rise and Fall of Palace Pictures*, London: Heineman, 1996.
2   *Heavy Mettle, The Film Festival Magazine*, Spring 2007, pp.34–35.

5 Sales and markets

1   Film London/UKFC/Skillset's 2009 'Market Place' sales training programme used these five headings for delivery of the course.
2   J. Pierson, *Mike, Spike, Slackers and Dykes*, New York: Hyperion, 1995.
3   A. Finney, 'A Dose of Reality: The State of European Cinema', *EFA/Screen International*, 1993, p.101

6 Film finance

1   T. Ilott, 'Fifty Theses about Film', Film Business Academy paper, Cass Business School, The City University, January 2008.
2   M. Beilby, 'Film Finance – The Alignment of Interests', Film Finance Workshop, Abu Dhabi Film Commission, September 2009.
3   See R. Phillips, 'The Global Export of Risk: Finance and the Film Business', Manchester Business School, Manchester University, UK, Online publication date: 1 June 2004. Phillips writes in excellent detail about risk transference and the off-setting of risk to 'foreign' to cash-flow the big-budget Hollywood production model.
4   P. Russo, 'Structured Film Finance', The Salter Group, presented at Film Finance Workshop, Abu Dhabi Film Commission, September 2009.

7 Co-production and the changing European film audience

1   A. Finney, *A New Dose of Reality: The State of European Cinema*, London: Cassell, 1996, p.93.
2   M. Kanzler, S. Newman-Baudaid and A. Lange, 'The Circulation of European Co-productions and Entirely National Films in Europe, 2001–2007', European Audiovisual Observatory, August 2008. The report studied sample data of 5,414 films with theatrical releases between 2001 and 2007 in 20 selected European markets.
3   A. Finney, op.cit.
4   Peter Aalbaek Jensen and Lars von Trier are paid €7,500 a month. Other senior producers are paid a similar level. Any further profits from films are put back into the company. For further reading, see Morten Piil and Liselotte Michelsen 'The Merchant of Zentropa', *Film* No.55, February 2007.
5   Aalbek Jensen announced in December 2009 that he was to step aside from the daily management of his group to concentrate on Zentropa's international activities. He also announced plans to layoff half of Zentropa's 80 staff members in Denmark, explaining that national productions (with the exception of Von Trier's *Antichrist*) were proving hard to make profitable, in part due to high Danish production costs.

8 Exhibition and the changing cinema experience

1   N. Gabler, *An Empire of Their Own: How the Jews Invented Hollywood*, New York: Doubleday, 1988.
2   G. Verter and A.M. McGahan, 'Coming Soon: A Theatre Near You', Harvard Business School, 24 September 1998, p.3.
3   J.E. Squire, *The Movie Business Book*, New York: Fireside, 3rd edn, 2004, p.394.
4   J.E. Squire, ibid, pp.386–400.
5   J. Eliashberg, A. Elberse and M.A.A.M. Leenders, 'The Motion Picture Industry: Critical Issues in Practice, Current Research and New Research Direction', Third Draft, The Wharton School, University of Pennsylvania, Harvard Business School, and Amsterdam School of Communications Research, University of Amsterdam, 23 February 2005.
6   T. Richards, British Screen Advisory Council conference, March 2008.
7   MSc class, Film Business Academy, Cass Business School, The City University, January 2008.

9 Users, consumer behaviour and market research

1   The average cost to make and market a major MPAA member company film was $100.3m in 2006. This includes $65.8m in negative costs and $34.5m in marketing costs. Source: MPAA Research and Statistics 2007/08.
2   A studio executive who has experimented actively on re-launching specific titles is Harvey Weinstein, former co-chair of Miramax Films. Two notable examples include *Into the West* (1992) and *Confessions of a Dangerous Mind* (2004). However, it should be noted that the reasons behind such action may have been connected to keeping talent satisfied as much as any potential commercial gain.
3   MPA, March 2007 Worldwide Market Research and Analysis. The top five films were 1. *Pirates of the Caribbean: Dead Man's Chest* ($423m); *Cars* ($244m); *X-Men: The Last Stand* ($234m); *Night at the Museum* ($219m); *The Da Vinci Code* ($218m).
4   Ibid.
5   MPA/*Variety* April 2007. The top five films were: 1. *Pirates of the Caribbean: Dead Man's Chest* ($642m); *The Da Vinci Code* ($540m); *Ice Age: The Meltdown* ($452m); *Casino Royale* ($339m); *Mission Impossible III* ($264m).
6   For an in-depth analysis of global cinema-going trends, see Charles Acland, *Screen Traffic, Movies, Multiplexes and Global Culture*, Durham, NC: Duke University Press, 2003. Acland examines the ways in which the post-1986 US commercial film business altered prevailing and audience conceptions of movie-going. Specifically, Acland demonstrates how the film industry's reliance on ancillary media markets has cultivated a global landscape of cross-marketed media commodities and led to the development of what he calls the megaplex cinema – a space of 'total entertainment' which focuses on 'up scaling, comfort, courteousness, cleanliness ... and prestige'.
7   P. Broderick, 'Maximising Distribution', *DGA Magazine*, January 2004. Broderick runs a Los Angeles-based consultancy and specializes in the independent production and distribution business. (Website: www.peterbroderick.com)
8   For more detailed examination of the marketing and distribution issues facing independent film, see Chapters 10 and 13.
9   The All Industry Marketing Committee was established in 1984.
10 Source: CAA, Nielsen EDI.
11 H. Bakhshi, 'The Plateau in Cinema Attendances and Drop in Video Sales in the UK: The Role of Digital Leisure Substitutes', UKFC, October 2006.

11 Digital production

1   M. Figgis, *Digital Filmmaking*, London: Faber and Faber, 2007.
2   F. Coppola, Eleanor, F. Bahr and G. Hickenlooper (directors), *Hearts of Darkness: A Filmmaker's Apocalypse*, Paramount, 1991.
3   For the purposes of this book the definition of a low- or micro-budget film is any film with a cash budget below £1m, as defined by the UKFC. See: M. Kelly, 'Low and Micro-Budget Film Production in the UK', a Northern Alliance report for the UKFC, June 2008.
4   M. Behar, 'A Star is Born', *Wired*, September 2008.
5   M. Behar, 'Analog Meets Its Match', *Wired*, 18 August 2008.
6   M. Behar, 'A Star is Born', op.cit.
7   M. Figgis, op.cit., p.43.
8   M. Kelly, op.cit.

12 Digital distribution

1   A. Currah, 'Managing Creativity: The Tensions between Commodities and Gifts in a Digital Networked Environment', *Economy and Society*, 36(3), 2007, pp.467–494.
2   P. Broderick, 'Maximising Distribution', *DGA Magazine*, January 2004.
3   S. Zeitchik, *Hollywood Reporter*, 20 March 2009, pp.10–11.
4   'Briefing: Hollywood and the Internet', *The Economist*, 23 February 2008, pp. 85–87.
5   S. Cunningham, 'Rates of Change: Online Distribution as Disruptive Technology in the Film Industry', keynote address, What is Film? Change and Continuity in the 21st Century, University of Oregon, Turnbull Center, Portland, Oregon, 7 November 2009.
6   Ibid.
7   S. Zeitchik, op.cit.
8   M. Kelly, 'New Stars and Old Dogs', a paper prepared for Cass Business School's Film Business Academy, January 2009.
9   NESTA, Take 12 Document, June 2009, pp.7–8.

13 Film marketing through the Internet

1   M. Franklin, 'Does the Use of the Internet Represent a Paradigmatic Shift in Film Marketing', MSc dissertation, Cass Business School, The City University, London, August 2008. See Elberse, Deighton and Barwise; Peppers and Rogers; and Wietz and Wensley in Franklin's bibliography.
2   D. Peppers, D and M. Rogers, *The One to One Future*, London: Piatkus, 1993; *Enterprise One to One*, London: Piatkus,1997.
3   J. Deighton, E. Salama and M. Sorrell, 'Interactive Marketing: Perspectives', *Harvard Business Review*, November–December 1996, pp.151–152.
4   J. Hazelton, 'Jetset Studios – Online High Flyers', *Screen International*, 15 February 2008.
5   'It Costs $500k to $1m a Day to Take Out a Sponsored Takeover of the My Space Homepage', *Screen International*, 14 December 2007.
6   Seth Godin, 'Unleashing the Ideavirus', www.ideavirus.com
7   David Meerman Scott, 'The New Rules of Viral Marketing – How Word of Mouse Spreads your Ideas for Free', e-book, 2008.
8   Source: adapted from www.Baekdal.com, 23 November 2006 edition (web magazine).
9   Movie Marketing Madness, www.moviemarketingmadness.com

15 Entrepreneurs and investors in the film industry

1   Leonardo da Vinci, *Prophecies*, London: Hesperus, 2002, p.3.
2   A. Finney interviewed Mark Gill at Film London's Production Finance Market, October 2007, where Gill delivered a keynote address.

16 The challenge of creative management

1   M. Stibbe, www.Stibbe.net/Writing/Games_Industry/Managing_Creativity.htm
2   M. Iansiti and R. Levien, 'Strategy as Ecology', *Harvard Business Review*, 82(3), 2004, pp.68–78, cited in H. Mintzberg, B. Ahlstrand and J. Lampel, *Strategy Safari*, London: Prentice Hall, 2nd edn, 2009, p.127.
3   P. Bloore, 'The Creative Producer: Leading and Managing Creative People', University of East Anglia, Lecture Notes 2008, delivered for the South West Screen Producer Training Cohort in March 2008.
4   R. Goffee and G. Jones, 'Leading Clever People', *Harvard Business Review*, 85(3), 2007, pp.72–79.
5   T. Amabile, *The Social Psychology of Creativity*, New York: Springer-Verlag, 1983, p.91.
6   M. Stibbe, op.cit.
7   E. Catmull, 'How Pixar Fosters Collective Creativity', *Harvard Business Review*, 86(9), 2008, pp.64–72.
8   E. Catmull, ibid.
9   For example, Bloore (P. Bloore, op.cit.) cites as a case study the company Sixteen Films, where director Ken Loach and producer Rebecca O'Brien work with long-term collaborator and writer Paul Laverty on an equal footing and he has a position in their company. The director and producer (along with long-standing script consultant Roger Smith) spend long periods of time with Laverty during the development period. The key motivator and contributor to success is not necessarily the amount spent on Laverty's fees, but the amount of time spent with him as the writer. Bloore points out that it is vital to maintain trust and regular channels of communication within the creative triangle of the writer, director and producer, in order to develop and preserve the central vision of the film. Loach and Laverty have co-operated on nine feature films (to 2009), and all the screenplays they have developed together have been converted to production: a remarkable track record.

17 Project management

1   W. Goldman, *Adventures in the Screen Trade: A Personal View of Hollywood and Screenwriting*, New York: Grand Central Publishing, reissue edition, 1989. The title is a parody of Dylan Thomas's *Adventures in the Skin Trade*.
2   A. Finney, 'Learning from Sharks: Lessons on Managing Projects in the Independent Film Industry', *Long Range Planning*, 41, 2008, p.108.
3   B. Mechanic, Independent Film & television Alliance (IFTA) Keynote Address, Los Angeles, September 2009.

18 Business models 2.0

1   P. McKenna, BAFTA Annual TV Lecture, 24 September 2008.
2   M. Rappa, 'Managing the Digital Enterprise – Business Models on the Web', 1 January 2008. http://digitalenterprise.org/models/models.html
3   W. Buffett, Annual letter to Berkshire Hathaway shareholders, 2009.

4   A. Currah, 'Managing Creativity: The Tensions between Commodities and Gifts in a Digital Networked Environment', *Economy and Society*, 36(3), 2007, pp.467–494.
5   BSAC 'Blue Skies' report, 2008.
6   M.W. Johnson, C.M. Christensen and H. Kagermann, 'Reinventing Your Business Model', *Harvard Business Review*, December 2008.
7   *The Economist*, 21 March 2009.
8   BSAC transcript, 2 October 2008.
9   C. Anderson, *The Long Tail: Why the Future of Business is Selling Less of More*, New York: Hyperion, 2006.
10 A. Elberse, 'Should You Invest in the Long Tail', *Harvard Business Review*, July–August 2008.
11 S. Till, 'Factors Impacting Films' Transition from Old to New Media', Cass Business School address to Film Distributors Association Cohort, 3 December 2009.
12 McKenna, op.cit.
13 A. Finney, *A New Dose of Reality: The State of European Cinema*, London: Cassell, 1996, p.155.
14 A. Finney interviewed Le Pogam for the keynote address at the Film London Production Finance Market, London, 21 October 2009. Quotes are from that interview and an earlier interview in Paris, in July 2009 in person.

20 The new looking glass: a changing wonderland

1   Leonardo da Vinci, *Prophecies*, London: Hesperus, 2002, p.33.
2   Angus Finney, *Developing Feature Films in Europe: A Practical Guide*, London: Routledge, 1996.
3   Henry Mintzberg, Bruce Ahlstrand, and Joseph Lampel, *Strategy Safari*, (2nd edn), Edinburgh: FT Prentice Hall, 2009.
4   M. Porter, *Competitive Advantage: Creating and Sustaining Superior Performance*, New York: Free Press, 1985, pp.33–38.

Bibliography

For a summary of academic articles relating to the film industry, please see Allegre L. Hadida's excellent comprehensive literature review of empirical studies of motion picture performance published from 1977 to 2006 ('Motion Picture Performance: A Review and Research Agenda, *International Journal of Management Reviews*, Volume 10, Issue 3, 2008).

Adler, T. (2004) *The Producers*, London: Methuen Drama.
Anderson, C. (2006) *The Long Tail: Why the Future of Business Is Selling Less of More*, New York: Hyperion.
Bach, S. (1986) *Final Cut*, London: Faber & Faber.
Bart, P. (1990) *Fade Out*, London: Simon & Schuster.
Bilton, C. (2006) *Management and Creativity: From Creative Industries to Creative Management*, London: Wiley-Blackwell.
Biskind, P. (1998) *Easy Riders, Raging Bulls*, New York: Simon & Schuster.
Biskind, P. (2004) *Down and Dirty Pictures*, New York: Simon & Schuster.
Boorman, J. (1985) *Money into Light*, London: Faber & Faber
Brown, M. K., Huettner, M. and Char James-Tanny, B. (2007) *Managing Virtual Teams: Getting the Most from Wikis, Blogs, and other Collaborative Tools*, Plano, TX: Wordward Publishing.
Burke, R. and Barron S. (2007) *Project Management Leadership: Building Creative Teams*, London: Burke Publishing.
Burns, P. (2007) *Entrepreneurship and Small Business* (2nd edn), Hampshire: Palgrave Macmillan.
Caves, R. E. (2000) *Creative Industries: Contracts between Art and Commerce*, Cambridge, MA: Harvard University Press.
Collins, J. (2001) *Good to Great*, New York: Harper Collins.
Corman, R. (1990) *How I Made 100 Movies in Hollywood and Never Lost a Dime*, London: Random Century Group.
Dale, M. (1997) *The Movie Game: The Film Business in Britain, Europe and America*, London: Cassell.
Durie, J. (Ed.), Pham, A. and Watson, N. (1993) *The Film Marketing Handbook: A Practical Guide to Marketing Strategies for Independent Films*, London: Media Business School.
Eberts, J. and Ilott, T. (1990) *My Indecision is Final: The Rise and Fall of Goldcrest Films*, London: Faber & Faber.
Epstein, J. E. (2005) *The Big Picture: The New Logic of Money and Power in Hollywood*, New York: Random House.
Figgis, M. (2007) *Digital Filmmaking*, London: Faber & Faber.

Finney, A. (1993) *A Dose of Reality: The State of European Cinema*, London/Berlin: European Film Academy/Screen International.

Finney, A. (1996) *The State of European Cinema: A New Dose of Reality*, London: Cassell.

Finney, A. (1996) *The Egos Have Landed: The Rise and Fall of Palace Pictures*, London: Heinemann.

Finney, A. (1996) *Developing Feature Films in Europe: A Practical Guide*, London: Routledge.

Gabler, N. (1988) *An Empire of Their Own: How the Jews Invented Hollywood*, New York: Doubleday.

Gregory Dunne, J. (1997) *Monster: Living off the Big Screen*, New York: Random House.

Hanson, S. (2007) *From Silent Screen to Multi-Screen: A History of Cinema Exhibition in Britain since 1896*, Manchester: Manchester University Press.

Hark, I. R. (2001) *Exhibition, The Film Reader* (1st edn), London: Routledge.

Henry, J. (2001) *Creative Management*, London: Sage Publications.

Ilott, T. and Puttnam, D. (1996) *Budgets and Markets: Study of the Budgeting of European Films*, London: Routledge.

Jackel, A. (2003) *European Film Industries*, London: British Film Institute.

Jancovich, M. (2008) *The Place of the Audience: Cultural Geographies of Film Consumption*, London: British Film Institute.

Kent, N. (1991) *Naked Hollywood: Money and Power in the Movies Today*, London: St Martin's Press.

Kula, S. (2002) *Appraising Moving Images: Assessing the Archival and Monetary Value of Film and Video Records*, Lanham, MD: Scarecrow Press.

Lampel, J., Shamsie, J. and Lant, T. K. (Eds) (2006) *The Business of Culture: Strategic Perspectives on Entertainment and Media*, Hillsdale, NJ: Lawrence Erlbaum.

Litvak, M. (1986) *Reel Power*, Los Angeles, CA: Silman-James.

McClintick, D. (1982) *Indecent Exposure*, New York: Dell.

Mintzberg, H., Ahlstrand, B. and Lampel, J. (2008) *Strategy Safari* (2nd edn), London: Prentice Hall.

Moore, S. M. (2007) *The Biz: The Basic Business, Legal and Financial Aspects of the Film Industry*, Los Angeles, CA: Silman-James.

Moul, C. (Ed.) (2005) *A Concise Handbook of Movie Industry Economics*, New York: Cambridge University Press.

Neumann, P. (2002) *The Fine Art of Co-Producing*, Madrid: Media Business School.

Pardo, Alejandro (Ed.) (2002) *The Audiovisual Management Handbook*, Madrid: Media Business School.

Pierson, J. (1995) *Spike, Mike, Slackers & Dykes*, New York: Hyperion.

Schatz, T. (1988) *The Genius of the System: Hollywood Filmmaking in the Studio Era*, New York: Metropolitan.

Scott Berg, A. (1989) *Goldwyn*, London: Hamish Hamilton.

Silber, L. (1999) *Career Management for the Creative Person*, New York: Three Rivers Press.

Soros, G. (2003) *The Alchemy of Finance*, Hoboken, NJ: John Wiley & Sons.

Squire, J.E. (2004) *The Movie Business Book* (3rd edn), New York: Fireside.

Sweeney, J. (2007) *Successful Business Models for Filmmakers*, Bloomington, IN: AuthorHouse.

Tapscott, D. and Williams, A. D. (2006) *Wikinomics: How Mass Collaboration Changes Everything*, London: Atlantic.

Thomson, D. (1993) *Showman: The Life of David O. Selznick*, London: Andre Deutsch.

Tolkin, M. (1988) *The Player*, London: Faber & Faber.

Torr, G. (2008) *Managing Creative People: Lessons in Leadership for the Ideas Economy*, Chichester: Wiley.

Vickery, G. and Hawkins, R. (2008) *Remaking the Movies: Digital Content and the Revolution of the Film and Video Industries*, Paris: OECD Publishing.

Vogel, H. (2007) *Entertainment Industry Economics: A Guide for Financial Analysis* (7th edn), Cambridge: Cambridge University Press.

Walker, A. (1985) *National Heroes*, London: Harrap.

Waller, A. G. (2001) *Movie Going in America: A Sourcebook in the History of Film Exhibition*, Oxford: Wiley-Blackwell.

Wasko, J. (2003) *How Hollywood Works*, London: Sage Publications.

Wasko, J. and McDonald, P. (1982) *Movies and Money: Financing the American Film Industry*, London: Sage Publications.

Wasko, J. and McDonald, P. (2008) *The Contemporary Hollywood Film Industry*, London: Blackwell Publishing.

Index

Note: Page numbers in **bold** relate to figures and tables.

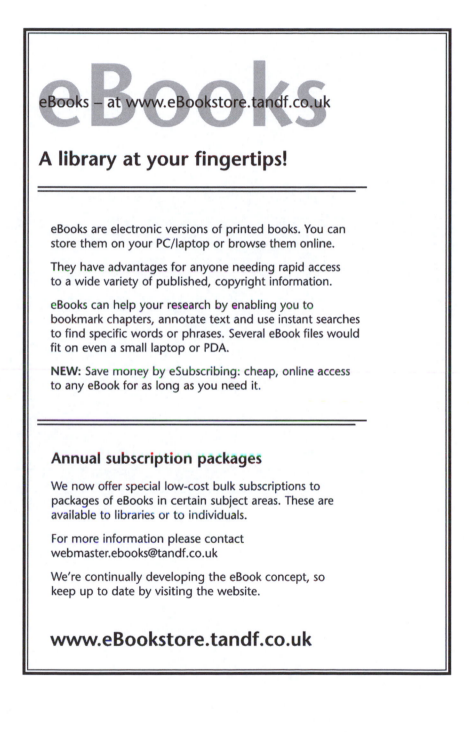